Environmental Regulation and Economic Growth

Environmental Regulation and Economic Growth

Edited by

A. E. BOYLE

CLARENDON PRESS · OXFORD
1994

Oxford University Press, Walton Street, Oxford OX2 6DP
Oxford New York
Athens Auckland Bangkok Bombay
Calcutta Cape Town Dar es Salaam Delhi
Florence Hong Kong Istanbul Karachi
Kuala Lumpur Madras Madrid Melbourne
Mexico City Nairobi Paris Singapore
Taipei Tokyo Toronto
and associated companies in
Berlin Ibadan

Oxford is a trade mark of Oxford University Press

Published in the United States
by Oxford University Press Inc., New York

British Library Cataloguing in Publication Data
Data available

Library of Congress Cataloging in Publication Data
Environmental regulation and economic growth / edited by A.E. Boyle.
(Oxford law colloquium)
Includes index.
1. Environmental law. 2. Pollution—Law and legislation.
3. Economic development—Environmental aspects.
I. Boyle, Alan E. II. Series.
K3585.6.E59 1994 344.73'046—dc20 [347.30446] 94–30754
ISBN 0–19–825910–7

1 3 5 7 9 10 8 6 4 2

Set by Hope Services (Abingdon) Ltd.
Printed in Great Britain
on acid-free paper by
Biddles Ltd.
Guildford & King's Lynn

Contents

Foreword

In 1991 the Oxford University Law Faculty and The Norton Rose M5 Group held their first Oxford Law Colloquium, a projected series of colloquia in which leading practitioners would join with academics in exploring trends and policy issues in particular fields of law of mutual interest. That highly successful joint venture led to the publication of *Commercial Aspects of Trusts and Fiduciary Obligations*, the collection of colloquium papers edited by my colleague Ewan McKendrick, which was very favourably received.

The present volume, which reproduces the papers presented at the 1993 Oxford Law Colloquium, is devoted to a subject of universal importance: the safeguarding of the environment and the impact of protective measures on national economies. It is hardly surprising that this has become a major field of legal practice and academic study, for it concerns the very future of life on earth. The ten contributors to this volume, all experts in their fields, embrace a wide diversity of interests and expertise. They include practising lawyers, academics, regulators, and leading figures in industry and commerce.

Massive claims and settlements for clean-up costs of large-scale pollution have become a feature of modern life. They expose the innate tension between the need to protect life, property and natural resources and the equally important need to ensure that the cost of prevention and cure does not become so large as to cripple industrial and commercial activity. The label 'sustainable development' accurately conveys the balance to be achieved but gives no guidance as to what is sustainable or how the concept is to be achieved. It is fundamental issues of this kind, their implications for legal liability, and the way that different regulators have sought to address them in particular fields, that is the focus of the present volume. The problems are fascinating and complex. They are admirably addressed in the ten papers collected here and skilfully edited by Professor Alan Boyle, whose colleague I was privileged to be for many years and whose own contribution to the debate reflects the perspective of a leading international lawyer.

In warmly commending this publication, which will be invaluable to all those with a serious interest in environmental regulation, I should like to express the appreciation of the Oxford Law Faculty to Alan Boyle, to all the contributors, to the partners and staff of The Norton Rose M5 Group, whose friendship and collaboration we greatly value, and to our own Oxford University Press for all their work in the publication of this attractively produced volume. I hope that it will be as widely read as its predecessor.

St. John's College
Oxford,
1 October, 1994

Roy Goode

List of Contributors

WILLIAM BIRTLES, Barrister, 15 Old Square, London

ALAN BOYLE, Professor of Public International Law, The University of Edinburgh

MARGARET BRUSASCO MACKENZIE, Head of Unit, DG XI-C1, Commission of the European Communities, Brussels

STEPHEN CHRISTY, the Norton Rose M5 Group, Mills & Reeve, Norwich

MARTIN COLEMAN, the Norton Rose M5 Group, Norton Rose, Brussels

JOHN CRIDLAND, Director of Environmental Affairs, Confederation of British Industry, London

BRIAN GREENWOOD, the Norton Rose M5 Group, Norton Rose, London

MICHAEL I. JEFFERY, QC, partner and Head, Environmental Law Group, Fraser & Beatty, Toronto

BENEDICT KINGSBURY, Duke University School of Law and the University of Oxford

LOGAN G. ROBINSON, Vice-President and General Counsel, Chrysler International corporation, Michigan

DAVID SLATER, Chief Inspector and Director, Her Majesty's Inspectorate of Pollution, London

Abbreviations

AC	Appeal Cases
ACP	Africa, Caribbean, Pacific
AJIL	*American Journal of International Law*
All ER	All England Reports
Alta LR	Alberta Law Reports
APC	Air pollution control
ASEAN	Association of South-East Asian Nations
BATNEEC	Best available technology not entailing excessive cost
BCLC	Butterworth's Company Law Cases
BISD	Basic Instruments and Selected Decisions (GATT)
BJIBFL	*Butterworth's Journal of International Banking and Financial Law*
BNFL	British Nuclear Fuels Ltd.
BPEO	Best practicable environmental option
BYIL	*British Yearbook of International Law*
CA	Court of Appeal
CBAO-CLE	Canadian Bar Association for Ontario-Council of Legal Education
CBI	Confederation of British Industry
CBLN	*Canada Banking Law News*
CBR	Canadian Bankruptcy Reports
CCC	Canadian Criminal Cases
CELR	Canadian Environmental Law Reports
CERCLA	Comprehensive Environmental Response Compensation and Liability Act
CFC	Chlorofluorocarbon
CFL	Compact fluorescent lightbulbs
Ch.D.	Chancery Division
CIMAH	Control of Industrial Major Accident Hazard Regulations 1984
Cir.	Circuit
CITES	Convention on International Trade in Endangered Species of Wild Fauna and Flora, 1973
CMLR	*Common Market Law Review*
CNG	Compressed natural gas
Col. JIEL	*Colorado Journal of International Environmental Law and Policy*
Comm. LJ	*Commercial Law Journal*

COSHH	Control of Substances Hazardous to Health Regulations 1988
CSCE	Conference on Security and Co-operation in Europe
CSD	Commission on Sustainable Development
Div. Ct.	Divisional Court
DLR	Dominion Law Reports
D.o.E.	Department of the Environment
DSB	Dispute Settlement Body
DSD	*Duales System Deutschland*
DTC	Dominion Tax Cases
EBF	Environment Business Forum
EC	Economic Community
ECJ	European Court of Justice
ECR	European Court Reports
EEA	European Environment Agency
EEC	European Economic Community
EFTA	European Free Trade Association
EL	*Environmental Law*
ELA	*Environmental Law Alert*
ELQ	*Ecology Law Quarterly*
ELR	*European Law Review*
EPA	Environmental Protection Agency
EPA90	Environmental Protection Act 1990
ERC (BNA)	Environmental Reporter Cases
ERCB	Energy Resources Conservation Board
EU	European Union
FAO	Food and Agriculture Organization
FDIC	Federal Deposit Insurance Corporation
Fed. Reg.	*Federal Register*
Fla. SUJTLP	*Florida State University Journal of Transnational Law and Policy*
GATT	General Agreement on Tariffs and Trade
GCC	Gulf Co-operation Council
GDP	Gross Domestic Product
GEF	Global Environmental Facility
GEO	Global Environmental Organization
GNP	Gross National Product
Harv. ELR	*Harvard Environmental Law Review*
HBFC	Hydrobromofluorocarbon
HCFC	Hydrochlorofluorocarbon
HICLR	*Hastings International and Comparative Law Review*
HL	House of Lords
HMIP	Her Majesty's Inspectorate of Pollution

HMSO	Her Majesty's Stationery Office
HRQ	*Human Rights Quarterly*
ICJ Rep.	International Court of Justice Reports
IFLR	*International Financial Law Review*
IL	*The International Lawyer*
ILM	*International Legal Materials*
ILO	International Labour Organization
IMO	International Maritime Organization
IPC	Integrated pollution control
IRLR	Industrial Relations Law Reports
ITO	International Trade Organization
ITTO	International Tropical Timber Organization
IUCN	International Union for the Conservation of Nature
JEL	*Journal of Environmental Law*
JELL	*Journal of Environmental Law and Litigation*
JELP	*Journal of Environmental Law and Practice*
JPEL	*Journal of Planning and Environmental Law*
JWT	*Journal of World Trade*
LMELR	*Land Management and Environmental Law Report*
LNTS	League of Nations Treaty Series
LR	Law Reports
MAFF	Ministry of Agriculture, Fisheries, and Food
MARPOL	1973/8 Convention for the Prevention of Pollution by Ships
MB	*Moniteur Belge*
Mich. LR	*Michigan Law Review*
Minn. JGT	*Minnesota Journal of Global Trade*
MFN	Most[-]favoured[-]nation
MLR	*Modern Law Review*
MMPA	Marine Mammal Protection Act
MTIDC	Malaysian Timber Industry Development Council
NAFTA	North American Free Trade Agreement
NAPE	National Agency for the Protection of the Environment
NCDR	*National Creditor/Debtor Revue*
NCJICR	*North Carolina Journal of International and Commercial Regulation*
NPL	National Priorities List
NRA	National Rivers Authority
OAC	Ontario Appeal Cases
OECD	Organization for Economic Co-operation and Development
Offer	Office of the Director-General of Electricity Supply
Ofgas	Office of the Director-General of Gas supply

Ofwat	Office of Water Services
OJ	Official Journal
Ont. CA	Ontario Court of Appeal
Ont. HC	Ontario High Court
OPEC	Organization of Petroleum Exporting Countries
OR	Ontario Reports
PPMs	Processes and production methods
Prov.J.	Provincial Judge
PRP	Potentially responsible party
QBD	Queen's Bench Division
RSC	Revised Statutes of Canada
RSO	Revised Statutes of Ontario
RTC	Resolution Trust Corporation
s., ss.	section, sections
SARA	Superfund Amendments and Reauthorization Act 1986
SCC	Supreme Court Cases (Canada)
SEA	Single European Act
SJE	*Swedish Journal of Economics*
Stan. JIL	Stanford Journal of International Law
STEP	Service and Technology for Environmental Protection
SW	South Western Reporter
SWQOs	Statutory Water Quality Objectives
UCCLJ	*Uniform Commerical Code Law Journal*
UKTS	United Kingdom Treaty Series
UNCED	United Nations Conference on Environment and Development
UNDP	United Nations Development Programme
UNEP	United Nations Environmental Programme
UNGA	United Nations General Assembly
UNICE	Union of Industrial and Employers' Confederations of Europe
UNTS	United Nations Treaty Series
USCA	United States Code Annotated
USCCAN	*US Code Congressional and Administrative News*
UTLJ	*University of Toronto Law Journal*
UWWTD	Urban Waste Water Treatment Directive
WD	*World Development*
WE	*The World Economy*
WIA	Water Industries Act 1991
WLLR	*Washington and Lee Law Review*
WLR	Weekly Law Reports
WRA	Waste Regulation Authority
WRA91	Water Resources Act 1991

WTO	World Trade Organization
WWF	World Wildlife Fund
WWR	Western Weekly Reports
Yale LJ	*Yale Law Journal*
Yb. IEL	*Yearbook of International Environmental Law*

Table of Cases

CANADA

CENTRAL AMERICAN COURT OF JUSTICE

EUROPEAN COURT OF HUMAN RIGHTS

EUROPEAN COURT OF JUSTICE AND COURT OF FIRST INSTANCE

UK

US

European Community Treaties

Table of European Community Secondary Legislation

DIRECTIVES

REGULATIONS

DECISIONS

International Treaties and Agreements

Table of National Legislation

NEW ZEALAND

SWEDEN

UK

US

Introduction

ALAN BOYLE

The papers collected as chapters in this book were originally presented at a colloquium sponsored by the Oxford University Law Faculty and the Norton Rose M5 Group of Solicitors which was held in September 1993. Their theme, somewhat broadly put, is the relationship between environmental law and economic growth, as viewed by lawyers, regulators, and industry in Europe and North America. The confines of the colloquium and of this book did not permit the inclusion of environmental economists, whose contribution to the general theme is certainly as important as that of lawyers and regulators. Nor could any attempt be made to consider the issues from the perspective of the developing world, where there have long been strongly held, if not always fully thought out, views on the supposedly harmful economic effect of environmental concerns. It does not, therefore, pretend to be a comprehensive treatment of the relationship between environmental regulation and economic growth.

What this book does try to do is to identify several themes, trends, and issues of general importance to all those involved in environmental law. One theme is apparent throughout: the inextricable interplay of domestic, European, and international environmental law. It is simply no longer possible to view these topics in splendid isolation. Developments at one level are increasingly influenced by, and influence, developments at other levels of law-making. This is particularly evident with issues such as the 'polluter pays' principle, a concept which has been taken up at all three levels. As the editor points out in his chapter, principles adopted internationally are often so open-textured as to leave much discretion to governments and regional organizations when it comes to implementation and interpretation. Key concepts such as 'sustainable development', and the 'polluter pays' principle, although at the heart of international environmental policy following the 1992 Rio Conference on Environment and Development, are very much of this kind. They acquire content and practical importance only when implemented nationally or regionally. This is one reason why European Community environmental law and policy are so important.

Several chapters bring out the increasing sophistication and scope of European community action on the environment. Margaret Brusasco Mackenzie argues that the Community has adopted a more 'holistic' approach than before, which, it is hoped, 'will bear fruit nationally and at the Community and international levels, by ensuring a more profound involvement of administrators, industrialist, NGOs and the general public with the aim of achieving more widely based and sound environmental policies'. Like sustainable development, these policies are not concerned solely with environmental protection, but with the broader idea of 'growth management'. For the Community, therefore, the guiding principles of environmental policy are the integration of environmental and other policies, shared responsibility, and subsidiarity, and the mechanisms on which it relies include market forces and economic instruments to internalize environmental costs, in addition to more traditional forms of 'command and control' through regulation. But Community regulation remains important, she argues, in view of the need for common environmental rules in a common market.

Brian Greenwood shares this assumption that common rules are necessary in a common market. He observes the difficulty of translating it into practice, however, when considering some of the problems affecting Community regulation of packaging and urban waste water. He sees Community harmonization of environmental liability as desirable if it leads to greater certainty, and favours strict liability for this reason, but cautions that liability is not the answer to all problems. This point is picked up by several other chapters, and given topical importance by the *Cambridge Water Case*.[1] But John Cridland's belief that industry is opposed to strict liability is not wholly borne out by other chapters, including Greenwood's, nor was it supported in discussion by industrialists present at the Oxford Conference.

But Cridland's concern with the extent of environmental liability is shared by Stephen Christy and Michael Jeffery. Their arguments suggest that the key issue in the *Cambridge Water* case is not the principle of strict liability as such, which the House of Lords endorsed, but its retrospective application by the Court of Appeal[2] to harm that was not reasonably foreseeable at the time the pollution was first introduced. The importance of the House of Lords' reversal of the Court of Appeal on this point can clearly be observed in the debate over liability for clean-up of historic pollution in contaminated land. Jeffery shows how governments in North America have sought to address this problem by extending liability for clean-up costs to lenders through a broad definition of ownership or operation of the property in question. He argues that 'deep pocket' liability has been taken to untenable extremes in North America, and that there is a need to protect the legitimate interests of institutions funding activities which lead to pollution. Cridland, speaking for the CBI, echoes this point, while Greenwood points out the need to decide whether

[1] *Cambridge Water Co.* v. *Eastern Counties Leather plc* [1994] 1 All ER 53.

[2] Ibid.

the objective is to repair damage *per se* or merely to offer remediation sufficient for future use of the land.

The problem of contaminated land aptly illustrates the difficult choices which remain even when a 'polluter pays' policy has been adopted in principle. As Christy points out, we still have to decide who the 'owner' is, and who should pay if the owner cannot. The House of Lords has given a restricted answer to these questions in *Cambridge Water*, which minimizes and focuses the scope of liability at common law, but leaves broader solutions to the legislature at national or European level. One interesting feature of this case is the extent to which the judgments have visibly been influenced by experience in other jurisdictions and an appreciation of developments in European and international law. But it demonstrates also that while environmental liability is undoubtedly important, it can only be part of a system of environmental law.

This point is evident in the chapters by Stephen Christy, David Slater, and William Birtles. Stephen Christy makes the obvious point that despite the flexibility and adaptability of the common law, a move to statutory regulation is essential if environmental problems are to be addressed adequately. Once regulation becomes the central tool of environmental protection, administrative agencies are needed to formulate and police it. These agencies will then have to respond to pressures from differing groups seeking to influence their judgment. Christy poses the question: 'Is proper environmental regulation altogether a more altruistic goal than any of us will ever be able to achieve in the face of so many conflicting interests?' David Slater, Chief Inspector at Her Majesty's Inspectorate of Pollution, is well placed to try to answer. He accepts Christy's point that there are conflicting interests, and sees HMIP as holding the ring between government, industry and public. 'Stewardship' is, for him, the concept which best describes the role of HMIP. But he does not regard regulation as a strait-jacket for industry. The statutory requirements of integrated pollution control (IPC) and 'best available technology not entailing excessive cost' (BATNEEC) are, he argues, flexible and sophisticated concepts, facilitating progressive implementation of higher environmental standards, and allowing industry to decide how to meet them. They represent one way of trying to reconcile economic growth and care for the environment.

This gives us a picture of stewardship which involves making choices, balancing conflicting objectives, and trying to satisfy competing claimants. Such is probably inevitable and necessary in a complex society. It is, however, a picture which is plausible only to the extent that it is seen to involve open, fair, and responsive decision-making. As William Birtles makes clear, 'a state that does not provide its citizens with as much environmental information as is possible is likely to find that it increasingly lacks credibility and legitimacy as public concern continues to grow and the millennium approaches'. It is for this reason that freedom of information is an important element of environmental policy in a democratic society. European Community law has grasped this essential point with its directive on access to environmental information. But as Birtles shows, there is no simple model for access to information, but instead a range of overlapping possibilities. Moreover, implementation of the EC directive in the United Kingdom is not without difficulties when it comes to interpretation and knowing what to ask for. Public participation is undoubtedly desirable, but it is less certain how far freedom of information in the United Kingdom has advanced this goal.

Democratic legitimacy is thus one criterion for judging a system of environmental law. Another is enforcement and effectiveness. It is fair to say that these questions could not be explored to any significant extent in this book. But a third criterion is expressed at the beginning of this introduction, which goes to the heart of the notion of sustainable development: the relationship between environmental law and economic growth. Five chapters address this topic directly. Alan Boyle observes that sustainable development, as defined internationally, does not mean no growth, but neither does it mean that there are no limits on growth, nor that existing levels of economic activity are necessarily sustainable. The concept, while nebulous in some degree, nevertheless represents a complex combination of values rather than a straightforward economic equation. Since interpretation and implementation are to a large extent left to individual governments, it will largely be their own choices which determine the impact of environmental policy on growth within their own economy.

But this will not be so in all cases. The increasing globalization of environmental law and policy are matched by the globalization of the world economy and international trade. Regional trading blocs in Europe and elsewhere are also part of an expanding economic system based on the General Agreement on Tariffs and Trade, to which significant amendments were agreed early in 1994.[3]

Benedict Kingsbury and Martin Coleman address the relationship between free trade policy, as represented by GATT and the EEC, and environmental protection. Kingsbury observes the varying ability of international institutions engaged with the law and policy of free trade to take account of the environment. This is a particular problem for GATT, which has tended to view environmental protection as simply another form of protectionism or subsidy. GATT thus poses particular problems for unilateral trade measures intended to protect the global commons or to address transborder problems, although it is easier to reconcile with

[3] For details see Benedict Kingsbury's chapter.

multilateral measures promoting participation in and compliance with environmental agreements. But integrating environmental considerations more fully into the GATT system remains difficult, Kingsbury argues, because it lacks an adequate conflict resolution structure, and the necessary expertise, to have regard to substantive principles of environmental policy and law in its operation. The danger in this situation is that considerations of free trade will always outweigh other values, including those of environmental protection, and may indeed exacerbate some environmental problems because of the economic specialization GATT tends to favour. By removing autonomy over an important area of decision-making from individual states, moreover, GATT undermines the emphasis on decentralization and public participation which many environmentalists see as important elements in promoting sustainable development.

Martin Coleman does not accept that this thesis is necessarily accurate, however. He argues instead that 'Whilst environmental legislation may restrict trade, it does not necessarily follow that the interests of free trade conflict with those of environmental protection. It may be that free trade is good for the environment . . . As the income of a country rises, it is more likely to increase expenditure on limiting damage to the environment.' Coleman observes, like many industrialists, that business often sharpens its competitive edge by 'going green' and that setting high environmental standards, far from being economically harmful, can be a route to increasing market share and enhancing industrial competitiveness. Even where this is not the case, EEC policy predicates harmonization of standards and the integration of environmental policy with competition policy in an effort to even out market distortion. But he also accepts that while this strategy may work within the EEC, it is harder to square with the rest of the world, where lower standards may remain, and where GATT does not offer the prospect of easing the inherent tensions.

The final two chapters move away from specific legal problems and address in conclusion the broader issue: What are the effects of environmental regulation on business? John Cridland of the CBI is wary of regulatory solutions to environmental problems, and opposed to stronger liability laws or more harmonization. He sees the risk of securing some environmental improvements at disproportionate cost. His preferred solution, alone among contributors to this book, is one of relying on voluntary action, emphasizing the responsibility of boards of directors for environmental matters. Business should, in his view, be part of the solution to the problem of sustainable development. But while favouring the use of market forces wherever possible, he warns of the need for a realistic appreciation of the costs, benefits, and trade-offs in any environmental policy. Cridland's views are by no means universally held by industry. An alternative view stresses the importance of setting clear standards, universally applied, so that business knows what it must aim at and knows that there is one standard for everyone. This of course will generally require greater regulatory intervention by government than Cridland's market solution would favour.

Logan Robinson addresses this issue from the perspective of the Chrysler Corporation of America. He plots, graphically, the costs to the car industry of environmental regulation, and the serious impediments regulation can pose to technological innovation and economic goals. Regulation, he believes, is often too inflexible, it distrusts the market, even though customers demand cleaner cars and factories, and produces conflict with government instead of co-operation. These criticisms are important, since they do reflect limitations which regulatory solutions sometimes encounter, not just in environmental matters. But it is as well to remember at this point the arguments of David Slater and Margaret Brusasco Mackenzie. It is possible to design regulatory systems that minimize or avoid altogether the inflexibility, the adversarial conflict, and the distrust of alternatives identified by Robinson. It is also possible to be too optimistic in believing the market will always deliver even those things that consumers do want.

There are, then, no easy answers and no clear-cut ways of analysing the relationship between economic and environmental goals. Sustainable development is a useful working description of what is desired, but like motherhood and virtue, it is not easy to define, and there are various ways to get there.

1

Environmental Regulation in the United Kingdom

STEPHEN CHRISTY

1.1. AN OVERVIEW

1.1.1. The United Kingdom Tradition

Perhaps the United Kingdom always has been peculiar. Maybe one of the concerns of those who fear greater European integration is that the United Kingdom will not be permitted to remain peculiar. In any event, it is not possible to understand the present system of environmental regulation without looking at its peculiarly English roots and so seeing it in its historical context.

The United Kingdom is a common law jurisdiction. That is to say, the law of the land comprises statute law and law made by judges through the decisions of the courts which act as binding precedents. The potential significance of that, for those who are not from common law jurisdictions, is perhaps best demonstrated by noting that the entire law of negligence has been developed by the courts from one case in the House of Lords in 1932. This is not the time to consider the relative merits and disadvantages of a common law system as opposed to other systems. However, the development of environmental regulation has been influenced—and, arguably, very strongly influenced—by common law traditions of flexibility and adaptation.

Many of the roots of what has now come to be called 'environmental law' are found, in the United Kingdom at least, in the second half of the nineteenth century. From then can be discerned two fundamental threads—the periodic concern of the legislature with social matters (housing, health and safety at work) and the recurrent preoccupation of the courts with protection of what might loosely be called 'property interests'. In 1875 the first of a series of Public Health Acts was passed, directed at safeguarding health and securing minimum standards of housing. Seven years before that, in 1868, the House of Lords formulated what has since become known as the rule in *Rylands* v. *Fletcher*[1]—that a person who brings on to his land and collects and keeps there anything likely to do mischief if it escapes, must keep it in at his peril and, if he does not do so, is prima facie answerable for all the damage which is the natural consequence if it escapes.

The common law has developed three main areas of law which have an impact in environmental matters: the rule in *Rylands* v. *Fletcher* just mentioned, nuisance, and negligence. This is not the place for a detailed examination of English civil law but one point ought to be stressed: the general rule of English law that civil cases are actionable only on proof of damage. In the environmental arena, that rule at present prevents, for example, civil law actions by environmental groups not affected by pollution. In essence, the rights and remedies developed by the courts are designed to protect those with some vested interest in the subject-matter of the action. They are, in general, available to individuals rather than to classes or groups of individuals.

That being said, the significance of common law remedies should not be overlooked. The potential flexibility and adaptability of judge-made law is in many ways well suited to confronting the changing demands of a developing and somewhat amorphous area of regulation which in many ways can be argued to defend property interests. The flexibility of the common law in environmental matters is demonstrated by *Cambridge Water Co.* v. *Eastern Counties Leather Plc*,[2] where the Court of Appeal held that the water company had a 'natural right' to have 'such of the water [as comes beneath an owner's land by percolation and] as [it appropriated] by abstraction come to [it] in an uncontaminated condition', following the 1885 decision of *Ballard* v. *Tomlinson*.[3] Further, the court held that liability was strict (i.e. without proof of fault):

> *Ballard* v. *Tomlinson* decided that where the nuisance is an interference with a natural right incident to ownership then the liability is a strict one . . . The actor acts at his peril in that if his actions result by the operation of ordinary natural processes in an interference with the right then he is liable to compensate for any damage suffered by the owner.

It is interesting to note that the water company lost at first instance, in a decision which stressed the inadequacies of *Rylands* v. *Fletcher* as an environmental weapon—only to win on appeal on a ground not considered in the lower court. The Court of Appeal decision on strict liability has now been upheld by the House of Lords,[4] although their Lordships allowed the defendant's appeal on the ground that harm of the relevant type had not been foreseeable.

[1] [1868] LR 3HL 330. [2] [1994] 2 WLR 53 (CA & HL). [3] [1885] 26 Ch.D 194.
[4] [1994] 2 WLR 53.

1.1.2. The Statutory Framework

Since the passing of the Control of Pollution Act in 1974 the United Kingdom has seen a clear move towards a statutory framework for environmental regulation. That move has been seen by some as a belated acknowledgment that the environment itself has rights and by others as craven subservience to the whim of Brussels' Eurocrats. In a very English way, the truth is an admirable compromise between the two extremes. Thus, there are today at least twelve major statutes dealing with matters related to environmental protection—what might be called 'primary legislation'. They include the Public Health Act 1961, the Factories Act 1961, the Transport Act 1968, the Fire Precautions Act 1971, the Control of Pollution Act 1974, the Health and Safety at Work etc. Act 1974, the Consumer Protection Act 1987, the Environmental Protection Act 1990, the Town and Country Planning Act 1990, the Planning (Listed Buildings and Conservation Areas) Act 1990, the Planning (Hazardous Substances) Act 1990, the Water Industry Act 1991, and the Water Resources Act 1991. In addition to the primary legislation there is the usual plethora of secondary legislation—rules, orders, and regulations, such as (to name but a few) the Asbestos (Licensing) Regulations 1983, the Classification, Packaging, and Labelling of Dangerous Substances Regulations 1984, the Control of Substances Dangerous to Health Regulations 1988, the Town and Country Planning (Assessment of Environmental Effects) Regulations 1988, and the Dangerous Substances (Notification and Marking of Sites) Regulations 1990.

1.1.3. The Administrative Framework

Administration of environmental law in the United Kingdom is carried out by a large number of central and local government departments, agencies, and statutory undertakings. These include the Department of the Environment, the Department of Energy, the Department of Transport, the Ministry of Agriculture, Fisheries, and Food, Her Majesty's Inspectorate of Pollution, the Health and Safety Executive, the National Rivers Authority, metropolitan, county, and district council planning departments, county and district council environmental health departments, the Transport Commission, and the UK Atomic Energy Authority. In this context, perhaps the medium is the only comprehensible message. Let us look briefly at hazardous substances, statutory nuisances, water, contaminated land, waste, and then at IPC and APC.

1.1.3.1. Hazardous Substances

The Planning (Hazardous Substances) Act 1990, which came into force on 1 June 1992, regulates the presence on, over, or under land of any hazardous substance in excess of the controlled quantity of that substance. Hazardous substances and their respective controlled quantities are prescribed by regulation.[5] The relevant authority for the purpose of issuing consents for storage of hazardous substances is usually the district council, but is the county council in relation to land used for mineral work or waste disposal and is the appropriate minister in the case of operational land of statutory undertakings. Control of hazardous substances during transport is the subject of a different set of regulations,[6] policed by the Health and Safety Executive. Regulation of hazardous substances on land is linked closely, historically and in terms of the regulatory authority, to planning law.

The Health and Safety at Work etc. Act 1974 imposes a general duty on employers to take reasonable care to protect their employees from risk of foreseeable injury, disease, or death at work. The Control of Substances Hazardous to Health Regulations 1988 (COSHH Regulations) extend and clarify the duty of employers under the 1974 Act in relation to hazardous substances in the workplace and impose duties to monitor health risks, workplace hazards and health of employees. They are enforced by the Health and Safety Executive or the local authority, depending on the type of activity.

1.1.3.2. Statutory Nuisances

Local authorities are responsible for policing statutory nuisances, which are set out in the Environmental Protection Act 1990 (EPA90). They include emissions of smoke, smells, and noise from, and from activities on, property which cause a nuisance or are prejudicial to health. A nuisance may occur where there is interference with the comfort of others even if no physical injury to health results. It is a defence to show that the 'best practicable means' were used to prevent or to counteract the effects of the nuisance.

1.1.3.3. Water

The primary legislation for England and Wales (Scotland has different provisions) is contained in the Water Resources Act 1991 (WRA) and the Water Industries Act 1991 (WIA), both of which replaced the short-lived Water Act of 1989. In very broad terms, the WRA deals with the National Rivers Authority (NRA) and its powers and duties, and the WIA covers water and sewerage undertakers and their powers and duties.

The NRA has developed a reputation for being the most aggressive—

[5] Planning (Hazardous Substances) Regulations 1992.

[6] Road Traffic (Carriage of Dangerous Substances in Road Tankers and Tanker Containers) Regulations 1992 and Road Traffic (Carriage of Dangerous Substances in Packages, etc.) Regulations 1992.

although it might prefer the word 'proactive'—of the United Kingdom's environmental enforcement agencies to date. It has succeeded in obtaining the imposition of substantial fines in proceedings against offenders who have polluted the ground water, streams, rivers, estuaries, and coastal waters for which it is responsible. It has extensive statutory powers to stop unauthorized discharges, to clean up pollution, to prosecute offenders, and to recover clean-up costs from them. The NRA is responsible for the issue of discharge consents to any person wishing to discharge polluting matter into waters controlled by the NRA.

There are close links between the NRA and HMIP, which administers integrated pollution control under the Environmental Protection Act 1990. HMIP consents for 'prescribed processes', for the purposes of IPC, which involve discharges into watercourses will be given, if at all, only after consultation between HMIP and the NRA. Implementation of water quality standards—a rather contentious subject in the United Kingdom—is imposed, in domestic legislation, through the WIA, which places water undertakers under a duty to provide drinking water and water used for food production to specified standards. Enforcement of the provisions is the responsibility of the Secretary of State for the Environment. Discharge of trade effluent into a sewerage undertaker's sewers is also governed by the WIA, and discharge without a consent from the sewerage undertaker is an offence.

There are a number of other detailed provisions which relate to protection of water resources[7] and the 1991 and 1992 Acts also give powers to the NRA and statutory undertakings to take steps to prevent pollution from occurring (for example, by compulsorily acquiring land). The Secretary of State for the Environment has the power, under ss.93 and 94 of the WRA, to designate water protection zones, and also nitrate-sensitive areas (designed to reduce the amount of nitrate leaching from agricultural land to watercourses).

1.1.3.4. Contaminated Land and Waste

Contaminated land is perhaps the area where regulation in the United Kingdom is least satisfactory. That is not necessarily a criticism of the legislation or of those who enforce it, but does highlight, perhaps more than any other issue, the basic conflict between those who wish to regulate and those who argue against regulation. It is sometimes very difficult to see that argument, at least in the context of contaminated land, other than as a conflict between commercial business interests on the one hand and responsibility to a wider community on the other.

It is also useful to look at disposal of waste with contaminated land.

[7] e.g. the Salmon and Freshwater Fisheries Act 1975; s.38, Countryside Act 1968.

Operation of waste disposal sites was, until very recently, governed by provisions in the Control of Pollution Act 1974, but is now covered by provisions contained in the EPA90. The EPA90 prohibits any unauthorized deposit, treatment, or disposal of household, industrial, or commercial waste. A business dealing with waste disposal, treatment, or storage must have a waste management licence which, if granted, remains in force until the licensing authority is satisfied that the site has been closed and reclaimed without any foreseeable continuing environmental risks. Licences are not transferable without the consent of the licensing authority (which is normally the county council). The EPA90 also establishes a duty of care which covers those persons importing, producing, carrying, keeping, treating, or disposing of household, industrial, or commercial waste. There are other provisions in the EPA90 which regulate collection, treatment and disposal of waste by waste-collection authorities and waste-disposal authorities.

Regulation of contaminated land in the United Kingdom is, to put it politely, in a state of flux. The EPA90 contained detailed provisions (in ss.61 and 143) relating to clean-up of contaminated land and the preparation of public registers of the most contaminated land in the country. In response to considerable pressure from commercial organizations and other pressure groups neither of those provisions was brought into force by the Government as originally proposed and both are the subject of continuing consultations between the Government and interested organizations. It is clear neither provision will now see the light of day in the form originally intended. What is not yet clear is how the Government will actually tackle the question of contaminated land. The two original sections go to the heart of the matter—the ability to make a polluter pay for clean-up and the ability of members of the public to know what land is contaminated. Both those issues have proved to be political dynamite. Many questions are raised when the detailed issues are considered. Who is 'the owner' of land who should be liable for clean-up costs? (The EPA90 used the term 'the owner' without further definition or explanation—much to the horror of the banks, among others.) What is 'contaminated land'? (Under s.143 it was nothing more than land which had at some time in the past been subject to one or more of a list of contaminative uses specified in regulations made under the section—irrespective of whether the land was actually contaminated or whether, if it was, any attempt was ever made to clean up the land.) What do you actually *do* about historically contaminated land apart from putting it on a register? (There was no provision in the EPA90 for establishment of anything like the United States' 'superfund'.)

1.1.3.5. IPC and APC

Part I of the EPA90 establishes two pollution control regimes—integrated pollution control and local authority air pollution control. IPC is operated by Her Majesty's Inspectorate of Pollution in England and Wales and by Her Majesty's Industrial Pollution Inspectorate in Scotland. The essence of IPC is that it is a system which applies to the major, most polluting industrial processes (which are called 'prescribed processes') under which the operators of those processes have to apply to HMIP for prior authorization to operate the processes. HMIP, in granting authorizations, has a duty to include conditions which ensure:

- That the operator uses the best available techniques not entailing excessive cost (known as BATNEEC);
- That if the process is likely to involve releases into more than one medium the operator must ensure that BATNEEC is used to minimize pollution to the environment as a whole, having regard to the best practicable environmental option (BPEO);
- Compliance with any direction given by the Secretary of State for the Environment to implement EC or other international obligations, or any statutory environmental quality standards or objectives, or other statutory limits, plans, or other requirements.

Where any of those requirements gives rise to a conflict the highest standard is to apply.

APC is enforced and administered by district and borough councils and is a regime designed to enforce the control of emissions to air alone from generally less polluting processes. APC authorization also requires compliance with BATNEEC.

1.2. CONFLICTS, PRESSURES, AND THE FUTURE

1.2.1. The Contaminated Land Dilemma

The problems of the Government in relation to ss.61 and 143 of the EPA90 has highlighted a number of contemporary problems which can be more generally associated with environmental regulation. One of the major questions is: what is the cost of environmental harm and who should pay for it? One of the other major questions is: what do you do if you cannot—or do not want to—answer a major question like that? The EPA90 left open the question of who was liable for clean-up costs of contaminated land. It did not define the 'owner' whom it sought to make liable. The banks thought an 'owner' meant a lender in possession when a borrower was in default. Pension funds thought an 'owner' was a landlord, who would be liable for the defaults of his tenant. The accountants worried about liability in receiverships and liquidations. Insurers revised, yet again, the terms of their pollution cover. One of the results was a powerful lobby against the Government that in the end persuaded it to reconsider.

One way of trying to avoid establishment of a national fund to pay for emergency clean-up work following pollution incidents is to seek to make as many people as possible liable for any incident of pollution in the hope that someone will have sufficient money to pay for the clean-up. That may well be what the Government wished when s.61 was originally drafted. Certainly establishment of anything akin to the United States' 'superfund' has not commended itself to the Government. The declared principle here is that the polluter pays—but what happens if the polluter has no money, or is able to pass on the cost to his customers through higher prices?

It is, of course, entirely arguable that the proper and efficient way to tackle environmental problems is to make as many people as possible potentially liable for them, in the knowledge that someone is then likely to remedy the problem. Whether that should be an excuse for not having available a fund to tackle emergency clean-up work is another matter, however. It is also fair to say that the EPA90's failure to define 'owner' may have been a calculated genuflection to our common law tradition, with the idea that in no time at all (and, doubtless, at considerable expense to the litigants involved) we would have had a body of case-law explaining what Parliament actually meant when it referred to 'owner'.

Our contaminated land problems in the United Kingdom highlight another problem which is obvious but worth stressing. A significant amount of pollution works on the time-bomb principle—you do not know it is there until it actually causes a problem. When it is discovered it may not be possible to find the polluter and even if it is possible he may be in no position to pay the clean-up costs. Further, it is quite possible that someone has carried out some activity on the land in the intervening period, which has exacerbated the position. Who should then be liable?

The third problem highlighted by our contaminated land saga is the thorny issue of public registers. Aside from what should actually be entered on the registers of contaminated land, it was clear that there was a substantial and powerful body of opinion (perhaps, more correctly, a powerful lobby of opinion) which felt there should be no new public records of contaminated land at all. All necessary information could be obtained by examination of existing maps and records, unjustifiable blight would be caused by the registers, the innocent would suffer . . . As is so often the case in environmental matters, the organized commercial lobby appears, for the time being at least, to have won the day and the question of the registers in being reconsidered.

The 'polluter pays' principle is by no means lacking in sense, but it cannot be a complete philosophy. The polluter may not have the means to pay or may have disappeared. There is a potential conflict between public availability of information—which may help to police the 'polluter pays' principle—and the proper interests of those who might be commercially affected by the disclosure of the information. Is proper environmental regulation altogether a more altruistic goal than any of us will ever be able to achieve in the face of so many conflicting interests?

2

The Role of Her Majesty's Inspectorate of Pollution

DAVID SLATER

2.1. HMIP: LINCHPIN OR FULCRUM?

Is HMIP the linchpin of Integrated Pollution Control? That is an interesting view, and not a bad one. Perhaps 'fulcrum' captures rather better the notion of HMIP as providing the balance point between two apparently opposing interests. Whether they are actually strongly opposed is a moot point. Economic growth is essential if we are to maintain and improve living standards around the world, and to afford the care for the environment that sustainable development demands. But it is important to emphasize that HMIP appreciates that IPC is only one device which the Government has available to implement its overall strategy for environmental protection. There are other devices; some are already in place; others may come in the future.

Central to this strategy for environmental protection is the principle of *stewardship* which arises from acknowledging that we do not inherit the earth from our parents, we borrow it from our children. We must pass our environment on to future generations in a state which allows them to meet their own needs. This lies at the heart of the principle of *sustainable development*, which is widely accepted by governments around the world as a foundation for living in harmony with our environment. Much thought is being given to this concept at the moment, but it does not mean zero growth or an end to consumption. The Department of the Environment's recently published consultation paper on the strategy for sustainable development is stimulating strong debate, which it is hoped will put flesh on the bones of the idea.

The Government has also embarked on the exercise of identifying those pieces of legislation which place unnecessary burdens on industry, and the regulatory framework as a whole is being scrutinized from this angle. However, while the opportunities and strengths of all the various options have to be clearly identified, it is rather limiting if we take too compartmentalized a view of the situation. Regulation is not necessarily a strait-jacket, and this will be expanded on when IPC is discussed in more detail. It may be that other options offer less freedom, or are less effective, than we might at first imagine. The objectives must be very clearly identified, and, once that is done, we should view the range of these options as a continuum which must be tuned and focused in a skilful way so that the objective is achieved.

As a regulator—*especially* as a regulator—I believe there is no point in regulation for the sake of regulation. That is demoralizing not only for industry, but also for the enforcers who would not wish to work for a body whose brief and powers they did not find credible. HMIP sees IPC as only one means to achieve an end, and it is upon that end that it must remain focused in order to discharge its responsibilities in the most closely targeted and effective manner.

So—linchpin or fulcrum? HMIP does see itself as very much 'holding the ring', through its role as regulator, between government, industry, and the public. The introduction of the system of IPC, embodied in the Environmental Protection Act 1990, marked an important milestone in the development of the legislative philosophy and framework in this country. For the first time it provided a mechanism and a legal basis for looking at the impact which a process *as a whole* has on the environment *as a whole*, and for balancing the imperative of protecting the environment against the reality that this protection has a financial cost.

From that starting point sound decisions can be made on priorities for environmental protection, and, equally important, sound decisions on investment to deliver those priorities. The Environmental Protection Act 1990 is very much in the Anglo-Saxon tradition of 'Clapham Omnibus Reasonableness'. Contrast this with the Water Industry Act 1991 which is very Napoleonic in its stringent criteria and inflexibility. Internally, the analogy of radar guns and speed traps versus governors and tachographs for controlling vehicle speeds is used. The latter system is more effective, more sophisticated (flexible), and, we think, more intelligent.

2.2. OBJECTIVES OF IPC

2.2.1. Environmental Protection Act

Part I of the Environmental Protection Act 1990 sets out a series of 'reasonableness' objectives which must be met in the operation of prescribed processes. These objectives are:

- to use the best available techniques not entailing excessive cost (BATNEEC) for preventing releases, or where that is not practicable, for minimizing and rendering them harmless;

- to ensure that BATNEEC is used to minimize the pollution which may be caused to the environment as a whole by the releases—the best practicable environmental option (BPEO);
- to comply with any Directions, limits, or quality standards set by the Secretary of State.

These objectives fall into two categories:

- those that are within the purview and discretion—subject to any appeal to the Secretary of State—of the Chief Inspector;
- those that are determined directly by the Secretary of State and which HMIP is required to implement.

The BATNEEC provision applies only to those objectives set by HMIP: there is no economic consideration in the implementation of quality standards, national plans etc.

2.2.2. Meaning of BATNEEC

Best refers purely to the effect of the technique on the environment, that is, it is that technique (or those techniques, for there may be more than one set of techniques with comparable effectiveness) that is most effective in preventing, minimizing, or rendering harmless polluting releases. *Available* means procurable by the operator in question. This does not imply that the technique has to be in general use in the United Kingdom or overseas, but it does recognize that novel techniques, proven only at pilot-plant scale, require a degree of business confidence before they can be said to be available. *Techniques* is defined in the Act. It embraces not only the plant and equipment in the process, but also the way it is operated, the manning and supervision levels, the training and qualifications of the staff, et cetera. *Not entailing excessive cost* needs to be taken in two contexts, depending on whether it is applied to new processes or existing processes. Nevertheless, in all cases BAT can properly be modified by economic considerations, where the costs of applying the best available techniques would be excessive in relation to the nature of the industry and to the environmental protection to be achieved.

What we seek to achieve, through IPC, is the right balance between cost to industry of better processes and abatement equipment, and cost to the environment in terms of the damage caused by releases. Superimposed on this is the objective of identifying and achieving the best practicable environmental option—ensuring that any substances which are released are released in such a way as to minimize the overall harm.

2.3. RESPONSIBILITIES THAT IPC BRINGS

We have looked briefly at the basic tenets of IPC, but it is important to recognize where the responsibilities lie in delivering them. The key point is that the onus is on the operator. The regulator does not assume responsibility by detailed prescription (compare the German system).

2.3.1. The Operator's Responsibilities

The primary responsibility lies with the operator of the process. It is up to him to conceive, design, build, and operate his process in such a way as to meet the requirements of the law. He must use the best available techniques not entailing excessive cost (BATNEEC) to prevent release of prescribed substances to the environment, or, where that is not practicable, to minimize their release and render it harmless, and to render harmless any other substances released. He must also achieve the best practicable environmental option (BPEO) for the process, ensuring that its overall adverse impact on the environment is minimized.

2.3.2. HMIP's Responsibilities

HMIP plays a dual role in supporting industry. First, it provides a regulatory service that endeavours to ensure that these requirements are met in each case. It seeks to treat companies even-handedly both in determining authorizations and in enforcing their conditions. Second, it undertakes research to support decision-making, and ensures that the results of this research are made publicly available.

HMIP has high expectations of IPC, and great confidence in it. It *will* deliver. However, we must not expect delivery overnight. Implementation alone is happening over a five-year timescale, after which HMIP is required to review each authorization not less frequently than every four years. Truly scientific methods of looking at 'harm', for example, are being developed. The 'critical loads' approach is one which HMIP is using to aid its determinations. But there is a long way to go, and again, a balance is being sought between the right level of caution and the need to ensure that industry is not overburdened.

Part of HMIP's research effort is being concentrated upon developing methodologies for determining BPEO for a process, and for achieving the balance which BATNEEC requires. This work recently reached a stage at which it could be shared with industry and other interested parties, for whom, it is hoped, it will prove a useful tool in decision-making.

2.3.3. Three-Pronged Approach

Three important threads of Government policy are woven into IPC—and indeed are common to much recent environmental legislation. First, IPC takes a holistic approach, ensuring that substances which are unavoidably released to the environment are released to the medium to which they will cause least damage. Second, it embodies the precautionary principle: prevention is better than cure. The tontine goes: prevent, minimize, render harmless. Third, the regulatory process, from application, through authorization, to regular returns of releases to the environment, and, where appropriate, to the enforcement action taken by HMIP, is open to public scrutiny and comment.

2.3.4. The Public

HMIP is also very clear that the obligation upon it is to serve the public:

- by taking into account specific comment on individual applications for authorization;
- by ensuring that operators provide data which demonstrate their compliance with the terms of their authorizations; and
- by the provision and maintenance of the public registers.

This is no less important than the obligation to provide a good regulatory service to industry, and is one which HMIP endeavours to meet with the same high level of commitment. The increased use being made of its public registers provides an interesting indication of the way in which the public is responding to the wider role and greater involvement which the regulatory process provides, and this is very encouraging.

2.3.5. The Government's Responsibilities

Part I of the Environmental Protection Act 1990 also doubles as a vehicle through which the Government can delegate a variety of other obligations, particularly international ones, which are laid upon it. A major example of this is the United Kingdom's obligation under the Large Combustion Plant Directive. This provides for a phased reduction of SO_2 and NO_x releases from a number of specified processes. The Secretary of State has, in response to this Directive, made a National Plan for its delivery, and HMIP, using powers given to it in the EPA90, translates this into limits for individual processes, and monitors and enforces these limits. Delivery of these obligations is quite separate from the BATNEEC and BPEO requirements of IPC, although they are written seamlessly into the authorization documents for the processes concerned.

2.4. SOPHISTICATION AND FLEXIBILITY

It is very easy, both for HMIP and for industry, to be so close to the system and so involved with the job that they fail to see wood for trees. IPC is an extremely sophisticated concept, and it requires an equal degree of sophistication from both regulators and industry to get the very best out of it. This sophistication stems from the inherent flexibility in the system.

IPC is not prescriptive. It leaves management decisions which are rightly the preserve of managers firmly in their hands, while providing them with a framework on which their decisions must be based, and a set of objectives which they must meet. HMIP, through the Chief Inspector's Guidance Notes to Inspectors, provides indicators of the performance standards which can be achieved for particular processes using BATNEEC. It is up to industry to decide for itself how to meet—or improve on—those performance standards, and to demonstrate to HMIP and the public how this will be done, and that it *is* being done. If the process is already in existence, then it is up to industry to show HMIP their plans for bringing it up to the higher standards which a new plant could—and would be required to—achieve now.

HMIP has found that there are organizations which fail to demonstrate these things in their applications, and are reticent about their improvement programmes. In these cases it must ensure fair play for other companies, for the environment, and for the public, and is likely to impose requirements upon the operator which he might find unpalatable. The choice is entirely his.

The application process provides a shop-window for industry. Provided the process is meeting the essential IPC objectives, it is for management to decide how much better they want to be. They can use the authorization to make commitments, to be inspected in regard to those commitments, and to demonstrate to the world that they are meeting them.

2.5. LEGAL ASPECTS

IPC is, of course, by no means the only regulatory regime which HMIP has to deliver. The other main area of its work is the implementation and enforcement of the Radioactive Substances Act 1960 (as amended, and now consolidated into the Radioactive Substances Act 1993). In addition, HMIP acts on behalf of the Secretary of State under the Water Industry Act 1991 in respect of discharge of certain prescribed substances to the sewerage system. There are one or two other pieces of environmental legislation which also fall to HMIP, and it is bound by Regulations (SI 1991

No. 507) in respect of making available to the public that information on the environment that it holds.

HMIP's decisions as regulator are being challenged in a number of ways. Applications for IPC authorization are placed, in their entirety, upon the public registers unless the Secretary of State deems that to do this would prejudice the interests of national security, or unless the Chief Inspector accepts an applicant's case for exclusion on the grounds that 'its being contained in the register would prejudice to an unreasonable degree the commercial interests of that individual or person'. In this latter situation the applicant has the right to appeal to the Secretary of State if his case is rejected. At the next stage, process operators sometimes feel it necessary to appeal against the imposition of a condition in an authorization. It is possible for many of these to be resolved without resorting to the full panoply of an appeal—which may be by written representation, or a hearing. But there are cases in which the procedure follows its full course. Anyone can seek judicial review of an HMIP decision, as Greenpeace has done in respect of decisions concerning the Sellafield site.

HMIP retains in-house legal expertise, and does not hesitate to augment this with external legal assistance when necessary. In an area of law where so many of the decisions must be based on scientific evidence interpreted with professional judgment, it is not surprising that challenges are made. The fact that it is challenged, and that these challenges come from both sides of the equation, suggests that HMIP is treading a difficult path with a fair measure of success.

2.6. CONCLUSION: THE FUTURE

Environmental legislation and indeed environmental policy is in an evolutionary phase. A range of options and opportunities is open to the Government. Some are fairly well defined—such as the proposals for an Environment Agency, to provide a more efficient 'one-stop-shop' service than is presently possible. Others are still at the thinking stage—such as, how do we really tie down this nebulous concept of sustainable development and turn it into the nuts and bolts of a workable mechanism? As far as IPC is concerned, there are further opportunities. An important one lies in the interface with planning. Can the two systems be made to fit and work more synergistically together, for the benefit of industry, the public, and regulators—and the environment?

3

Environmental Information and Audit

WILLIAM BIRTLES

3.1. INTRODUCTION

This chapter is concerned with freedom of access to information on the environment. The United Kingdom still does not have a freedom of information statute for central government although one now exists for local government.[1] The recent EC Directive on Freedom of Access to Information on the Environment[2] as well as the most recent United Kingdom legislation referred to below has started an irresistible move to confirm the right of the citizen, pressure group, company, or state agency to know much more about the environment. The concept of a 'right' to environmental information is crucial because it improves environmental monitoring systems, increases the quality of environmental information which is gathered, and makes much of that information available to the public. These effects will, in turn, increase public participation in the procedures to control pollution, including the enforcement of environmental laws.[3] What follows is a modest attempt to set out some of the developments in the last few years in this crucial area of environmental law.

3.2. REGISTERS

The provision for the keeping of registers of environmental information which are available to the public is one now well established in English law. Thus local planning authorities are required to keep registers of all planning applications[4] and conditions imposed on planning permissions

[1] Local Government (Access to Information) Act 1985. There is a substantial amount of UK literature on the general issue of freedom of information. The best general survey is P. Birkinshaw, *Government and Information: The Law Relating to Access, Disclosure and Regulation* (London: Butterworths, 1990).

[2] The Directive was adopted by the Council of Ministers on 7 June 1990 (90/313/EEC: OJ 1990 L158/56, 23 June 1990).

[3] See P. Sands, 'European Community Environmental Law: Legislation, the European Court of Justice and Common-Interest Groups' (1990) 53 *MLR* 685 at 689.

[4] Town and Country Planning Act 1990 s.69.

are registrable in the Local Land Charges Register.[5] Furthermore, what is now s.100A–K of the Local Government Act 1972 (introduced by the Local Government (Access to Information) Act 1985) makes minutes of committee decisions available to the public, together with reports and documents relating to the decision-making process. Section 20 of the Environmental Protection Act 1990 (EPA90) requires each local authority to set up a register giving details of all integrated pollution control (IPC) and local authority air-pollution-controlled processes in its area. These must include prescribed particulars of applications, authorizations, notices, directions issued by the Secretary of State, revocations, appeal decisions, process data, convictions for certain offences, and other particulars as prescribed by regulation of, or relating to, the matters set out in the Act. Local authorities must also supply the information under their own control in respect of local authority air-pollution control applications. Information relating to IPC processes is supplied to local authorities by HMIP. The information is to be kept from the register only on grounds of national security or commercial confidentiality.[6] Information on noise data can also be obtained from local authority environmental health departments under the Control of Noise (Measurement and Registers) Regulations 1976 (SI 1976 No. 37). Information on air emissions can be obtained by virtue of the Health and Safety (Emissions into the Atmosphere) Regulations (SI 1989 No. 319) and the Control of Industrial Air Pollution (Registration of Works) Regulations 1989 (SI 1989 No. 318). Section 143 of the EPA90 enables the Secretary of State to make regulations requiring local authorities to maintain a register of contaminated land within their area. However, as a result of the consultation process and pressure from industry, a further round of consultation is in progress and it is doubtful that the section will be implemented.

Section 20 also requires HMIP to keep a register of all applications made under Part I of the EPA90 as it is responsible for granting authorizations for the largest and most complex industrial plants. One of the ten copies of an IPC application and relevant materials is given to the National Rivers Authority (NRA) for inclusion in its register. A local authority whose area adjoins that of a Port Health Authority must include in its register corresponding information contained in the Port Authority's register. So far as water discharges are concerned, the local authority's register must also contain prescribed particulars with such information as is contained in any register maintained by the Chief

[5] Local Land Charges Act 1975 s.1(1)(b)(i). As to conditions imposed by planning permissions before 1 Aug. 1977, see s.2(e).

[6] EPA90 ss.21–2; the Environmental Protection (Applications, Appeals and Registers) Regulations 1991 (SI 1991 No. 507) and GGN3—Applications and Registers (D.o.E./HMSO).

Inspector of HMIP as relates to the carrying on in the area of the local authority of a prescribed process in relation to which the Chief Inspector has functions under Part I of the EPA90.

The NRA has a statutory duty to maintain registers containing prescribed particulars of abstraction and impounding licences, for the purposes of works discharges, detail of persons and premises, prescribed particulars of water quality objectives, applications for consents, consents given, and information produced by analysis of water samples, amongst other matters.[7]

Waste regulation authorities are required by ss.64–6 of the EPA90 to maintain a register containing prescribed particulars of or in relation to current or recently current licences granted by that authority or current or recently current applications to the authority along with modification applications, notices issued by the authority, appeals, certificates of completion, convictions for any offence under Part II of the EPA90, and various other matters. There are detailed provisions relating to the exclusion of information affecting national security and certain confidential information. There is a separate duty on each waste regulation authority to establish and maintain a register of carriers of controlled waste which is open to public inspection free of charge, and indexed and arranged in such a way as to enable members of the public readily to trace information contained in it.[8]

Water and sewerage undertakers are under a duty by s.196 of the Water Industry Act 1991 to keep records about trade effluent discharge consents in respect of discharges into public sewers. Finally, every hazardous substance authority is under a duty to keep a register with prescribed particulars relating to hazardous substances consents.[9]

There has been very little reported empirical research into the operation of the register system. T. P. Burton of the University of Hull found that there was not much use of water registers.[10] Recent empirical research in which the present writer was involved showed few difficulties but varying practices by different bodies.

The most important exception to the register system is the category of 'confidential information'. Unfortunately there has been little authoritative guidance as to what this term means. On 9 November 1992 the Secretary of State decided two appeals under Part I of the EPA90. He allowed an appeal by National Power that details of future emissions at

[7] WRA91 ss.189–91; The Control of Pollution (Registers) Regulations 1989 (SI 1989 No. 1160).

[8] The Controlled Waste (Registration of Carriers and Seizure of Vehicles) Regulations 1991 (SI 1991 No. 1624).

[9] Planning (Hazardous Substances) Act 1990 s.28.

[10] T. P. Burton, 'Access to Environmental Information: The UK Experience of Water Registers' (1989) 1 *JEL* 192.

eighteen of its power stations should not be made public. This would reveal future needs for fuel and choice of fuel. The basis for the decision appears to be that the information required by HMIP was not directly relevant to the application under Part I of the EPA90. On the same date he also decided an appeal by PowerGen.

3.3. THE ENVIRONMENTAL REGULATIONS 1992

3.3.1. Introduction

Following a D.o.E. Consultation Paper,[11] the Secretary of State for the Environment made the Environmental Information Regulations 1992 (SI 1992 No. 3240).[12] These Regulations are designed to implement EC Directive 90/313/EEC (OJ 1990 L158/56, 23.06.90).[13] They differ little from the draft Regulations sent out for consultation on 29 October 1992 (apart from widening the exemption relating to legal proceedings discussed below). The Regulations came into force on 31 December 1992 and apply to Great Britain only. As yet they appear to have made no impact whatsoever, which may be due to the fact that neither the Government nor the media appear to have provided much public information about them. Catch-22 yet again!

3.3.2. The Effect of EC Law

Before discussing the Regulations in detail it is important to bear in mind what effect EC law has on their application and construction. First, the courts must give effect to the EC Directive in construing the Regulations.[14] Second, in any event the Directive may be directly applicable and an aggrieved person would have a separate cause of action against the United Kingdom Government under the Directive itself.[15] Finally, under EC law the United Kingdom Government is liable to pay compensation to an aggrieved party for its failure fully to implement an EC Directive.[16]

[11] *The Government's Proposals for the Implementation in UK Law of the EC Directive on the Freedom of Access to Information on the Environment* (London: D.o.E., Jan. 1992). The best commentary on these proposals is D. Hughes, (1992) 4(3) *LMELR*, 73–108. I am greatly indebted to this article.

[12] See W. Birtles, 'A Right to Know: The Environmental Information Regulations 1992' (1993) *JPEL* 615.

[13] See W. Birtles (1991) *JPEL* 607; L. Krämer, *Focus on European Environmental Law*, ch. 14 (London: Sweet and Maxwell, 1992).

[14] *Litster* v. *Forth Dry Dock and Engineering Co.* [1990] 1 AC 546.

[15] *Van Duyn* v. *Home Office* [1974] ECR 1337.

[16] *Francovich and Bonifaci* v. *Italy* [1992] IRLR 84.

3.3.3. Application of Regulations

By Regulation 2(1) the Regulations apply to any information which

(a) relates to the environment;
(b) is held by a relevant person in an accessible form and otherwise than for the purposes of any judicial or legislative functions; and
(c) is not (apart from these Regulations) either—
  (i) information which is required, in accordance with any statutory provision, to be provided on request to every person who makes a request; or
  (ii) information contained in records which are required, in accordance with any statutory provision, to be made available for inspection by every person who wishes to inspect them.

Regulation 2(1) (a) is amplified by Regulation 2(2) which provides that:

information relates to the environment if, and only if, it relates to any of the following, that is to say—

(a) the state of any water or air, the state of flora or fauna, the state of any soil or the state of any natural site or other land;
(b) any activities or measures (including activities giving rise to noise or any other nuisance) which adversely affect anything mentioned in sub-paragraph (a) above or are likely adversely to affect anything so mentioned;
(c) any activities or administrative or other measures (including any environmental management programmes) which are designed to protect anything so mentioned.

Regulation 2(1) is based on Article 2a of the EC Directive which defines 'information relating to the environment' as meaning:

any available information in written, visual, aural or data-base form on the state of water, air, soil, fauna, flora, land and natural sites, and on activities (including those which give rise to nuisances such as noise) or measures adversely affecting or likely so to affect these, and on activities or measures designed to protect these, including administrative measures and environmental management programmes.

Although wide, this definition does not include climatic changes nor human conditions in the aftermath of an environmental disaster, for example, the Camelford water pollution case. It does, however, cover environmental damage which is likely to occur as well as that which has already occurred. It would not cover activities where there is no *adverse* impact, or where it is considered unlikely there will be an adverse impact.[17] Furthermore, a literal reading of the listed media would

[17] As Hughes cogently puts it: 'When CFCs were initially developed and utilised as propellants, etc., is it not true that their ultimate impact on the ozone layer was not foreseen,

exclude, for example, microbial and bacteriological life-forms which may not be regarded as fauna but whose functioning may be essential to the environment.[18]

Regulation 2(1)(b) is amplified by Regulation 2(3) which defines relevant persons as:

(a) all such Ministers of the Crown, Government departments, local authorities and other persons carrying out functions of public administration at a national, regional or local level as, for the purposes of or in connection with their functions, have responsibilities in relation to the environment; and
(b) any body with public responsibilities for the environment which does not fall within sub-paragraph (a) above but is under the control of a person falling within that sub-paragraph.

The word 'as' in the third line of Regulation 2(3) is assumed to be a misprint for 'and' which is the word used in the draft Regulations sent out for consultation.

While paragraph (a) is clear the same cannot be said for (b). This is provided to implement Article 6 of the EC Directive. The D.o.E. Consultation Paper Annexe D listed a substantial number of 'public bodies' with responsibilities for the environment. There are some obvious omissions, for example, BNFL, and the privatized water and sewerage companies are not *public* bodies but do have public environmental responsibilities. The water companies are also subject to considerable supervision by the Secretary of State and Ofwat. Other supervisory bodies are National Power, PowerGen, and British Gas. A literal interpretation of the phrases, 'any body with public responsibilities for the environment' and 'under the control of a person' within subparagraph (a) means the exclusion of these bodies. In some cases the regulatory agency itself, for example, Ofwat, Ofgas, and Offer, is included while the private bodies they regulate are not. Given the massive effect which the activities of the bodies named above can have on the environment it makes no sense at all to exclude them. Whether they are excluded will become a matter for the Courts.[19]

Regulation 2(1)(c) is further amplified by Regulation 2(4) which provides:

and indeed they were hailed as highly useful and beneficial chemicals? The problem is that some activities are initially recognisable as likely to adversely affect the environment, but does not the application of the precautionary principle demand that there should be openness over the development of new processes and materials where details are known to governmental agencies and where it is considered that there is the potential in the process, etc., to affect the environment? These processes which can be shown to be "innocent" surely have little to fear from disclosures being made.' Hughes, *Land Management*, 76.

[18] Ibid.

[19] Ibid. 77.

(4) In these Regulations—
'Information' includes anything contained in any records;
'records' includes registers, reports and returns, as well as computer records and other records kept otherwise than in a document; and
'statutory provision' means any provision made by or under any enactment.

It is not clear whether this covers precisely the same ground covered by Article 2a set out above, but as the Regulations have to be interpreted to conform with the EC Directive attempts to exclude, for example, visual or aural forms must be included within the word 'information'.

3.3.4. The Duty to Make Environmental Information Available

Every relevant person who holds any information to which the Regulations apply 'shall make that information available to every person who requests it' (Regulation 3(1)). The duty is owed to the person requesting the information (Regulation 3(6)), and it is that person who will have the legal interest to take proceedings to enforce the right.

That primary duty is made effective by Regulation 3(2), which imposes a further duty on every relevant person to make arrangements to give effect to the primary duty to ensure:

(a) that every request made for the purposes of Regulation 3(1) is responded to as soon as possible;
(b) that no such request is responded to more than two months after it is made; and
(c) that, where the response to such a request contains a refusal to make information available, the refusal is in writing and specifies the reason for the refusal.

The Regulations themselves do not give any further guidance as to how these arrangements are to have effect in practice. The guidance notes issued by the D.o.E. with the Regulations[20] say that such guidance is impossible to give in a way which will cover all situations. General guidance is given to the extent that each relevant person is advised to report what information is available by means, for example, of an annual report, and consideration should be given to publishing reports of information. The public register system is again commended (para. 26) and the necessity for answering personal requests is emphasized (para. 27). However, if it is not known what information exists it is extremely difficult to know what information may be asked for! Complaints to councillors or MPs, or the time-consuming process of judicial review are not a substitute for a legal duty imposed upon all relevant persons to index and

[20] D.o.E., 'Guidance on the Implementation of the Environmental Information Regulations 1992 in Great Britain', 21 Dec. 1992.

publish the environmental information held by them indicating for what categories of information exemption is claimed.[21]

Provision is made in Regulation 3 to enable the relevant person:

(a) to refuse a request for information in cases where a request is manifestly unreasonable or is formulated in too general a manner: Regulation 3(3).

A literal interpretation of this provision could drive a coach and horses straight through the Regulations. If there is no clear published index of information on the environment by the relevant person concerned, how on earth can an interested person know what to ask for? The relevant person decides whether or not the request is 'manifestly unreasonable' or 'is formulated in too general a manner'. Such an administrative decision could only be challenged by political pressure or by way of judicial review. What this provision implies—as do others in the Regulations—is the need for a statutory appeals tribunal to deal with the multiplicity of points which these Regulations could give rise to if they are widely known and, it is hoped, used:

(b) to include provision for the imposition of a charge in respect of the costs reasonably attributable to the supply of information: Regulation 3(4)(a);
(c) to make the supply of any information conditional on the payment of such a charge: Regulation 3(4)(b); and
(d) to make the information available in such form, and at such times and places, as may be reasonable: Regulation 3(5).

3.3.5. Exceptions to Disclosure

Regulation 4(3) lists the cases under which requested information must be treated as confidential.[22] They are as follows:

1. the information is capable of being treated as confidential and its disclosure in response to a request would (apart from Regulation 3(7)) contravene any statutory provision or rule of law or would involve a breach of any agreement: Regulation 4(3)(a).
2. the information is personal information contained in records held in relation to an individual who has not given his consent to its disclosure: Regulation 4(3)(b).

The D.o.E. guidance notes make it clear that personal information should not be withheld when there are provisions to the contrary, for

[21] Hughes, *Land Management*, 77.

[22] For the general law of breach of confidence see F. Gurry, *Breach of Confidence* (Oxford: Clarendon Press, 1984); S. Mehigan and D. Griffiths; *Restraint of Trade and Business Secrets: Law and Practice*, 2nd edn. (London: Longmans, 1991); *The Law Commission, Breach of Confidence* (Law Com. 110 Cmnd. 8388 (1981); For a comprehensive Australian survey see R. Dean, *The Law of Trade Secrets* (Sydney: Law Book Co. Ltd., 1990). For an academic analysis see M. J. Trebilcock, *The Common Law of Restraint of Trade* (London: Sweet & Maxwell Ltd., 1986).

example, information supplied under the Environmental Protection (Stray Dogs) Regulations 1992 (SI 1992 No. 288).[23] The D.o.E. guidance notes go on to say that unless there is provision to the contrary, information containing the addresses of individual dwellings should be restricted in order to safeguard the property against possible blighting (the standard property information form used by solicitors tends to incorporate such information when it becomes publicly available). Examples would be radon tests (where householders are told the test results will not be released) and the quality of drinking water supplies serving single dwellings for domestic purposes only. In such cases it should be possible to release summary information or remove reference to the actual address and release the remaining information.[24]

3. the information is held by the relevant person in consequence of having been supplied by a person who was not under, and could not have been put under, any legal obligation to supply it to the relevant person and has not consented to its disclosure: Regulation 4(3)(c).

The justification for this exception is that it would inhibit the 'present open and constructive discussion between environmental control authorities and industry and the gathering of information on which environmental studies are based'. Given the criticisms which have long existed about the close and far too friendly relationships between environmental regulators and polluters this exception would cover up enormous quantities of environmental information which those affected could properly be said to have a right to know. It is difficult to see how the honest exchange of information and views between government and industry can be inhibited by the publication of that kind of information. In the writer's view this exception smacks of the old law of Crown privilege which was frequently used to cover up the incompetence of ministers and civil servants. The D.o.E. guidance notes show some awareness of the problem and state that suppliers of information should be encouraged to waive this exception.

4. the disclosure of the information in response to that request would, in the circumstances, increase the likelihood of damage to the environment affecting anything to which the information relates: Regulation 4(3)(d).

The examples given in the D.o.E. guidance notes are non-contentious: information about the location of nesting sites, rare habitats, or endangered/protected species. Also included is information about possible Sites of Special Scientific Interest not being made available until a formal notice is served, thereby avoiding the risk of pre-emptive damage being caused to the site before it was protected.[25] However the phraseology of

[23] D.o.E., 'Guidance on Implementation', para. 65.
[24] Ibid. 66.
[25] Ibid. 70.

the exception would enable a much broader view to be taken by a relevant person in refusing to grant disclosure of information.

3.3.6. Information Which May be Treated as Confidential

Regulation 4(2) sets out the following additional cases where requested information *may* be treated as confidential. These are:

1. information relating to matters affecting international relations, national defence or public security: Regulation 4(2)(a);
2. information relating to, or to anything which is or has been the subject of, any legal or other proceedings (whether actual or prospective): Regulation 4(2)(b). This definition is greatly extended by Regulation 4(5) which defines 'legal or other proceedings' as including 'any disciplinary proceedings, the proceedings at any local or other public inquiry and the proceedings at any hearing conducted by a person appointed under any enactment for the purpose of affording an opportunity to persons to make representations or objections with respect to any matter'.

While there are clearly strong arguments in favour of some limitation on the disclosure of information in relation to prospective (particularly criminal) proceedings and proceedings which are actually taking place, it is difficult to see what justification there can be for refusing to release information which relates to proceedings which are completed. Even where proceedings have not yet been commenced it is difficult to see why, for example, a government ministry such as MAFF should be entitled to refuse to disclose information which will assist one or either party in civil litigation in which MAFF itself is not involved. Such information would be discoverable if MAFF itself were a party to the litigation.

3. information relating to the confidential deliberations of any relevant person or to the contents of any internal communications of a body corporate or other undertaking or organization: Regulation 4(2)(c).

Under the Local Government Act 1972, s.100A-K, the public has rights of access to council, committee, and subcommittee meetings and to the papers and background papers relating to those meetings. The information relating to the confidential part of such meetings may be released by a local authority. No such rights of access exist in relation to central government. Internal communications cover a wide variety of matters and according to the D.o.E. guidance notes could include classified documents, information passed between officials in the course of their duties, deliberations during the decision-making process, and advice on policy and recommendations given to ministers and members. It does not need much imagination to realize how much information could be kept secret under this exception. Once again the comparison with the United States is striking.

4. information contained in a document or other record which is still in the course of completion: Regulation 4(2)(d).

Again, it is difficult to see the logic of this exception. The D.o.E. guidance notes say this:

Bodies may carry out their own studies including inspection, testing, evaluation, monitoring and research; data may be collected in the process. It is reasonable that access to the documents and data should await the completion of the study so that analysis and interpretation can proceed *unhindered.*[26] (Emphasis added.)

Quite why the disclosure of data should impede its analysis is beyond the present writer. In the case of a major public inquiry into, for example, a nuclear power station or a road widening scheme it is important that objectors have early access to the database upon which the proposer's case is based. Experience at such inquiries suggest that a proposer is often unwilling to provide early access to such information precisely because it undermines the case put forward. There is the added complication that a relevant person can always say that a document or record is still in the course of completion;

5. information affecting matters to which any commercial or industrial confidentiality attaches or any intellectual property: Regulation 4(2)(e).

The D.o.E. guidance notes suggest that there are two ways of proceeding when the information has been received from a third party under contract or statute: to classify information when it is received or to classify it when access is first requested. Some guidance is given as to the procedure to be followed when adopting either approach.[27]

3.3.7. Existing Rights to Information

Regulation 5 deals with information which is not covered by these Regulations but which is required under any other statutory provision to be made available to any person. There is now a duty on any relevant person to make arrangements to implement such statutory duty so as to provide a similar procedure for that required for information covered by the Regulations so as to secure:

1. that every request for information relating to the environment which is made for the purposes of that provision is responded to as soon as possible;
2. that each request is responded to within two months of being made;
3. that, where the response to such a request contains a refusal to make information available, the refusal is in writing and specifies the reasons for the refusal; and
4. that no charge that exceeds a reasonable amount is made for making information relating to the environment available in accordance with that provision.

[26] Ibid. 53. [27] Ibid. 56–61.

3.3.8. Rights of Appeal

Where a relevant person refuses a request to make information available the refusal must be in writing and specify the reasons for the refusal: Regulation 3(2)(c). Examples given in the D.o.E. guidance notes are:

1. that the organization does not consider itself a relevant person and thus subject to the requirements of the Regulations;
2. that the relevant person does not consider that the information requested is 'environmental' as defined by the Regulations;
3. that the information requested is not held by the person;
4. that the information is used by the person acting in its judicial or legislative capacity; or
5. that one of the exemptions apply.[28]

There is no new statutory right of appeal given by these Regulations. Any applicant dissatisfied with the refusal by a relevant person to make information available, or who considers that a request for information has been inadequately answered or delayed may seek a remedy through judicial or administrative review, for instance, by utilizing an MP, local councillor, or board member, or by way of complaint (in appropriate cases) to the local or parliamentary ombudsman. On the matter of European law it may ultimately be necessary to go to the European Court of Justice.

3.4. OTHER EC DEVELOPMENTS

It is not always easy to follow the development of EC law because there is not always clear and open reporting-back of the progress of measures. Recently two waste measures went to the Council of EC Ministers and were agreed, their final forms requiring consultation with the European Parliament. Without warning, the directive suddenly appeared in the Official Journal. This happened with the amendments to the Framework Directive,[29] and a similar situation has been reached with an amendment to the Directive on Toxic and Dangerous Waste, the final form of which was agreed at a Council meeting in December 1990.[30]

A directive has now been proposed by the Commission to make the Directive on Freedom of Access to Information on the Environment applicable to the Commission itself and it is to be hoped that this will inspire the EC authorities to provide better information on the progress of legislation.

[28] D.o.E., 'Guidance on Implementation', para. 71.

[29] OJ L194/39 15 July 1975. For the amendment see OJ L78/32 26 Mar. 1991.

[30] See OJ L084/43 31 Mar. 1978 for the original Directive. The amendment is OJ L353/59 17 Dec. 1990.

A second development is the establishment of EC Environmental Databases. This initiative was the result of the Council's CORINE Decision.[31] Initially this was for a demonstration project until the end of 1988. In 1990 the CORINE Decision was extended for two more years.[32]

A third development is the European Environment Agency Regulation[33] which is intended to provide the EC and the Member States with objective, reliable, and comparable information at the European level to enable environmental protection measures to be taken, to assess the results of such measures, and to ensure that the public is properly informed. The Agency will be an autonomous entity having separate legal personality, and it will be run by a management board, an executive director, and a scientific committee. The Agency's principal task will be to act as a monitoring body, gathering information, establishing the network, providing the EC and Member States with objective information, and recording, collating, and assessing data on the state of the environment. The Agency will also ensure that environmental data at European level are comparable, providing European environmental information to appropriate international bodies, ensuring broad dissemination of reliable information (including a report on the state of the environment every three years), and stimulating the development of environmental forecasting techniques and methods for assessing environmental costs. The Agency's assessment function relates to the pressure on and quality and sensitivity of the environment, and is directed to certain priority areas which are to include 'trans-frontier, plurinational and global phenomena' and the socio-economic dimension. Subject to certain conditions the Agency may publish information and make it available to the public. Significantly the Agency is open to countries which are not members of the EC and it may turn out to be a model for environmental monitoring arrangements at the international level. The Regulation will enter into force the day after the location of the Agency seat has been decided.

Finally, although it may not seem immediately relevant, the Broadcasting Directive[34] may have an effect on freedom of environmental information. The Directive itself is aimed at establishing the minimum rules needed to ensure freedom of transmission in broadcasting, breaking down national barriers by allowing broadcasters to transmit and retransmit across EC national boundaries and by creating an obligation on

[31] Council Decision of 27 June 1985 (OJ 1985 L176/14).

[32] Council Decision 90/150 (OJ 1990 L81/38).

[33] Council Regulation 1210/90/EEC of 7 May 1990 on the establishment of the European Environment Agency and the European Environment Information and Observation Network (OJ 1990 L120/1).

[34] Council Directive 89/552/EEC of 3 Oct. 1989 on the co-ordination of certain provisions laid down by law, regulation, or administrative action in Member States concerning the pursuit of television activities (OJ 1989 L298/23).

Member States to receive such transmissions and retransmissions except in certain limited circumstances set out in the Directive. The Directive establishes minimum standards in respect of, *inter alia*, television programme and television advertising content. In respect of advertisements, the Directive now provides in Article 12 that 'television advertising shall not . . . (e) encourage behaviour prejudicial to the protection of the environment'.[35] This establishes the possibility that, following the adoption of the Directive into the national laws of the Member States (to be achieved by 3 October 1991), legal actions could be brought in national courts seeking to prohibit the broadcast of advertising encouraging the public to buy cars, or beverages sold in containers which might be considered to be harmful to the environment.[36]

3.5. INTERNATIONAL TREATIES

This paper is not the place to discuss the position relating to international treaties on environmental law.[37] However, it should be noted that the EC has entered into a number of co-operation agreements with third countries on research and development in the field of environmental protection. Agreements with Norway[38] and Finland,[39] for example, involve an already established community environmental programme covering matters such as: health and ecological effects of pollutants, assessment of chemicals, air, soil, and water quality, eco-system and waste research, and reduction of pollution. The third countries contribute funds and expertise through a framework of shared-cost research contracts in order to implement this Community-administered programme.

Recent agreements with the USSR[40] and Poland[41] provide for environmental co-operation, and suggest that environmental protection objectives are increasingly being integrated into the EC's economic policy objectives.

[35] Council Directive 89/552/EEC of 3 Oct. 1989. For the meaning of the phrase, 'behaviour prejudicial to the environment', see the *Danish Bottles Case*, Case 302/86; [1989] I *CMLR* 619 and P. Kromarek, 'Environmental Protection and, the Free Movement of Goods: The Danish Bottles Case' (1990) 2 *JEL* 89.

[36] P. Sands, 'EC Environmental Law', 696–7.

[37] For a discussion from the standpoint of the European Community (see P. Sands in *EC Environment and Planning Law*, 17–28 (London: Butterworths, 1991)). More generally see T. C. Hartley, *The Foundations of European Community Law*, 2nd edn. (Oxford: Oxford University Press, 1988), 153–82. See generally, P. W. Birnie and A. E. Boyle, *International Law and the Environment* (Oxford: Clarendon Press, 1992).

[38] OJ L304/1 10 Oct. 1989.

[39] OJ 304/9 10 Oct. 1989.

[40] OJ L68/1 15 Mar. 1990.

[41] OJ L339/1 22 Nov. 1989. In June 1991 the Commission submitted a Proposal for a Council Decision concerning the Conclusion of Bilateral Co-operation Agreements on Service and Technology for Environmental Protection (STEP) between the EEC and Austria, Finland, and Norway (OJ C179/10 10 July 1991).

Under parts entitled 'Economic Co-operation', the agreements require contracting parties to foster co-operation in environmental protection and the management of natural resources, as well as to encourage environmentally sound policies.

If the need for public access to environmental information is accepted then international treaties could be made which provide for shared access to and dissemination of that information.

3.6. ENVIRONMENTAL AUDITING

This section is concerned with a number of different kinds of audits all of which have implications for access to and dissemination of information on the environment.[42]

3.6.1. Company Audits

The company audit has been defined as:

> partly a management tool comprising a systematic, documented, periodic and objective evaluation of how well organisations, management and equipment are performing in the environmental area with the aim of helping to safeguard the environment by facilitating management control of environmental practices and assessing and verifying compliance with company policies which would include meeting regulatory requirements. It is also a risk assessment tool for use in negotiating updated consent conditions. It highlights issues—what is at stake. It helps to give quality assurance in TQM programmes by standard setting—what can be achieved. It is the audit of existing activities and can therefore be distinguished from the environmental assessment which is a kind of audit of proposed activities. It is much wider than the compliance audit which merely looks at a detailed operating facility; it identifies areas where environmental improvements may be achieved and savings made. It tests company performance as against company policy. It can review what competitors are doing. It is undertaken with reference to performance of personnel, technology, systems and documentation and how those relate to relevant standards of practice. It is quite different from a due diligence audit consisting of procedures which lawyers use on the acquisition, disposal and merger of companies. It is also quite different from a property

[42] This section relies heavily on the analysis in John R. Salter, *Corporate Environmental Responsibility: Law and Practice* (London: Butterworths, 1992), ch. 8. See generally R. Gray, D. Owen, and K. Maunders: *Corporate Social Reporting* (London: Prentice Hall, 1987); J. Elkington, *The Environmental Audit: A Green Filter for Company Policies, Plants and Products* (London: Sustainability, 1990); R. Gray, *The Greening of Accountancy: The Profession After Pearce* (London: Certified Accountants Publications, 1990); *ICC Guide to Effective Environmental Auditing* (Paris: International Chambers of Commerce, 1991); British Standards Institution, *Draft British Standard Environmental Managers & Systems* (London: British Standards Institution, 1991).

environmental audit which lawyers use in connection with the purchases and sales of property. It should also be distinguished from an environmental risk assessment which is often used in connection with insurance matters to assess a production process in order to identify potential liabilities. The Environmental Audit is therefore in the nature of a Corporate Policy Audit.[43]

Before an environmental audit can be commissioned there must be a corporate environmental policy in place and available. If not, then such a policy will need to be established first. Pre-environmental audit action requires the establishment of such corporate policies and procedures by identifying key policy areas and aims and objectives, the agreement of the scope of the audit, and a timetable, setting up legal measures to ensure confidentiality and the method of reporting. The audit questionnaire will need to be agreed and the audit team given as much information as possible about site operations and conditions before arriving on site. Part of pre-environmental audit action is a records review. This is a review not only of the legal position in fact but also of all compliance measures taken by the company including health and safety, training, and insurance.

This chapter is not the place to consider best practice for the carrying out of an environmental audit. There is a wealth of information obtainable through the environmental audit process, which may cover many fácets of a company's activities. Some of this information will be of use to competitors and some of it may be of use to individuals or pressure groups who object to the impact of a process or a product.

3.6.2. Eco-Audit

EC Regulation 880/92[44] came into force on 2 May 1992 with formal compliance for Member States by 2 November 1992. The Regulation establishes a voluntary scheme for the award of eco-labels to products with reduced environmental impact, as assessed against uniform Community criteria. The scheme's objectives are to promote the design, production, marketing, and use of such products and to improve the information available on their environmental impact to consumers, without compromising product or worker safety or significantly affecting a product's essential useful properties.

Under the Regulation manufacturers or importers may apply for the award of an eco-label to products which meet the scheme's basic objectives and EC health, safety, and environmental requirements. Food, drink, and pharmaceuticals are excluded. Products manufactured by processes likely to significantly harm man and/or the environment are not eligible; neither are products which are classified as dangerous substances

[43] Salter, *Corporate Responsibility*, 148.

[44] OJ L99, 11 Apr. 1992.

or preparations under Directive 64/548 or 88/379. The eco-label may be awarded to products containing such a substance or preparation in so far as they meet the scheme's basic objective. In the United Kingdom the Eco-labelling Board was established in July 1992 and it is the United Kingdom's competent body under the scheme.[45] It is to the Eco-labelling Board that applications for the eco-label are to be made by the manufacturer or importer. The Eco-labelling Board consults the registers of applications maintained by the EC Commission. If the product falls within an established product group, its environmental performance is assessed by reference to the scheme's general principles and relevant product group's criteria. If a competent body decides to award an ecolabel it notifies the Commission of the full results and a summary of its assessment. The Commission circulates the decision and summary to all the competent bodies of the Community. If no objections are received within thirty days the Eco-labelling Board may award an ecolabel. There are procedures within the Regulation for dealing with conflicts between Member States.

The information gained in the course of assessing applications must not be divulged, although after the award of an eco-label, the name of the product, its manufacturer or importer and the reasons for awarding the eco-label may not be kept secret. The Commission must publish the following information in the Official Journal:

1. product groups and ecological criteria, with their periods of validity;
2. a list of products awarded an eco-label, with their manufacturers or importers and expiry dates (to be published at least annually);
3. names and addresses of all the competent bodies;
4. a consolidated list of all products awarded an eco-label.

In addition, Member States are required to ensure that consumers and undertakings are informed about the eco-label award scheme. References to eco-labels in advertising may be made only after their award and only in relation to the specific products concerned. Fake or misleading advertising, or the use of a label or logo which leads to confusion with the EC eco-label is banned. The scheme is to be reviewed after five years from its implementation.

3.6.3. Resources Audits

The EC Energy Directorate has put forward proposals for requiring home-owners to carry out energy audits of their houses when they offer properties for sale. A graded energy certificate would be awarded after

[45] The UK Eco-labelling Board Regulations 1992 (SI 1992 No. 2383) in force 1 Nov. 1992.

the audit. The grade would reflect insulation and efficient energy use. A similar proposal has been mooted for industrial installations.

3.6.4. Acquisition Audits

An acquisition audit is undertaken by lawyers and consists of procedures used on acquisitions, disposals, or mergers of companies. Its main objective is to identify potential liability exposure problems. The result of such an audit should result in a well-drawn disposal or merger agreement containing warranties and indemnities covering likely environmental risks.[46]

3.6.5. Property Audits

These are audits carried out on the sale and purchase of land. They are quite specific, but otherwise procedures are very much the same except that a detailed questionnaire is put by way of preliminary inquiries to the vendor's solicitors. The Environmental Information Regulations 1992 discussed above should give much greater access to environmental information to a prospective purchaser from bodies such as the British Coal Corporation which keeps information about mining under or in relation to a site and Conservancy Councils which publish a range of ecological information about a site and its surroundings.[47]

3.6.6. Risk Audits

A risk audit leads to an assessment of, for example, a production process, to identify potential liabilities and problems, and is linked to an action plan resulting from the audit. It examines impairment or claims arising from environmental pollution. Such an audit would include obtaining details of general liability insurance cover with copies of declarations made to the insurer, copies of environmental risk assurance cover, environmental reports, history of accidents, health and safety records under COSHH,[48] CIMAH,[49] and the EPA90 would be seen and reviewed.

[46] See J. Jarvis and M. Fordham, *Lender Liability* esp. chs. 9–11 (London: Cameron and May, 1993).

[47] See C. Deansley, C. Papanicolaou, and A. Turner, *Badlands: Essential Environmental Law for Property Professionals*, esp. chs. 10–12 (London: Cameron and May 1993).

[48] COSHH (SI 1988 No. 1657).

[49] CIMAH (SI 1984 No. 1902). See also D.o.E. guidance note, June 1991 and HS(R)21 (Rev.), 1990.

3.7. PRIVILEGE AND ENVIRONMENTAL AUDITS

The recent Canadian cases of *Gregory* v. *MNR*[50] and *R.* v. *McCarthy Tétrault*[51] have highlighted the difficulties of structuring environmental audits (eco-audits) and similar reports so that they are not susceptible to disclosure during the discovery process in litigation.

3.7.1. The Scope of Legal Professional Privilege[52]

3.7.1.1. 'Advice' Privilege

This may apply whether or not litigation is contemplated or pending. Advice privilege covers communications between a lawyer in his professional capacity and his client if they are confidential and for the purposes of seeking or giving legal advice. Those purposes have to be construed broadly, and will include communications in 'the continuum aimed at keeping [solicitor and client] informed' and 'must include advice as to what should prudently and sensibly be done in the relevant legal context'.[53]

3.7.1.2. 'Litigation' Privilege

This covers confidential communications made after litigation is commenced or even contemplated, between (*a*) a lawyer and his client, (*b*) a lawyer and his non-professional agent, or (*c*) a lawyer and a third party, for the sole or dominant purpose of such litigation (whether for seeking or giving advice in relation to it, or for obtaining evidence to be used in it).[54]

The test as to whether litigation is contemplated is simply whether litigation is 'reasonably in prospect'.[55] It should be noted that the contemplated litigation need not be the particular litigation in which the discovery is being sought, but may be other litigation, involving different parties and subject-matter.[56]

Given that an eco-audit may contain potentially sensitive information about, say, a company's compliance record, it is clearly important that companies are aware of how eco-audits fit into the framework of legal professional privilege. In *R.* v. *McCarthy Tétrault*, Tétrault (a law firm)

[50] (1992) 92 DTC 6518.

[51] (1993) 9 CELR (NS) 12.

[52] I am indebted here to N. Stewart QC, C. Pugh, and D. Oudkerk, 'Confidentiality and Environmental Audits' (1993) *Environmental Liability* 137.

[53] *Babel* v. *Air India* [1988] Ch. 317 at 331.

[54] *Wheeler* v. *Le Marchant* (1881) 17 Ch.D. 675 at 681; *Re Highgrade Traders Ltd.* [1984] BCLC 151, CA; *Ventouris* v. *Mountain* [1991] 3 All ER 472 at 475–6.

[55] *Waugh* v. *British Railways Board* [1980] AC 521 at 544A.

[56] *Bullock & Co.* v. *Corry & Co.* (1878) 3 QBD 356.

was retained to advise Lafarge Canada Inc. on matters of environmental law. A solicitor from the law firm attended a meeting at Lafarge. According to the affidavit filed by him, the purpose of that meeting was to receive confidential information and provide legal advice concerning the compliance of Lafarge with applicable environmental statutes, regulations and policies. The solicitor further deposed that during the course of the meeting confidential discussions took place regarding a potential prosecution of Lafarge in relation to a coal storage settling pond. The only notes of the meeting were taken by the solicitor. He deposed that, 'the documents for which Lafarge claims privilege are notes and memoranda prepared by me of confidential communications between me and my client, and confidential communications from my client, which were prepared for the purpose of receiving information and providing or recording the provision of . . . legal advice'.

In holding that privilege attached to the notes and advice, MacDonnell Prov.J. quoted, with implicit approval, this excerpt from Edwards, 'Confidentiality and Environmental Auditing': 'in order for the [solicitor–client] privilege to attach, the report must have been created for the purpose of obtaining legal advice or assistance'.[57] The decision appears to be authority for the proposition that if an environmental audit is prepared by either a solicitor or an environmental consultant it may be covered by advice privilege, provided that it is commissioned for the purpose of providing legal advice.

However, in *Gregory* v. *MNR*, an environmental audit report had been obtained by the solicitor from a consultant on behalf of the client in order to provide legal advice. It was conceded that the report was not obtained for the purposes of litigation or in contemplation of litigation. Teitelbaum J. held that privilege did not attach to the report as it was a third-party communication not prepared for purposes of litigation or in contemplation of litigation:

> It is my understanding . . . that all communication between the client and his or her solicitor wherein a legal opinion is given is subject to the solicitor–client privilege. Documents, not account documents, prepared by third parties, for and on behalf of a solicitor would be subject to the privilege only if the documents were prepared for the purposes of litigation or in contemplation of litigation.[58]

This accords with the position in English law (set out below) and it would seem that, in so far as the decision in *R.* v. *McCarthy Tétrault* supports the proposition that an eco-audit prepared by a consultant, that is, a non-professional third party, for the purpose of giving legal advice could be covered by advice privilege, it was decided *per incuriam*.

[57] (1991) 1 *JELP* 1 at 5–6.

[58] (1992) 92 DTC at 6524.

However, it should be noted that *R.* v. *McCarthy Tétrault* was rightly decided on its facts, as the audit report in question was not a third-party communication (having been prepared by the solicitor) and the only question was 'whether the [audit] was truly conducted for the *bona fide* purpose of obtaining legal advice from [the solicitor]'.[59]

3.7.2. The position in English Law

The general principle is that documents embodying communications (including reports) between a solicitor and a non-professional servant, agent, or third party are privileged if and only if coming into existence for the purposes of obtaining legal advice in existing or anticipated proceedings.[60]

In *Wheeler* v. *Le Marchant*, Jessell MR held that documents communicated to the solicitor by third parties who are not agents of the clients seeking advice:

> are protected where they have come into existence after litigation commenced or in contemplation, and when they have been made with a view to such litigation, either for the purpose of obtaining advice as to such litigation, or of obtaining evidence to be used in such litigation, or of obtaining information which might lead to the obtaining of such evidence, but it has never hitherto been decided that documents are protected merely because they are produced by a third person in answer to an inquiry made by the solicitor.[61]

And Brett LJ said this:

> This applies to information such as a surveyor's report obtained by a solicitor with a view to giving his client legal advice, and such information is not privileged unless obtained with a view to contemplated or existing litigation.[62]

Similarly, in *Price Waterhouse (a firm)* v. *BCCI Holdings (Luxembourg) SA*,[63] reports prepared by bank accountants in the course of investigating problem loans were held not to be protected as (*a*) such were not communications between bank and its legal advisers and (*b*) were not documents produced in contemplation of litigation.

The position in English law as regards the circumstances in which privilege can be claimed for environmental audits is essentially the same as that elucidated by Teitelbaum J. in *Gregory* v. *MNR*.

3.7.3. Summary

The following propositions state the current position:

1. an environmental report prepared by a third party (e.g. an environmental consultant) will not be covered by legal advice privilege;

[59] (1993) CELR (NS) 12 at 23.
[60] *Seabrook* v. *British Transport Commission* [1959] 1 WLR 509.
[61] (1881) 17 Ch.D. 675 at 680–1. [62] Ibid. 683. [63] (1992) BCLC 583.

2. an environmental report prepared *by a solicitor* based on information obtained directly from the client may be covered by legal advice privilege if the report was prepared for the purpose of giving legal advice; and
3. an environmental report prepared by a third party (e.g. an environmental consultant) may be covered by litigation privilege if it was prepared after litigation is commenced or contemplated, for the sale or dominant purpose of such litigation.

3.7.4. Structuring Eco-Audits with a View to Privilege

Clearly it is desirable to hive off contentious matters to an eco-audit which is not susceptible to disclosure (e.g. a legal eco-audit). The legal advice and the documents on which it is based should be prepared by the solicitor using information taken directly from the client. It is imperative that the purpose of the report is to obtain legal advice and that unrelated matters are not incorporated. Any non-sensitive auditing (i.e. matters not related to compliance with regulations/assessing exposure to third party claims) should be carried out by independent auditors in a separate report to avoid the suggestion that the purpose of the legal eco-audit is other than to obtain legal advice. If litigation is pending or contemplated, a more comprehensive eco-audit can be carried out by a third party (e.g. an environmental consultant) which would then, provided it was carried out for the sole or dominant purpose of litigation, be privileged.

3.8. COMPANIES

In the United Kingdom at present the shareholders of a company—who are best placed to influence a company's policy—have no legal right to be informed of its safety and environmental record. One obvious place for publication of such information would be in the annual report. Unfortunately, few companies actually do this. Even when environmental information is included in the annual report it is often selective and inadequate.

By s.234(4) and Schedule 7 Part 4 of the Companies Act 1985, the Secretary of State for Trade and Industry is empowered to make regulations obliging companies to set out information on health and safety in their annual report. However, no regulations have been made and there does not seem to be any immediate prospect of any such regulations being made. Furthermore, no provision exists in English law by which to order the disclosure of such environmental information.

3.9. ENVIRONMENTAL INFORMATION, MARKETS, AND PRICES

So far we have considered legal obligations on companies to disclose information about the environment. But there is another, equally important, source of information about environmental values. Within a market economy, a prime source of information is prices. Consumers obtain information about the relative value of goods from their relative prices.

What we have learnt in Western market economies is that environmental goods are, all too often, under-priced or indeed not priced at all. The result is that producers and consumers are not getting the right information about environmental values. For instance, if a company can dump waste in a river or in the sea at no cost to itself—if all the costs of that pollution are externalized, borne by other people living further down the river, or other people in other countries, or people in a generation not yet born—then the company will go on polluting. But if the value of the environment—the water, in this case—is reflected in a price, then the company has an incentive to find some other way of dealing with its waste, perhaps even not creating the waste in the first place. And those companies who carry on polluting will at least be paying a fee—creating revenue which can be used to clear up the waste.[64]

Environmental prices can be created in different ways. It is possible for local or national government literally to charge a price for dumping waste in the river. But direct regulation—a ban on dumping waste in the river, for instance—also creates a price.[65] If, for instance, there is a regulation against dumping waste but the regulation is hardly ever enforced and the fines against offenders are very low, then the effective cost of waste-dumping is so low that many companies will simply add the small risk of a small fine into their costs and carry on polluting. But effective enforcement of the regulation, with a high risk of detection and a high fine for offenders, means that, just as with an actual charge for dumping, companies face a cost for their pollution.

As noted earlier, markets have to be created. And creating markets involves government, particularly where environmental goods are concerned. Where there is a private owner, it will set the price of the goods it produces. But the environment—the air, the rivers, the sea, the wildlife in

[64] An early study of environmental pricing in market economics is W. Beckerman, *Pricing for Pollution: Market Pricing, Government Regulation, Environmental Policy*, (London: Institute for Economic Affairs, 1975). The general economic theory underlying the case for environmental taxes was set out by A. C. Pigou, *The Economics of Welfare*, 4th edn. (London: Macmillan, 1932). A review of environmental taxes in OECD countries is contained in J. B. Opschoor and H. B. Vos, *Economic Instruments for Environmental Protection* (Paris: OECD, 1989).

[65] See e.g. W. Baumol and W. Oates, 'The Use of Standards and Prices for Protection of the Environment' (1971) 73 *SJE* 42.

undeveloped areas, the ozone layer—all these have no private owners. If the value of these environmental goods is to be reflected in their price, then government has to create the appropriate framework, government has to help create the market. Whether it does so by literally imposing a price on polluting, or whether it does so by regulation, is a secondary question: both are a restructuring of a market which would otherwise ignore the value of the environment. By setting the environmental boundaries of the market, government is in fact ensuring that producers and consumers both get information about the environment—information which is ultimately carried through prices.

Of course, there are problems in valuing the environment—in setting a price on the value of rare species, or unpolluted air, or clean water. A huge amount of technical work is available on the subject,[66] which it is not possible to review here, save to draw attention to the all-too-often overlooked fact that prices convey information, that environmental prices convey environmental information, and that environmental costs need to be incorporated within the structure of markets, whether they already exist or whether they are being created afresh.

3.10. CONCLUSION

This has been a brief attempt to survey a subject which has many aspects to it. There is no simple legal model for making access to environmental information readily available. Different legal systems will approach the problem in different ways. One thing is certain: a state that does not provide its citizens with as much environmental information as is possible is likely to find that it increasingly lacks credibility and legitimacy as public concern continues to grow and the millennium approaches.

[66] See e.g. D. Pearce, A. Markandya, and E. B. Barbier, *Blueprint for a Green Economy* (London: Earthscan, 1989) (a report initially commissioned by the British Government). An introduction to some German thinking will be found in G. Hunermann, *Fiscal Charges and Taxes as Economic Instruments for Environmental Policy* (1988) (Forschungsstelle für Umweltpolitik, Freie Universität Berlin).

4

Environmental Liability: A Continuing Concern for Lenders

MICHAEL I. JEFFERY, QC

4.1. INTRODUCTION

Although environmental liability has long been a concern to those directly responsible for or associated with polluting activities under a plethora of environmental statutes and common law causes of action, such as nuisance, negligence, and trespass, financial institutions until recently paid little attention to factors unrelated to the fiscal well-being or creditworthiness of their borrowers. Financial risk was minimized by lenders insisting that adequate security was available to satisfy indebtedness in the event that the borrower failed to repay the loan in accordance with its terms.

The accepted role of the lender underwent a traumatic transformation in the latter half of the 1980s as the result of a rather dramatic policy shift on the part of governments—a movement initiated primarily by the United States. In response to the public's demand for a cleaner environment, governments sought to transfer the rapidly increasing costs of remedial action to the private sector, and gave birth to what has been euphemistically referred to as the 'deep pocket' theory of liability. Legislation embodying to a greater or lesser degree some of the principles associated with the infamous 'Superfund' statute in the United States appeared in several jurisdictions, and subjected any person who owns or has the charge, management, or control of a 'hazardous substance' to financial liability for the full costs of clean-up.

This chapter will trace the evolution of lender liability in Canada and the United States and its extension in many situations to trustees in bankruptcy, receivers/managers, insurers, and even shareholders, and attempt to outline and comment upon a number of recent developments which have served to temper what many lenders were beginning to describe as an 'open season' on those sufficiently well-heeled to take the financial burden.

This chapter has been adapted in part from an earlier paper by M. I. Jeffery, QC, entitled 'Environmental Liability for Lenders: A Canadian Perspective' (1991)23/2 *The Urban Lawyer*.

4.2. LENDER LIABILITY IN THE UNITED STATES

4.2.1. The Comprehensive Environmental Response Compensation and Liability Act[1] (CERCLA) and the Superfund Amendments and Reauthorization Act of 1986[2] (SARA)

The Draconian CERCLA or Superfund Statute enacted by Congress in 1980 was born out of the ashes of the 'Love Canal' débâcle, and placed the clean-up of severely contaminated sites throughout the United States at the top of the national environmental agenda.

The basic scheme of the Superfund legislation is relatively straightforward. Under CERCLA, the federal Environmental Protection Agency (EPA) is empowered to evaluate the nature of the contamination or suspected contamination, decide upon appropriate remedial action and compel certain parties within the statutorily defined categories of 'owners and operators' (referred to as potentially responsible parties—PRPs) to undertake clean-up of the contaminated site at their own expense and under government supervision. The EPA may also elect to clean up the site itself, drawing the necessary funds from the proceeds of a tax on feedstocks used by the chemical industry (the Superfund), and then sue to recover these costs from PRPs, whose liability may be characterized as strict as well as joint and several.

Initially, CERCLA established a trust fund of $1.6 billion, which was later increased by SARA in 1986 to $8.5 billion.

The basis for liability under CERCLA is found in s.9607(a), which defines the persons liable for clean-up and associated costs as:

1. the current owner and operator of a vessel or facility;
2. any person who formerly owned or operated a facility at the time of disposal of any hazardous substances;
3. generators or any persons who arranged for disposal or treatment of a hazardous substance at any facility owned or operated by another person; and
4. transporters of such substances to a facility.[3]

[1] 42 USCA § 9601 (1980).

[2] Act of 17 Oct. 1986, Publ. L. 99–499, 1986 *US CCAN* (100 STT. 1613). Note that although CERCLA allowed what became known as the 'innocent landowner' defence under s.107(b)(3), SARA amended this Act by adding s.101(35(A)(ii), which extended the defence to government entities, including government-appointed conservators and receivers in involuntary acquisitions or transfers. The EPA in its Final Rule, discussed later in this chapter, clarified what is meant by the term 'involuntary acquisition or transfer'.

[3] The term 'person' has a broad meaning and includes an individual, firm, corporation, association, partnership, consortium, joint venture, commercial entity, United States government, state, municipality, commission, political subdivision of a state, or any interstate body: 42 USCA § 9601(21) (1980). 'Facility' includes any site or area where a hazardous

The term 'owner or operator' was defined to mean any person owning or operating such a facility, but does not include a person who, without participating in the management of the facility, holds indicia of ownership primarily to protect his security interest.[4]

It follows, therefore, from the above definition that a lender who does participate in the facility's management is potentially liable as an owner or operator, and that the key issue in determining lender liability under CERCLA revolves around the element or degree of control attributed to the lender.

At first glance the exclusionary provision contained in the definition of the term 'owner or operator' was thought adequate to place financial institutions outside the CERCLA liability net, for surely the primary purpose of the lender's efforts to realize his security by taking possession and/or title to the debtor's property was to protect his security interest and recover the borrowed funds—that is, after all, one of the fundamental tenets of the financial services industry.

In one of the earliest United States lender liability cases under CERCLA, *United States* v. *Mirabile*,[5] the Government sued the current owners of real property, the Mirabiles, to recover its clean-up costs for contamination created by a prior owner, Turco. The Mirabiles joined the former lenders to Turco (American Bank and Mellon Bank) as third-party defendants, claiming such lenders to be 'owners and operators'. The two banks counterclaimed against the United States Government because of the involvement of its agency, another former lender, the Small Business Administration. The court dismissed the actions against two of the three financial institutions and allowed the claims against the Mellon bank to go to trial. The court drew a distinction between participation in the financial aspects of the business versus the actual operation of the facility, finding that financial ability to control waste-disposal practices is not sufficient for the imposition of liability. In the case of Mellon Bank, after its loan was in a 'workout position'* the court found that one of the bank's officers had become sufficiently involved in the day-to-day operation of Turco's business as to fall within CERCLA's definition of 'operator' at the time of disposal of hazardous substances, and thus denied this lender's motion for summary dismissal.

substance has been deposited, stored, disposed of or placed, or otherwise come to be located: ibid. § 9601(9).

[4] Ibid. § 9601(20(A).

[5] 15 Envtl. L. Rep. 20,992 9ED. Pa. 4 (Sept. 1985); see also *State National Bank of El Paso* v. *Farah Manufacturing Co. Inc.* 678 SW 2d 661 (Tex. App. 1984).

* Editor's note: this term is used where the lender's loan is in default and the lender is co-operating with the debtor to recover its loan. Often a loan is in a 'workout position' prior to the debtor seeking formal relief under, e.g., US Chapter 11 bankruptcy.

In *United States* v. *Maryland Bank & Trust Company*[6] which followed shortly thereafter, the court held that a mortgagee who buys property at a foreclosure sale does not hold indicia of ownership to protect its security interest, but instead to maximize the amount of its recovery.[7] Further, the court, in commenting on the *Mirabile* decision, and in particular upon the dismissal of the action against the American Bank, stated that the *Mirabile* decision pertained to a situation in which the mortgagee-turned-owner (American Bank) promptly sold the property.[8] More ominously, the court went on to state that 'mortgagees . . . have the means to protect themselves by making prudent loans. Financial institutions are in a position to investigate and discover potential problems . . . [and] CERCLA will not absolve them from responsibility for their mistakes of judgment'.[9]

To this point, the liability of a lender appeared dependent on both the lender's period of ownership and the degree of involvement in the borrower's business undertaken by the lender once having gained possession or title.

Lenders were by and large unprepared for the *Fleet Factors*[10] decision of the United States Court of Appeals for the Eleventh Circuit in 1990 (*Fleet Factors II*), which suggested that a secured creditor may incur liability 'if its involvement with the management of the facility is sufficiently broad to support the inference that it *could* affect hazardous waste disposal decisions if it so chose'.[11] The court in this case extended the risk for lenders by stating that it was 'not necessary for the secured creditor actually to involve itself in the day-to-day operations of the facility in order to be liable—although such conduct will certainly lead to the loss of the protection under the statutory exemption'.[12] The court concluded that 'creditors' awareness that they are potentially liable under CERCLA will encourage them to monitor the hazardous waste treatment systems

[6] 632 F. Supp. 573 (D. Md. 1986); see also M. S. Cohen, 'Hazardous Waste: A Threat to the Lender's Environment' (1986) 19 *UCCLJ* 99 for a more detailed discussion of this case and *United States* v. *Mirabile, supra.*

[7] 632 F. Supp. 579.

[8] Ibid. 580.

[9] Ibid.

[10] *United States* v. *Fleet Factors* 901 F. 2d 1550 (11th Cir., 1990) (*Fleet Factors II*); see also *Fleet Factors IV*, 821 F. Supp. 707 (SDG, 12 May 1993) wherein the US District Court dealt with the issues at trial *subsequent* to the EPA's Final Rule interpreting the CERCLA secured creditor liability exemption. At trial the court held, *inter alia*, that CERCLA liability may attach on any person who 'arranged for' disposal or treatment of hazardous substances at a facility owned by another, even if the potentially responsible party did not intend to dispose of hazardous substances. There must, however, be a sufficient nexus between the potentially responsible party and the items disposed, which may be established by showing actual involvement in the decision to dispose of by showing an obligation to control the hazardous substances.

[11] Emphasis added; *US* v. *Fleet Factors* 901 F. 2d 1558; note that some actual involvement by a holder is a necessary precedent to voiding the exemption, a point that was specifically underlined in the case of *In Re Bergsoe Metal Corp.* 910 F 668 (1990).

[12] *Fleet Factors II*, ibid. 1557–8.

and policies of their debtors and insist upon compliance with acceptable treatment standards as a prerequisite to continued and future financial support'.[13] However, in doing so, a lender must be cognizant of the fact that it cannot involve itself in the day-to-day activities of the facility.

The *Fleet Factors* decision caused an immediate outcry of concern on the part of both lenders and borrowers in many jurisdictions, including Canada. Not surprisingly, there was genuine outrage over the realization that the courts were now prepared to join forces with the Government and enlist the aid of lenders in the effort to curb pollution by placing them in a new, unfamiliar role—that of 'environmental cop'.

The suggestion, in the view of a large segment of the business community, that lenders could be held directly liable for the clean-up costs of the debtor, particularly in circumstances where the lender had not been involved in the management decisions which were responsible for the pollution, went far beyond what was considered fair and in keeping with the accepted business practices of the financial services industry. Regulatory authorities in jurisdictions which did not have analogous CERCLA legislation were also nervously following the developments in the United States closely to see if the imposition of lender liability would have a significant impact upon the waste-management practices of industry which could ill afford a more stringent credit environment, for the prospect of other governments adopting legislative measures having similar effect was considered a distinct possibility by many financial institutions.

The Court of Appeals for the Ninth Circuit had the opportunity to confirm the 'ratio' of *Fleet Factors* in the case of *In Re Bergsoe Metal Corp.*,[14] but declined to do so. The court in the *Bergsoe* case stated that 'it is clear from the statute that, whatever the precise parameters of 'participation', there must be some *actual* management of the facility before a secured creditor will fall outside the exception'.[15] In *Bergsoe* there was no actual management, and thus the court expressed no need to 'engage in line drawing'.[16]

As mentioned earlier, CERCLA liability may be characterized as joint and several, allowing the EPA to recover its entire claim against one defendant, where the liability cannot be apportioned properly among a number of defendants, or where defendants who should properly bear a

[13] Ibid.

[14] 910 F. 2d 668 (1990).

[15] Ibid. 672; see also *United States* v. *Nicolet*, 29 ERC (BNA) (1851) (ED Pa. 1989) and *Guidice* v. *B.F.G. Electroplating and Manufacturing Co.* 732 F. Supp. 556 (WDPa 1989) 556, which held that a secured creditor's involvement in financially related matters will not void the exemption.

[16] 910 F. 2d 672 (1990); see also *O'Neil* v. *Q.L.C.R.I. Inc.*, 750 F. Supp. 551 (DRI 1990) and *Friends of the Sakonnet* v. *Dutra*, 738 F. Supp. 623 (DRI 1990) for a discussion of circumstances wherein it was argued that a lender 'aided and abetted' the borrower in the alleged polluting activity.

portion of the liability are financially unable to pay or in some cases cannot be located.[17] The obvious advantage to the EPA in focusing their recovery efforts on banks or other large financial institutions has left them in the unenviable position of being prime targets in circumstances where the elements of lender liability are present.

A review of the CERCLA case-law in the United States confirms the determination of the courts to interpret the legislation in a manner which permits few to escape its wide-ranging tentacles.

Examples can be found of courts willing to lift the corporate veil in certain circumstances to impose personal liability on officers and shareholders,[18] and both parent and successor corporations have been held liable for the environmental activities of subsidiary and predecessor corporations respectively.[19]

In addition to the federal CERCLA liability outlined above, lenders may also be subjected to the risk of having repayment of their loans jeopardized by states which are able to assert liens on the borrower's property pursuant to 'superlien' statutes designed to allow states to recover the costs of a state-funded environmental clean-up. A number of states have enacted superlien statutes, and most afford the state priority over lenders with respect to certain specified types of property.[20]

4.2.2. Lender Liability under CERCLA Clarified: EPA Final Rule

On 29 April 1992 the United States Environmental Protection Agency issued its Final Rule[21] (as stated in the explanation provided by the Agency) to define and interpret the provisions of CERCLA as they affect persons maintaining indicia of ownership in a facility primarily to protect a security interest (which includes private and governmental lending institutions or entities), or which guarantee loans secured by a facility contaminated by or containing hazardous substances, or which acquire title to or ownership of contaminated property by an involuntary transfer or acquisition.

[17] *United States* v. *Wade*, 577 F. Supp. 1361 (DNH 1985); note that some courts have refused to impose joint and several liability on PRPs where there is a basis for apportioning liability. See e.g. *United States* v. *Chem-Dyne Corp.* 572 F. Supp. 802 (SD Ohio, 1983).

[18] *United States* v. *Northeastern Pharmaceutical & Chemical Co. Inc.* 810 F. 2d 276 (8th Cir. 1986); see also *State of New York* v. *Shore Reality Corp.* 759 F. 2d 1032 (2nd Cir. 1985).

[19] See *State of Idaho* v. *Bunker Hill Co.*, 635 F. Supp. 665 (D. Idaho, 1986); *United States* v. *Shell Oil Co.* 605 F. Supp. 1064 (D. Colo. 1985). For a more detailed discussion of these issues see G. Klotz and E. Siakotos, 'Lender Liability Under Federal and State Environmental Law: Of Deep Pockets, Debt Defeat and Deadbeats' (1988) 92 *Comm. LJ* 275.

[20] See Cohen, 'Hazardous Waste', for a survey of the twelve states which had enacted Superlien Statutes as of 1986.

[21] The EPA published a draft version of its Lender Liability Rule on 24 June 1991 (56 *Fed. Reg.* 28798), and extensive public debate issued a revised Final Rule on 29 Apr. 1992 (57 Fed. Reg. 18344).

It became obvious to the EPA that the uncertainty that had been generated by the judiciary in its interpretation of the 'security interest' exemption provided in s.101(20)A, particularly with regard to the extent to which a secured creditor may undertake activities to oversee the affairs of a person whose facility is encumbered by a security interest for the purposes of protecting the security interest without sustaining CERCLA liability, had to be addressed by way of setting precise standards as to the nature and extent of involvement that would not void the exemption.

The uncertainty was of particular concern to the Government because of the activities of the Federal Deposit Insurance Corporation (FDIC) and the Resolution Trust Corporation (RTC), both of which acted as conservators and receivers of failing or failed insured depository institutions, and which were likely to own, possess, or have security interests in potentially contaminated properties transferred to them as a result of their appointment as the conservator or receiver of failed and insolvent lending institutions.

The potential for government entities such as the FDIC and RTC to incur significant CERCLA liability provided a strong motivating factor for the EPA to put an end to the uncertainty surrounding the 'security interest' exemption, while at the same time preserving the EPA's mandate to recover the costs incurred by the Fund from those liable under CERCLA.

It is beyond the purview of this chapter to examine in depth all the specific provisions of the EPA's Final Rule, and, accordingly, only a brief summary is provided herein. Under the Rule, the primary reason why indicia of ownership are held must be as protection for a security interest, and not for investment or for other purposes. The Final Rule defines the term 'participation in management' to be *actual* participation in the management or operational affairs of the borrower's facility, while the borrower is still in possession of the facility encumbered by the security interest only if the holder either:

(i) exercises decision-making control over the borrower's environmental compliance, such that the holder has undertaken responsibility for the borrower's hazardous substance handling or disposal practice; or
(ii) exercises day-to-day management control over the borrower's business enterprises with respect to environmental compliance or all, or substantially all, of the operational (as opposed to administrative) aspects of the enterprise other than environmental compliance.[22]

In such circumstances the security interest exemption will be lost. The lender will not be considered to be participating in management so as to jeopardize the security interest exemption when:

[22] 57 *Fed. Reg.* (1992) at 18383; the two situations set out above are referred to as the 'general test or standard of participation in a facility's management'; see also the discussion commencing at p. 18375. Note that the term 'holder' is defined as a person who maintains

(i) policing the loan;
(ii) undertaking financial work-out with a borrower where the obligation is in default or in threat of default;
(iii) foreclosing and preparing the facility for sale or liquidation;
(iv) monitoring the borrower's business;
(v) requiring or conducting on-site inspections and audits of the environmental condition of the facility or the borrower's financial condition; and
(vi) requiring certification of financial information or compliance with applicable duties, laws, or regulations or requiring other similar actions provided that the holder does not otherwise participate in the management of the facility as provided for in the Rule.[23]

Actions taken by a lender prior to or at the inception of a transaction are irrelevant with respect to the general test of participation in management and thus not considered evidence of participation in the management of the facility. Pre-loan activities which would not affect the exemption would include negotiations between a lender and borrower, environmental inspections or audits conducted by the lender or borrower, or the requirement by the lender that the borrower clean up the facility as a condition of the loan or other obligation.[24] Recognizing that foreclosure or sale is often the only practical remedy left to the lender on default by the borrower, the Rule provides that the mere foreclosure and taking of title does not void the exemption provided that the lender is actively attempting to sell or liquidate the secured assets. Where a holder's actions indicate that it is not seeking to sell or liquidate the secured assets, the exemption is voided.[25] Under the Rule a 'bright line' test is set out that, if followed, establishes that a lender is selling the assets in a reasonably expeditious manner.

In order to meet the test the lender must, within twelve months of taking title, list the property with a broker, dealer, or agent who deals with the type of property in question or advertise the property for sale or disposition on at least a monthly basis in a real estate or trade publication.[26]

There is no time limit set out in the Rule for the actual disposition of the property; however, the exemption will be lost if, at any time after six months following the acquisition of title, the lender rejects, fails to act upon within ninety days of receipt of a written, bona fide, cash offer of fair consideration for the property, or if the lender outbids others offering fair consideration.[27] It should also be noted that a lender may incur CERCLA liability independently of not having 'participated in management' under the circumstances referred to above if it arranged for the dis-

indicia of ownership and includes a lender, guarantor, surety, receiver, or any other person who acts on behalf of or for the benefit or a holder.

[23] 57 *Fed. Reg.* (1992) at 18377; see also 18383–4.

[24] Ibid. 18376–7.

[25] See *Guidice* v. *B.F.G. Electroplating and Manufacturing Co.*, 732 F. Supp. 556 (WPAa 1989) at 562–3; *United States* v. *Maryland Bank & Trust Co.*, 632 F. Supp. at 579.

[26] 57 *Fed. Reg.* 18378; see provisions of Rule set out at pp. 18383–4.

[27] Ibid. 18384.

posal or treatment of hazardous substances at the facility under s.107(a)(3), or by having transported hazardous substances for disposal under s.107(a)(4).[28] The Rule also clarifies the 'innocent landowner' defence as it applies to government entities where the harm was caused solely by the acts of third parties with which the government entity had no contractual relationship, provided that certain additional elements specified in ss.101(35)(A)–(B) are also established.[29]

Although the Final EPA Rule goes a considerable way to reducing the uncertainty created by the *Fleet Factors II* decision, the manner in which it will be applied in practice has yet to be determined. As noted earlier, the *Fleet Factors IV* trial decision issued on 12 May 1993 has created a further round of uncertainty with respect to the term 'arranged for' as used in the section under the CERCLA statute imposing liability on any person who arranged for the disposal or treatment of hazardous substances at any facility owned or operated by another.[30] The district trial court was clearly of the view that courts applying that section should interpret that phrase broadly to effectuate CERCLA's remedial goals. The Rule's effectiveness in creating a less troubling climate for lenders will also have to await the outcome of the inevitable spate of judicial challenges which will emerge as lenders and the EPA explore the outer limits of the newly defined security interest exemption.

Note: On 4 February 1994 a federal Appeals Court invalidated the United States Environmental Protection Agency's lender liability Final Rule, holding that the EPA lacked statutory authority to curtail liability under CERCLA. See *Kelly* v. *EPA* Nos. 92–1312, 92–1314, 1994 U.S. App. LEXIS 1715 (DC Cir. 4 February 1994).

4.3. LENDER LIABILITY IN CANADA

4.3.1. Constitutional and Legislative Framework

Canada, although having a federal system of government as does the United States, is confronted with a very different constitutional basis to support its environmental regulatory regimes. Both the federal and provincial governments (and, by delegation from the provinces, municipal governments) have enacted a multitude of statutes, regulations, and by-laws to monitor and control activities which potentially cause harm to the environment. Since the authority to enact environmental legislation is not specifically given to either the federal or provincial governments in

[28] Ibid. 18384–5.

[29] Ibid. 18380 and 18385.

[30] *United States* v. *Fleet Factors (Fleet Factors IV)* 821 F. Supp. 707; *supra* at n. 10.

the constitution, that authority must be derived instead from the particular head of power within the jurisdiction of the federal or provincial governments to which it pertains.[31] Thus, in Canada, the provinces in a practical sense are primarily responsible for the enactment of environmental legislation which might affect lenders, by reason of having exclusive jurisdiction over 'property and civil rights'.[32] The federal government, through its jurisdiction over fisheries, bankruptcy and insolvency, and the regulation of trade and commerce has a more limited role,[33] and increasing attention in recent years has also been given to the federal government's ability and willingness to co-ordinate and set standards on a nation-wide basis.[34]

To date, none of the provinces in Canada have enacted a 'Superfund' statute along the lines of the United States model, relying instead upon regulatory legislation which, although varying from province to province, contains the following basic elements.[35]

1. a general prohibition against the discharge of pollutants (contaminants) which may cause environmental harm to the natural environment.[36] This often refers to specified permissive levels or concentrations set out in accompanying regulations;
2. definition of the persons or parties who may be held responsible and thus exposed to potential liability;[37]

[31] Canada's constitution traces its origins to the British North America Act of 1867, which predated the modern concepts of pollution and environmental impacts associated with pollution; see D. Gibson 'Constitutional Jurisdiction over Environmental Management in Canada' (1973) 23 UTLJ 54, and D. Tingley (ed.), *Environmental Protection and the Canadian Constitution* (Edmonton: Environmental Law Centre, 1987) for an excellent review of the Canadian constitutional framework.

[32] Other provincial heads of power which may be relevant in a lender liability context include: The Management and Sale of the Public Lands belonging to the Province and of the Timber and Wood Thereon (s.92(5)); Local Works and Undertakings (s.92(10)).

[33] The federal government, in addition to the overriding, 'Peace, Order and Good Government' power, also has exclusive jurisdiction over: Navigation and Shipping (s.91(10)); Criminal Law (s.91(27)); and Banking, Incorporation of Banks and the Issue of Paper Money (s.91(15)).

[34] See e.g. the Canadian Environmental Protection Act, RSC 1985, c.16 (4th Supp.).

[35] The Ontario Environmental Protection Act, RSO 1990, c.E.19 (referred to as the Ontario EPA) has been utilized herein as a typical example of the type of environmental regulatory legislation enacted by the provinces.

[36] See e.g. Ontario Environmental Protection Act s.6(1) 'No person shall discharge into the natural environment any contaminant, and no person responsible for a source of contaminant shall permit the discharge into the natural environment of any contaminant from the source of contaminant, in an amount, concentration or level in excess of that prescribed by the regulations.'

[37] Amendments to the Ontario Environmental Protection Act in June of 1990 expand the definition of PRPs to include 'previous' owners, occupiers, and those having the charge, management, or control of a source of contaminant (Ontario Bill 220, 1990 Ont. Stat. c.18, s.19); see D. Shand, 'Cleanup of Contaminated Sites: Will Lenders Be Implicated?' (1990) 3 *CBLN* 33, for an analysis of the Bill 220 amendments on lenders; see also J. Fordyce, J. Kofman, and D. Tay, 'Environmental Liability: A Gun at the Lender's Head' (1990) IX *IFLR* 19.

3. Provisions prescribing the statutory duties and responsibilities of both regulatory authorities and those having the charge, management, or control of a source of contaminant, including mitigative and/or remedial measures to be taken in the event of an unlawful discharge; and
4. A penalty regime, including fines and imprisonment, and liability for the costs of clean-up for breach of any statutory duty or obligation.

Within the context of a particular environmental statute, different categories of liability may attach to an ever-expanding list of PRPs. Thus, depending on the fact situation a PRP may be required to comply with one or more administrative orders issued by the applicable regulatory authority, such as stop orders, control orders, or orders of a restorative or preventive nature. Moreover, legislation now routinely provides the regulatory authority with the power to take effective remedial action in emergency situations or when a person is ordered to take such action in a timely fashion and fails to do so. In such case, the costs incurred by the regulatory authority may be recovered from the person held liable under the statute in question.[38]

In addition, a PRP may be subject to civil liability to third parties for both direct and consequential damages resulting from a discharge of contaminants including, in most cases, damages incurred by the Crown. Finally, as mentioned above, a person who is convicted of a statutory offence, most of which entail strict liability, will be subject also to increasingly stringent penalties involving substantial fines and/or imprisonment.

4.3.2. Ownership or Control

It is reasonably clear at the present time that the lender in Canada will not, generally speaking, risk environmental liability with respect to the borrower's business *without* assuming some form of ownership or control in the course of realizing its security held as collateral for the subject loan.[39] At the other end of the spectrum it is also relatively clear that the lender will probably incur potential environmental liability when it has acquired ownership through foreclosure, for, in such cases, the lender would fall within the definition of 'owner' under most environmental statutes, and the requisite obligations and liabilities attributable to owners would normally apply. The more difficult question involves the degree of

[38] Ontario Bill 220, 1990 Ont. Stat. c.18, s.19.

[39] Note that under the Ontario Environmental Protection Act personal liability may be incurred by directors or officers of a corporation for breach of their statutory duties under s.194. This liability may also extend to those individuals nominated by the lender to the borrower's board, even though such nominee directors will often have little to do with the day-to-day management of the business.

control which might be permitted the lender with respect to the appointment of a receiver/manager (herein called 'receiver') pursuant to the provisions of the loan instrument before the threshold is crossed and environmental liability incurred.

In Canada, there is an absence of statutory provisions which purport to exempt a lender from liability if it merely holds indicia of ownership primarily to protect its security interest, and does not participate in the management of the facility, such as is found in the United States CERCLA legislation. Furthermore, the absence of statutory defences, such as the 'innocent landowner' defence available under the United States statute, could potentially place the Canadian lender in a more vulnerable position. The point has been made by some Canadian commentators that by exercising control or, as the United States cases sometimes state, 'participating in the management of the borrower's business', a lender leaves itself open to a ministerial order to repair the injury or damage caused by the discharge of any contaminant which has caused an adverse effect upon the environment. The rationale underlying this view is the supposition that, by exercising such control, the lender may become 'a person who *causes* or *permits* the discharge into the natural environment of a contaminant that injures or damages land, water, property or plant life'.[40] In addition, by assuming control of the borrower's assets through a receiver appointed by the lender, the lender and the receiver (who will be considered the agent of the lender notwithstanding any language to the contrary contained in the security instrument) may find themselves designated as 'persons responsible' under provisions of the legislation and, as such, subject to control orders issued by the regulatory authority.[41]

The Canadian courts have only recently begun to address the subject of lender liability, and therefore the case-law provides only limited guidance. However, they have indicated that the element of control is a key factor in determining whether a person has caused or permitted a discharge in contravention of the legislation. It is therefore also instructive to review the case law dealing with control and ownership in *non-lender* liability situations.

[40] See e.g. D. Tay and D. Wakefield, 'Lenders Need Greater Awareness of Potential Environmental Liability' (1990), 4 *NCDR*, 95. See also *Re Mac's Convenience Stores Inc. and Minister of the Environment for Ontario; Re Suncor Inc. et al. and Minister of the Environment for Ontario* (1984) 48 Or (2d) 9 (Div. Ct.). The point is also made by Fordyce *et al.*, 'Environmental Liability', and R. B. Smith, 'Secured Lending Practice: The Impact of Environmental Law in Canada' (1990) 5 *BJIBFL* 1 at 16.

[41] See *Canada Trust Co.* v. *Bulora Corp. Ltd.* (1980) 34 CBR (NS) 145, *aff'd*, 39 CBR (NS) 162; *Peat Marwick Ltd.* v. *Consumers' Gas Co.* (1980) 35 CBR (NS) 1 (Ont. CA).

4.3.3. Summary of Canadian Case-Law

The following represents a brief summary of some of the most frequently cited cases, to provide the reader with an appreciation of the position the courts have taken on a number of issues which are germane to a discussion of lender liability in Canada.

In *R.* v. *Placer Developments Ltd.*,[42] on a charge of permitting the deposit of diesel fuel into water frequented by fish contrary to the Fisheries Act, the court found the defendant responsible for the activities of the independent contractor that directly led to the spill, because the contract between the parties empowered the defendant to supervise and influence the offending conduct.[43] The defendant had the opportunity and expertise to exercise its responsibility and failed to do so. The court adopted the following concept from *R.* v. *City of Sault Ste. Marie*.[44]

> The ability to influence the conduct of an independent contractor or any other party is measured by the power the accused may employ to affect the conduct in question. These powers may derive from legislation, financial control, executive control, expertise, ownership or contractual or legal rights, and from any other factor creating an influential bargaining power, position of authority, or ability to control offending activities.[45]

In *R.* v. *City of Sault Ste. Marie*[46] the Supreme Court of Canada considered the concept of 'control' in a prosecution under the *Ontario Water Resources Act*. The court stated that the control test is a factual one, based on an assessment of the defendant's position with respect to the activity it undertakes that causes pollution.[47] If the accused can and should control the activity at the point where pollution occurs, then it is responsible for the pollution.

In *In Re Mac's Convenience Stores, Suncor Inc., and the Minister of Environment for Ontario*,[48] the jurisdiction of the Ontario Minister of Environment to issue a repair order under then s.16 of the EPA was being challenged. Charges were laid against the operator of a service station, the property owner, and the supplier of the operator. The court found that extensive obligations were imposed on the operator in its agreement with its supplier. There were a number of provisions relating to the petroleum products of the supplier which would support an argument that the supplier exercised a degree of control over the operation of the premises. It is noteworthy that the court took the position that the Minister had a duty to determine the persons who have caused or

[42] (1983) 13 CELR 42 (Terr. Ct. of Yukon).
[43] Ibid. at 47.
[44] (1978) 40 CCC (2d) 353 (SCC).
[45] (1983) 13 CELR at 47.
[46] (1978) 40 CCC (2d) 353 (SCC).
[47] Ibid.
[48] (1984) 48 OR (2d) 9 (Ont. HC).

permitted pollution.[49] Where the Minister had done so in a reasonable manner with credible evidence to support the finding, the court should show deference and refrain from interfering. The Minister had no duty to hold an inquiry before issuing an order, as the consequent delay of such a procedure would frustrate the ability of the Minister to administer the statute.

Canada Trust Co. v. *Bulora Corp., Ltd.*[50] is instructive as to the attitude of Canadian courts regarding the position of a receiver of a property requiring repair. It is the only Canadian case dealing, albeit indirectly, with the lender. The case concerned a group of buildings in such a state of disrepair that they posed a fire hazard. The office of the local fire marshal issued an order under the Fire Marshal's Act requiring repair or demolition. The costs of demolition would exceed the market value of the properties. The court found that the receiver was indeed the proper person to receive service of the order for demolition, since the order appointing the receiver empowered the receiver to carry on the business of the debtor in all of its phases, including the prosecution of lawsuits that are deemed necessary for the protection of the property and assets.

In directing the receiver to comply with the demolition order, the Supreme Court of Ontario imposed a duty on the receiver to pay the costs of demolition where the safety of individuals was of vital concern. While noting the unfortunate consequences of a creditor's suffering the loss resulting from the demolition, the court was of the opinion that the management of an asset with a view to the safety of those residing in and beside the asset was paramount. The Ontario Court of Appeal upheld the trial judge's order on the grounds of the statutory duty imposed on the receiver under the legislation, and further indicated that it was unnecessary to consider the social implications of the order.[51]

Canada Trust Co. and *Peat Marwick Ltd.* v. *Consumers' Gas Co.*[52] pose concern for a lender in the event that it appoints a receiver to realize on assets. Notwithstanding the usual provisions in the lender's security documentation that its receiver is agent for the borrower, *Peat Marwick* indicates the clause has application in the case of a receiver conducting the business affairs of the debtor.[53] However, the court found that, in performing its task of realizing assets, the receiver wears a different hat in that it acts as agent for the lender. Arguably, it follows that if a receiver attracts liability under the environmental legislation in the course of realizing on security, then the lender may well find itself vicariously liable through the actions of its agent. Even the standard clause—providing

[49] (1984) 48 OR (2d) 9 (Ont. HC). at 12.

[50] (1980) 34 CBR (NS) 145 (SC), *aff'd*, 39 CBR (NS) 152 (CA).

[51] 39 CBR (NS) 153.

[52] (1980) 35 CBR (NS) 1 (Ont. CA).

[53] Ibid. at 11.

that any and all costs and expenses incurred by a lender in connection with the borrower's compliance with statutory duties imposed on the operation of his business will be added to the loan and secured by the security—will prove futile if the value of the collateral is largely reduced by environmental liability[54] or, as in *Canada Trust Co.* v. *Bulora*, the cost of the remedial measures under the environmental legislation exceeds the costs of the assets held.

The Ontario Divisional Court in the case of *Canadian National Railway Co.* v. *Ontario (Director, Environmental Protection Act)*,[55] known as the 'Northern Wood Preservers' case, held that a lender's (mortgagee's) liability could only arise once it had entered into actual possession or control of the source of contaminant. The court in this case concluded that in order to be an 'owner' within the meaning of the Ontario Environmental Protection Act, the mortgagee or any other potentially liable party must have 'possession and dominion over the facility'. Since the mortgagee in this case had not taken any steps to acquire possession or control of the facility, it could not be found to be a 'person responsible' for the source of contaminant. At best, the mortgagee had the right to obtain control in the future through its remedies under the mortgage, and was not actually in control of the facility at the time of the Ministry's control order. The principal findings in this case were affirmed on appeal.

In *Panamericana de Bienes y Servicos S.A.* v. *Northern Badger Oil and Gas Ltd.*,[56] the practical issue before the court was whether the $200,000 estimated costs of complying with an order by the Energy Resources Conservation Board (ERCB), made subsequent to receiverships but prior to bankruptcy, to abandon seven oil wells, should be paid out of the funds held by the receiver for secured creditors or funds payable to the trustee in bankruptcy. Since the order has been sanctioned by orders-in-council of the government, the court treated them as having the force of law in Alberta.

The court held that the receiver was bound by the abandonment order. Since a receiving order had been made under the Bankruptcy Act, the court was of the opinion that the receiver and all other creditors then became subject to the provisions of the Bankruptcy Act. It was the court's view that the ERCB was a creditor seeking to have its claim to

[54] See Tay and Wakefield, 'Lenders Need Greater Awareness' 94.

[55] (1992) 87 DLR (4th 603); 54 OAC 367 (CA). Note that the decision in this case was based on the wording of the Ontario EPA prior to the 1990 amendments.

[56] 75 Alta LR (2d) 185; the Alberta Court of Appeal agreed that the ERCB had the jurisdiction to issue the order and that the receiver had to pay for the costs of the abandonment from the proceeds of the receivership. In doing so, however, the Court of Appeal overturned the trial judge's decision that the ERCB held a provable claim as an unsecured creditor in the bankruptcy and concluded that the ERCB was not a creditor in the bankruptcy. See [1991] 5 WWR 577, 81 Alta LR (2d) 45. Leave to appeal to SCC refused 83 Alta LR (2d) IXvi.

have the seven wells abandoned preferred to the claim of the secured creditor and to the scheme of distribution set forth in s.107 of the Bankruptcy Act. Such a claim was provable in bankruptcy since it fell within the broad definition of s.121 of the Act: 'all debts, liabilities, present or future, to which the bankrupt is subject'. The court reached this conclusion by reasoning that the ERCB had the powers under the Oil and Gas Production and Conservation Act to abandon the wells and collect its costs so incurred. If the ERCB had pursued that route, it would only have a monetary claim against the bankrupt. The court stated that ordering the receiver to effect the abandonment was simply another form of the same claim. Thus the claim, whether done directly or ordered to be done, was a claim provable in bankruptcy. Such a claim, as a Crown claim, would be a preferred claim in bankruptcy subject to the prior claims of secured creditors. Accordingly, the court instructed the receiver not to proceed to abandon the wells out of the moneys held for the secured creditors.

In a subsequent case, *Re Lamford Forest Products Ltd. (Lamford)*,[57] the court dealt with the issue of who is responsible for environment damage in a bankruptcy. Prior to making a voluntary assignment in bankruptcy, Lamford had contaminated its sawmill site with heavy metals and a number of other toxic substances. Subsequent to the assignment the Ministry issued a clean-up order, and issue arose as to whether the trustee in bankruptcy was personally responsible for the cost of clean-up. The court held that the provisions of the Bankruptcy Act do not make the trustee liable for the costs of the clean-up any more than it makes the trustee liable for any of the other debts of the estate, although it did leave open the possibility that the trustee could be personally liable under the environmental legislation that may provide a broader definition of 'persons responsible'.

In addition, the court followed the *Panamericana* case in holding that the safety and health of society took precedence over the rights of creditors and that the Waste Management Act was a law of general application which was binding upon the trustee. Although concluding that the clean-up costs were not a claim in the bankruptcy, the court did allow the trustee's fees to have priority over the clean-up costs in the event of a deficiency in the funds available from the estate.

In the more recent case of *King (Township)* v. *Rolex Equipment Co.*,[58] the court once again held that the costs of removal of waste which had

[57] (1991) 63 BCLR (2d) 388; 86 DLR (4th) 534 (SC): for an excellent discussion of the cases involving insolvencies see J. Klimek, 'Liability for Environmental Damages in Insolvencies: Bulora, Panamericana and Lamford' (1992) 2 *JELP* 25.

[58] 90 DLR (4th) 442; 8 OR (3d) 457; see D. Saxe, 'Lender's Liability for Provincial Environmental Protection Requirements: Recent Developments' (1992) 14 CBR (3d) at p. 197.

been illegally dumped on lands subject to a mortgage had priority over the mortgagee's interest. In this case the mortgagee had refused to take possession of the contaminated property and the court announced that, if the mortgagee was unwilling to remove the waste itself, the court was prepared to appoint a receiver to remove the waste and sell the property, with the costs of removal being recoverable out of the proceeds of sale.

4.3.4. Limited Relief to Trustees in Bankruptcy

Recent amendments to the federal Bankruptcy and Insolvency Act[59] have provided a limited degree of comfort to trustees in bankruptcy with respect to environmental liability exposure. Section 14.06(2) of the revised Act absolves a trustee in bankruptcy from personal liability in respect of any environmental condition that arose, or any environmental damage that occurred, both before the trustee's appointment or after that appointment, except where the condition arose or the damage occurred as a result of the trustee's failure to exercise due diligence. In addition, the new amendments eliminate the hitherto preferred status of claims by both the federal and provincial Crown except in specific situations, thus placing a provincial claim or lien for recovery of clean-up costs behind those of secured creditors in a bankruptcy.

4.3.5. Curtailment of Open-Ended Liability for Court-Appointed Receivers

In *Bank of Montreal* v. *Lundigran's Ltd.*,[60] the court, faced with the reluctance of receivers to accept appointments with open-ended liability exposure for environmental clean-up costs in circumstances where the receiver assumes control of contaminated property, held that a receiver cannot be held responsible for clean-up costs of pre-existing contamination 'in excess of the value or moneys received from the sale of the individual asset which caused the environmental damage'. The court indicated that to impose unlimited liability on a receiver and manager, the legislation would have to be clear in its intent, which was not the case with existing environmental legislation.[61] In addition, the court noted that a superior court had the power to issue orders on whatever terms it considered just, and therefore it remained within the court's jurisdiction to limit the liability of the receiver in the order appointing him.

[59] RSC 1985, C-B-3 as amended. See D. Estrin and R. Jansen, 'Negotiating Agreements with the MOE: The Perspective of Secured Lenders, Receivers and Trustees in Bankruptcy', CBAO–CLE Program, 9 Mar. 1993.

[60] (1992) 12 CBR (3d) 170; 92 DLR (4th) 554.

[61] (1992) 12 CBR (3d) 178–180.

4.3.6. Limitations on Liability through Negotiated Agreements with Regulatory Authorities

Regulatory authorities in some Canadian jurisdictions, notably in Ontario, have recently shown a willingness to consider limiting the liability of secured lenders and receivers through negotiated agreements. By doing so the Ministry is assured that a party who is likely to recover funds at some point in time from the sale of the contaminated property will by agreement undertake a remedial programme satisfactory to the Ministry, which in turn will allow the secured creditor to retain a portion of the recovered funds even if the agreed work does not remedy all the environmental problems. In addition, the Ontario Ministry of the Environment will normally allow a lender to enter on the property for the purposes of carrying out a brief inspection to determine whether or not it is worthwhile to proceed further, provided that the lender is prepared to fund proper security on the property during the inspection period.

Although such agreements cannot protect the lender against claims from third parties, they do provide a practical means of placing some limits on a lender's environmental liability exposure in the absence of express statutory limitations, or the failure of the secured lender or receiver to obtain an appropriate court order limiting their environmental liability.[62] There may also be some question as to the enforceability of such agreements negotiated with the Ministry, although to date there have been no actions challenging their validity.[63]

4.4. MINIMIZING ENVIRONMENTAL RISK

The foregoing review of potential environmental liability exposure facing lenders in North America underlines the necessity for lenders and their professional advisers to consider implementing a thorough review of existing lending practices with a view to minimizing environmental risk. There is little doubt that the lender will be in a better position to avoid environmental liability by exercising appropriate caution and undertaking rigorous due diligence inquiries *prior* to entering into a loan transaction, particularly with respect to formulating both the loan commitment and documentation setting out the rights of the lender in the event of default

[62] For a definitive discussion of the Ontario Ministry's approach to negotiated agreements limiting lender's liability, see M. B. Jackson, 'Dialogue with the Regulators', Insight Seminar Program, 11 July 1991; a draft comprehensive agreement is found as an attachment to a further paper by M. B. Jackson, entitled 'Contaminated Sites: Negotiating with the Ministry', CBAO–CLE Program, 9 Mar. 1993.

[63] See H. Dahme and R. Jansen, 'Government Agreements with Receivers and Secured Creditors: Are they Enforceable?' (1992) 3 *ELA* 1–3.

on the part of the borrower. There are, however, a number of factors which should also be taken into account by the lender with respect to existing loans for which funds have been advanced and where the security for the loan is already in place. The following section will outline some prudent steps which might be taken to minimize the lender's environmental liability exposure in both situations.

4.4.1. Pre-Loan Due Diligence

1. At the very outset of the discussions with the borrower, the lender should ensure that it fully understands the nature of the borrower's business and take note of anything concerning the borrower's assets or activities which might give rise to environmental concerns. In many cases, the lender will have to formulate a series of specific questions tailored to the borrower's particular business enterprise.

The lender's account managers should be thoroughly trained to identify the environmental warning signs and request the following type of information at the time of initial discussions with the borrower:

(a) whether the borrower's business involves a hazardous substance in any form or manner (e.g. pesticides, herbicides, dust suppressants, PCBs, solvents, used oils or liquid wastes, paints, lacquers, dry cleaning fluids);
(b) whether the prior owner of the property had any connection with any hazardous substances;
(c) whether the structures on the property contain hazardous substances such as urea formaldehyde or asbestos;
(d) whether the property was ever used for industrial purposes;
(e) whether there is an order or approval outstanding relative to any environmental legislation or other government authority;
(f) whether the borrower stores waste in underground tanks, what quantities are stored, the type of construction used for the tanks, the age of the tanks; and
(g) whether the borrower is aware of any obvious physical signs of contamination such as stained soil or concrete, vegetation damage, odours, surface draining wastes, discoloration, etc.[64]

2. Although it is necessary to have representations and warranties in the loan commitment of the kind listed subsequently, there is no substitute for the lender's satisfying itself by way of due diligence, and perhaps even by way of a physical inspection of the property, that adverse environmental conditions do not appear to exist.

Where such environmental concerns are apparent or have been

[64] See Klotz and Saikotos, 'Lender Liability', 275 (discussing risk minimization).

discussed, the lender is well advised to consider a full-blown investigation of the environmental conditions of the borrower's business and assets and the potential costs associated with potential environmental liabilities. In order properly to assess the utility of granting the loan, the degree of risk should be factored into the lender's pricing decision. This investigation should be performed by an experienced environmental consulting firm under supervision of environmental counsel and should include soil and ground water sampling, if appropriate.

3. Provision should be made in the loan commitment for the borrower to produce to the lender warranties and representations, executed by a senior officer of the borrower,[65] that:

(a) to the best of his knowledge he is not aware of any present hazardous condition in or on the land or any building or structure on the land;
(b) to the best of his knowledge he is not aware of any present hazardous condition in or on other land owned or operated by the borrower, or any other building or structure on such land;
(c) neither the borrower nor any prior owner, to the borrower's knowledge, have created conditions which may give rise to environmental liabilities, and that no enforcement actions or civil actions relating to an environmental matter are pending or threatened;
(d) the use and condition of the assets of the borrower are not in breach of any regulation or order under existing legislation;
(e) the borrower has obtained all certificates, consents, permits, and approvals required for compliance under the applicable legislation;
(f) there have been no complaints of any kind whatsoever by any person relating to an environmental hazard;
(g) the borrower has or will have proper operations and management programmes, with regular reporting by an independent specialist that the programmes are being adhered to; and
(h) the borrower will immediately notify the lender if there is any type of environmental concern or if any complaint is received from any person alleging an environmental concern.

Notwithstanding the lender's due diligence, loan agreements should be structured in such a way that enables the lender to withhold funds if, prior to advancement, it discovers a material environmental concern in relation to the borrower's business and/or assets. In addition, lenders may wish to restrict the borrower's ability to lease the property to a tenant who might cause an environmental concern, and to include an indemnifi-

[65] See J. N. Berman, 'Lender's Environmental Concerns', in *Lender Liability and Responsibility* (Law Society of Upper Canada (Toronto, 1989)) (listing possible clauses to include in a loan commitment).

cation clause in the loan commitment for any cost incurred by the lender in undertaking environmental due diligence prior to advancing funds under its loan commitment.

In view of recent court decisions on the issue of ownership and control, lenders should exercise some degree of caution as regards how the loan is secured. In certain cases the lender may consider securing environmentally risky assets (or those with potential for environmental risk) by way of separate charges, in order more easily to facilitate the lender selectively realizing only those assets which are unlikely to expose the lender to environmental liability. Even if the borrower's assets were charged by a single debenture, the lender would still have the option of appointing a receiver to realize only part of the security. The lender could then execute a partial discharge with respect to the environmentally risky assets if it chooses to do so. The lender might also consider securing appropriate environmental indemnities or guarantees from other legal entities which may be related to or controlled by the borrower. However, the financial viability of any such indemnitor or guarantor and its legal right to provide such financial assistance must be considered carefully. In some jurisdictions, it may be possible for the borrower to obtain environmental liability insurance and/or surety bonds to underwrite environmental clean-up costs. Experience has shown, however, that even where such insurance is available it is often too expensive, and may not provide adequate coverage both in terms of amount and risk.

4.4.2. Existing Loans

1. Lenders must be extremely careful to avoid involvement in the management of their borrower's businesses. A major risk for lenders who become involved in the business operations of their borrowers is the potential liability of a *person who causes or permits* the discharge of a contaminant into the natural environment that injures or damages land, water, property, or plant life.
2. As soon as the lender becomes aware of a situation which might impair its security interest or give rise to potential environmental liability to the borrower, or, by implication, to the lender, the lender may wish to seek the advice of environmental counsel *prior* to embarking upon a course of action which may increase the lender's environmental liability exposure.
3. The lender should be vigilant in ensuring that the borrower is in full compliance with all environmental legislation. In this way the lender increases its chances of saving itself and the borrower from potentially crippling liability. However, in so doing, the lender walks a tightrope: the more it knows and participates in its borrower's

business, the more likely that it could be found to have '*caused or permitted*' the contamination.[66]

4. Once default has occurred and the lender is considering foreclosure on real estate that could be contaminated, the lender should think carefully about putting the borrower into bankruptcy, unless the value of the assets in the estate exceeds any cost of clean-up or any other remedial measures and litigation costs. In most cases, however, the lender will likely proceed by way of power of sale and, if possible, in appropriate circumstances should avoid going into possession.
5. In many cases the lender should consider appointing an agent to collect receivables and sell other assets, instead of appointing a receiver and manager to carry on the borrower's business.
6. In cases where a receiver has been appointed to carry on the borrower's business, it is important to ensure that all reasonable steps are taken to prevent pollution and to comply with all relevant environmental legislation. A competent environmental consultant should be retained by the receiver to provide ongoing professional advice.

4.5. CONCLUDING COMMENTS

It is difficult to do full justice to a very complex and ill-defined area of law, and this chapter only attempts to provide an overview of the inherent risks facing the key actors involved in the financial services industry in the United States and Canada. Although environmental liability will, most probably, be a continuing source of concern for lenders for the foreseeable future, it now appears that governments and regulatory authorities in both countries are prepared to exhibit a more reasoned and flexible approach to what had become an untenable situation for the lending community.

The degree to which the recent developments referred to above will advance society's pressing need to improve its sorry environmental record, while at the same time protecting the legitimate interests of those institutions funding (albeit indirectly) the polluting activities, will undoubtedly become clear, but for the jurisdictions which have yet to embark upon an area fraught with complexity and controversy, the North American experience may encourage an abundance of caution.

[66] See Fordyce *et al.*, 'Environmental Liability', 22.

5

European Community Law and the Environment

MARGARET BRUSASCO MACKENZIE

5.1. INTRODUCTION

European Communities environmental regulation dates in the main from 1973 when the first Environmental Action Programme was adopted by the Community, subsequent to the first United Nations conference on the environment in Stockholm in 1972. Over the past twenty years the EC has adopted five Action Programmes in the field of the environment. Within the framework of these programmes it has adopted more than 200 legally binding acts—regulations, directives, decisions covering water, air, and noise pollution, waste, chemical substances, and nature protection.

Emphasis during the first two programmes was on legislation aimed at clearing up existing black-spots caused by industrial pollution. The emphasis in the 3rd and 4th programmes has switched to a more preventive philosophy aimed at creating sound environmental policies, plans, and programmes from the outset by requiring prior environment impact assessment procedures, and freedom of access to information in environmental planning procedures.

A vast and comprehensive legislative arsenal has thus been created within the European Community and therefore in each of the Member States. However, the implementation of this legislation is still not achieving the hoped-for results. Having constituted this legislative bedrock, it was then possible to look for alternative or additional approaches to achieving environmental protection and therefore the Fifth Action Programme which was endorsed in December 1992—the same year as the Rio Conference—is a turning-point in environmental policy.[1]

It relies upon a series of instruments, not just the command and control approach but also on market forces through the use of economic instruments such as taxes and incentives. It also opens up the consultation

The author gratefully acknowledges the major contribution made to this paper by Mr. J. García Burgués, Deputy Head of Unit, International Affairs, DG XI.1.

[1] See B. Greenwood, *infra*, Ch. 6.

process to a much larger extent, involving industry, academia, and non-governmental organizations. Similarly, it is intended that much greater use will be made of voluntary codes of conduct on the part of industry. More emphasis will also be given to information, education, and training, so as to involve the general public at large in the common goal of protecting the environment of the European Community at local, national, and regional level.

5.2. THE GENERAL FRAMEWORK

5.2.1. Origins of Community Environment Policy

The Treaties establishing the European Communities did not contain specific provisions relating to Community action in the field of the environment. Only the health and safety provisions of the Euratom Treaty concerning the establishment of basic Community standards for the protection of workers and the general public against the dangers arising from ionizing radiation (Articles 30–39) were of some relevance for environmental purposes.

In the EEC Treaty some indirect references were made to environmental protection. In particular, Article 36 authorized the introduction of prohibitions or restrictions on imports, exports, or goods in transit justified on grounds of 'the protection of health and life of humans, animals or plants'. Similarly, according to the broad definition in Article 2, the general objective of the European Economic Community is 'to promote throughout the Community a harmonious development of economic activities, a continuous and balanced expansion, an increase in stability, an accelerated raising of the standard of living and closer relations between the Member States belonging to it'.

Although this comprehensive definition might well cover environmental goals and objectives, it is clear that for its founders environmental protection was not among the initial aims of the Community. This omission is, however, far from surprising, since in the late 1950s, when the Communities were created, the environment was not yet perceived as needing a specific policy to protect it.

Yet it soon became apparent that the establishment of the common market and, especially, the removal of restrictions on the import and export of goods, inevitably required the adoption of some common environmental rules. As a result, several environmental measures were enacted even before Community environment policy was officially launched. For example, a directive on the classification, packaging, and labelling of dangerous substances was adopted in 1967, and three years later the Council approved two directives on the sound level of, and emissions from, motor vehicles.

The real impetus for the creation of a comprehensive Community policy in the field of the environment came from an external factor. In July 1972 the UN Conference on the Human Environment took place in Stockholm. This Conference showed for the first time that effective measures were urgently needed in order to protect the world's environment from the increasing pressure resulting from human activities and economic growth. Accordingly, the Conference gave rise to numerous initiatives at national, regional, and international level.

In the Community, at a European summit held in Paris in November 1972, four months after the Stockholm Conference, the Heads of State and Government of the Community Member States and of the states which were about to join the Community, recognized that:

> Economic expansion is not an end in itself . . . It should result in an improvement in the quality of life as well as standards of living. As befits the genius of Europe, particular attention will be given to intangible values and to protecting the environment, so that real progress may really be put at the service of mankind.

The Heads of State and Government therefore invited the Community institutions to draft a programme of action for a Community environmental policy by the end of July 1973.

5.2.2. The Environmental Action Programmes

Following this invitation, the Commission drew up a first Environmental Action Programme whose basic guidelines were agreed by the Council in November 1973. This Programme defined the main principles and objectives of Community environment policy. It laid down, *inter alia*, that the best environment policy consists in preventing pollution at source rather than subsequently trying to remedy the damage, that environmental impact must be taken into account at the earliest possible stage in all decision-making processes, and that the cost of preventing and eliminating nuisances must in principle be borne by the polluter. Most of these principles still remain valid and were later incorporated into Article 130r of the EEC Treaty, as amended by the Single European Act.

Three subsequent Programmes adopted in 1977, 1983, and 1987 updated and reinforced the objectives and the philosophy set out in the first Programme. They reflected the evolution of environmental policy and thinking which occurred since 1973, by recognizing, in particular, the need to integrate environmental concerns and requirements into other Community policies and to develop a more integrated approach to pollution control in order to avoid the transfer of pollution from one environmental medium to another.

Even if they were not designed as legally binding for Community institutions, in the absence of specific provisions in the Treaties concerning Community action in the field of the environment, the successive Environmental Action Programmes provided the foundations and the policy framework for the development of such action and defined the agenda to respond to new environmental challenges as they arose. For example, the Fourth Action Programme called for harmonized legislation to manage the environmental risks associated with the use and release of genetically modified organisms, a problem which did not emerge until the 1980s with the development of biotechnology. Similarly, the priority given to the international dimension of Community environment policy has significantly increased over the years. The First Action Programme already recognized the need to reinforce international co-operation to address regional and transboundary environmental problems. As concern for global environmental challenges grew in the Community, the subsequent Programmes put particular emphasis on international action and on the promotion of a coherent and effective response to those challenges by the world community.

5.3. THE LEGAL BASIS

5.3.1. Articles 100 and 235 of the EEC Treaty

In the period between the adoption of the First Environmental Action Programme and the entry into force of the Single European Act in 1987, a large amount of environmental legislation was enacted in the Community. Two general provisions in the EEC Treaty—Article 100 and Article 235—provided, jointly or separately, the legal basis for the adoption of this legislation.

According to Article 100, 'the Council shall, acting unanimously on a proposal from the Commission, issue directives for the approximation of such provisions laid down by law, regulation or administrative action in Member States, as directly affect the establishment or functioning of the common market'. This article was used, in particular, to remove obstacles to intra-Community trade and to eliminate distortions of competition resulting from the existence of different national environmental regulations with a potential impact on production and marketing costs.

Article 235 lays down that 'if action by the Community should prove necessary to attain, in the course of the operation of the common market, one of the objectives of the Community and this Treaty has not provided the necessary powers, the Council shall, acting unanimously on a proposal from the Commission and after consulting the Parliament, take the appropriate measures'. Article 235, in conjunction with the reference contained in Article 2 to 'the improvement of the living and working conditions' as one of the objectives of the Community, was deemed enough to justify the adoption of specific measures in the sphere of environmental protection and improvement of the quality of life.

The jurisprudence of the European Court of Justice helped to clarify the remaining legal uncertainties as regards the Community's competence on environmental issues and the interpretation to be given to Articles 100 and 235 of the EEC Treaty. In Case 91/79,[2] and similarly in Case 240/83,[3] the court stated that environmental protection is 'one of the Community's essential objectives' and 'an object of general interest'.

5.3.2. The Single European Act

5.3.2.1. Articles 130r, 130s, and 130t

The Single European Act inserted into the EEC Treaty a separate title on the environment (Part III, Title VII), thus recognizing for the first time in explicit legal terms the Community's competence and responsibility in the field of the environment. The three articles included in this new title (Articles 130r, 130s, and 130t) defined the objectives, principles, and scope of Community environmental action, the decision-making procedures, and the relationship between Community and Member States environmental legislation.

Article 130r, 1, which constitutes the basic provision in this title, lists the three fundamental objectives of Community environmental action:

- to preserve, protect, and improve the quality of the environment;
- to contribute towards protecting human health;
- to ensure a prudent and rational utilization of natural resources.

According to Article 130r, 2, Community action 'shall be based on the principles that preventive action should be taken, that environmental damage should as a priority be rectified at source and that the polluter should pay'. Similarly, Article 130r, 2, stipulates that 'environmental protection requirements shall be a component of the Community's other policies'.

There is, however, an important aspect of the new rules on the environment introduced in the EEC Treaty by the Single European Act which should be noted. Article 130s lays down that 'the Council acting unanimously on a proposal from the Commission and after consulting the European Parliament and the Economic and Social Committee, shall

[2] Case 91/79 (*Commission* v. *Italy*), ECR 1980, pp. 1099–106.

[3] Case 240/83 (*Procureur de la République* v. *Association de défense des brûleurs d'huiles-usagées*), ECR 1985, pp. 531, 548.

decide what action is to be taken by the Community'. Although Article 130s also allows the Council to define by unanimity those matters on which decisions are to be taken by a qualified majority, six years after the entry into force of the Single European Act, the Council has never considered making use of this provision. As a result, the adoption of most decisions in the field of the environment still requires unanimity in the Council.

This legal requirement has undoubtedly slowed down the development of Community environment policy. In a Community of twelve Member States which very often have different priorities and diverging views on environmental issues, it is extremely difficult to make substantial progress if just one Member State can block the decision-making process. This is the reason why some proposals made by the Commission have been pending for years in the Council and, when finally adopted, the lowest common denominator has sometimes been the basis for compromise.

Against this background, the Treaty has explicitly recognized that Member States can, under certain conditions, reinforce the environmental standards established at Community level in order to achieve domestic environmental objectives. Article 130t allows Member States to maintain or introduce protective measures more stringent than those adopted in common, provided that these measures are compatible with the Treaty. This requirement means, in particular, that national measures may constitute neither a means of arbitrary discrimination nor a disguised restriction on trade between Member States.

In accordance with the jurisprudence of the European Court of Justice, as reflected, in particular, in the *Danish Bottles Case*,[4] intra-Community trade restrictive measures adopted by Member States on environmental grounds must fulfil three basic conditions:

- they must apply equally to domestic and to imported goods;
- the restrictions they introduce must be necessary in order to achieve legitimate environmental protection objectives;
- they must not be disproportionate or unreasonable.

5.3.2.2. Article 100a

The Single European Act similarly took into account environmental protection requirements as an integral component of the establishment and functioning of the internal market. In accordance with Article 100a.3, of the EEC Treaty, the Commission has to take as a basis a high level of protection in its proposals for the approximation of the provisions laid down by law, regulation, or administrative action by Member States which have as their object the establishment and functioning of the inter-

[4] Case 302/86 (*Commission* v. *Denmark*) ECR 1988, p. 4607.

nal market, when these proposals relate to health, safety, environmental protection, and consumer protection.

The definition of the respective fields of application of Articles 100a and 130s is a particularly controversial issue with important practical implications. In the first place, while Article 130s requires unanimity, those environmental measures relating to the completion of the internal market based on Article 100a are adopted by the Council by a qualified majority, in co-operation with the European Parliament. Further to that, a specific procedure has been established to verify that national measures more stringent than those adopted by the Community under Article 100a are not a means of arbitrary discrimination or a disguised restriction on trade between Member States. According to Article 100a.4:

> If after the adoption of a harmonisation measure by the Council acting by a qualified majority, a Member State deems it necessary to apply national provisions on grounds of major needs referred to in Article 36, or relating to protection of the environment or the working environment, it shall notify the Commission of these provisions.
>
> The Commission shall confirm the provisions involved after having verified that they are not a means of arbitrary discrimination or a disguised restriction on trade between Member States.
>
> By way of derogation from the procedure laid down in Articles 169 and 170, the Commission or any Member State may bring the matter directly before the Court of Justice if it considers that another Member State is making improper use of the powers provided for in this article.

These exceptional safeguards do not apply when, in accordance with Article 130t, Member States introduce protective measures more stringent than those adopted in common under Article 130s. The compatibility of such measures with the provisions of the Treaty can only be verified by the Court of Justice through the normal Article 169 and Article 170 procedures.

Despite these far-reaching practical implications, it is sometimes very difficult to decide whether a particular measure should be based on Article 130s or on Article 100a, since in practice environmental protection and completion of the internal market may appear as complementary, closely related objectives. Accordingly, over the past six years, the Council, the European Parliament, and the Commission have maintained different views on the definition of the respective fields of application of Articles 100a and 130s.

The Council has held a very restrictive interpretation on the scope of Article 100a, accepting this Article only as the legal basis for those measures which, while pursuing environmental objectives, are primarily aimed at removing obstacles to the functioning of the internal market, in particular as regards free movement of goods. On the other hand, the European Parliament and the Commission were in favour of using this Article as the legal basis for the adoption of other environmental measures which also contribute to removing distortions of competition.

The jurisprudence of the Court of Justice has brought some light into this complex matter, although some legal uncertainties still remain. In Case 300/89[5] (*Commission* v. *Council*), the court recognized that reliance on the double legal basis of Articles 100a and 130s is excluded in view of the different procedures applicable under both Articles. The court also stated that 'a measure intended to approximate national rules concerning conditions of production in a given industry with the aim of eliminating distortions of competition in this industry is such as to contribute to the achievement of the internal market and comes within the field of application of Article 100a'.

In case 155/91[6] (*Commission* v. *Council*) the court examined in the first place the objective of the litigious act—a directive on waste management—to conclude that Article 100a is not applicable as the legal basis for those measures which are primarily aimed at protecting the environment, even if they also contribute, as a secondary objective, to removing distortions of competition.

5.3.3. The Treaty on European Union

The new Treaty on European Union, which was signed by all the Member States on 7 February 1992 and came into force on 31 October 1993, contains a certain number of provisions which will significantly influence the development of Community environment policy in the coming years.

The new Treaty will, in the first place, amend Article 2 of the EEC Treaty, to include among the basic tasks of the European Community, as the European Economic Community will be known in the future, the promotion of 'a harmonious and balanced development of economic activities' and 'sustainable and non-inflationary growth respecting the environment'. Accordingly, Article 3 will provide that the activities of the Community shall include a policy in the sphere of the environment.

The Treaty on European Union will also introduce several important amendments in the Title on the environment which was inserted into the EEC Treaty by the Single European Act. In particular, the scope of Community policy on the environment will be significantly expanded, by including among its objectives, as listed in Article 130r, para. 1, the promotion of measures at international level to deal with regional or world-

[5] Case 300/89 (*Commission* v. *Council*) ECR 1991, pp. 28–67.

[6] Case 155/91 (*Commission* v. *Council*), not yet published.

wide environmental problems. The growing importance of the international dimension of this policy has thus been explicitly recognized.

At the same time, in accordance with Article 130r, para. 2, as it will be amended by the Treaty on European Union, 'Community policy on the environment shall aim at a high level of protection taking into account the diversity of situations in the various regions of the Community.' Similarly the precautionary principle is explicitly mentioned in this paragraph among the guiding principles of Community policy on the environment.

The most significant change to be introduced by the Treaty on European Union relates to the decision-making procedures. Article 130s will be substantially amended and, accordingly, environmental measures will, as a general rule, be adopted by the Council acting by a qualified majority, following the procedure of co-operation with the European Parliament referred to in Article 189c. Unanimity will only be required for the adoption of:

- provisions primarily of a fiscal nature;
- measures concerning town and country planning, land use with the exception of waste management and measures of a general nature, and management of water resources;
- measures significantly affecting a Member State's choice between different energy sources and the general structure of its energy supply.

It is also envisaged that general action programmes setting out priority objectives to be attained shall be adopted by the Council by a qualified majority, following the new codecision procedure referred to in Article 189b, where the powers of the European Parliament have been substantially reinforced. The codecision procedure will similarly be applicable for the adoption of those measures relating to the establishment of functioning of the internal market based on Article 100a and the Treaty.

The new system is certainly very complex, as three different procedures will be applicable for the adoption of environmental measures: Article 189c procedure (co-operation) will become the general procedure for the adoption of decisions based on Article 130s; Article 189b procedure (codecision) will be applicable for the approval of general action programmes and measures based on Article 100a; unanimity will only be required, as an exception, for those particular measures referred to in Article 130s para. 2.

The choice of the legal basis for the adoption of environmental measures will therefore remain, in all probability, a very controversial issue, especially as regards the interpretation to be given to the exceptions listed in Article 130s.2. It is clear, however, that the Treaty on European Union will significantly contribute to improving the efficiency and speed of the decision-making procedures in the field of the environment, and to reducing the democratic deficit by strengthening the role of the European Parliament.

5.4. ACHIEVEMENTS

5.4.1. Community Environmental Legislation

Despite all legal uncertainties and political obstacles, Community environment policy has achieved remarkable results, especially in the legislative area. Since 1973 the Community has adopted more than 200 legal acts in the field of the environment which cover a wider range of sectors, including water and air pollution, management of waste and chemicals, biotechnology, nuclear safety, and nature protection. Community environmental law includes standards applicable to a wide range of products, from detergents to subsonic aircraft, rules governing industrial processes, and environmental quality objectives. Further to that, several horizontal measures, relating, *inter alia*, to environmental impact assessment and access to environmental information, have been adopted.

Although it is not possible to examine in detail all aspects of existing Community environmental law, it is important to bear in mind that one of the principal strengths of the European Community, as distinct from traditional international organizations, is that it is a legislative body which has been given the power to enact legislation binding upon its Member States. Accordingly, the Community and its constituent Member States have developed a set of common environmental rules, which, though relatively young and still incomplete, have a mandatory character and ensure a high, uniform level of environmental protection in the twelve EC countries.

Most, though not all, Community environmental legislation is enacted by way of directives, which, according to the definition given in Article 189 of the EEC Treaty, are legally binding as to the result to be achieved, while leaving the choice of forms and methods of implementation to national authorities. By contrast, a Community regulation—another legal instrument also used in environmental legislation—has general application, is binding in its entirety, and directly applicable in all Member States.

The enforcement of Community directives is a national responsibility. Once transposed into national law in accordance with each country's constitutional rules, the implementation of a directive's provisions becomes a matter for national, regional, and local authorities. In practice, however, this process of transposition and implementation can give rise to several problems: there may be a delay in carrying over the provisions of a directive into national legislation; where national implementing provisions are put in place, they may be defective; or, notwithstanding national implementing provisions, the aims of a directive may be ignored in practice. In such cases, the Commission, as guardian of the Treaties, is empowered to take legal action against the Member States concerned. According to Article 169 of the EEC Treaty:

> if the Commission considers that a Member State has failed to fulfil an obligation under this Treaty, it shall deliver a reasoned opinion on the matter after giving the State concerned the opportunity to submit its observations. If the State concerned does not comply with the opinion within the period laid down by the Commission, the latter may bring the matter before the Court of Justice.

In recent years, the Commission has been resorting to legal action against Member States more frequently, as more and more problems concerning implementation of Community environmental law come to its notice. For example, according to the 10th Annual Report on the monitoring of the application of Community law, in 1992 the Commission sent to Member States 143 'Article 169' letters relating to infringements of environmental legislation, issued twenty-six reasoned opinions and referred nine cases to the Court of Justice. The court also delivered nine judgments in this area.

Yet, as an enforcement agency, the Commission suffers from several drawbacks. The multitude of infringements, the shortage of staff, and the lack of a Community environment inspectorate make it very difficult for the Commission to monitor closely the implementation of Community environmental legislation in Member States. Despite these shortcomings, the Commission operates a very effective complaints system, under which every individual citizen can request the Commission to initiate an investigation in cases of alleged infringement of Community law. The number of violations of Community law brought to the Commission's attention is rising faster in the environmental field than in any other area, having experienced a 30 per cent increase since 1991.

Once fully operational, the European Environment Agency is intended to remedy the existing gaps in this area, especially in view of the fact that, according to the Regulation establishing the Agency, its possible involvement in the monitoring of Community legislation should be examined after an initial phase.

5.4.2. Integration

The principle of integration of environmental considerations into the other policies was formulated for the first time in the Third Action

Programme, back in 1983. Since then, it has remained one of the basic guiding principles of Community action and in 1987 became a legal requirement in accordance with Article 130r para. 2, of the EEC Treaty.

The high priority attached to the integration principle is the result of two combined factors. In the first place, it is clear that some Community policies with a strong physical impact are likely to have significant effects on the environment. Hence the need to take preventive action, at an early stage of the decision-making process, to minimize such effects and also to ensure that environment policy and other relevant Community policies are mutually supportive and reinforce each other. Similarly, due to their growing complexity, many environmental problems can only be effectively dealt with through the definition and implementation of a comprehensive strategy, involving measures adopted under different Community policies.

Over the past few years, several initiatives aimed at integrating environmental considerations into the most important Community policies have been undertaken. There has been, for example, a clear shift of emphasis from productivity growth, as the primary goal of the Common Agricultural Policy, to new policy concerns which include, *inter alia*, respect for the environment and protection of rural living standards. The environmental dimension of the three Community structural funds—the European Regional Development Fund, the European Social Fund, and the guidance element of the European Agricultural Guidance and Guarantee Fund—has also been considerably reinforced in the reform carried out in the late 1980s. At the same time, environmental requirements are progressively being integrated into all Community programmes of assistance to developing countries, as exemplified by the provisions on environmental co-operation in the Lome IV convention which governs the relationship between the Community and the developing countries of Africa, the Caribbean, and the Pacific.

It is however important to bear in mind that there are many outstanding issues the Community has still to address in order to implement the integration principle. For instance, every year there are a large number of complaints regarding lack of conformity of projects financed from the Structural Funds with Community environmental law. Similarly, a report issued by the European Court of Auditors in September 1992 identified several important gaps in the environmental safeguards built into the European Regional Development Fund. It should also be noted that the implementation of the integration principle is a dynamic process. The integration of environmental requirements into all other relevant Community policies will therefore remain a priority objective for the foreseeable future, as recognized in the Fifth Environmental Action Programme.

5.4.3. Financial Instruments

In accordance with Article 130s.4, of the EEC Treaty, without prejudice to some measures of a Community nature, Member States have the primary responsibility for financing environmental protection measures. Further to that, financial interventions from the Community and national administrations must not result in diminishing the fundamental responsibility of all relevant economic actors in accordance with the 'polluter pays' principle. The Community has, nevertheless, established various financial mechanisms with the aim of supporting the achievement of some of the objectives of Community environment policy.

The Community's Structural Funds are undoubtedly the most important of these mechanisms. Funds allocated to environmental projects under the European Regional Development Fund have risen dramatically from around 100 million ECU per year in 1985–7 to some 700 million ECU per year at present. The Community has also earmarked 500 million ECU for a programme known as ENVIREG that enables beneficiary regions to finance environmental projects linked to economic development, in areas such as coastal sewage treatment, waste management, and protection of sensitive areas.

Similarly, environmental protection constitutes for the European Investment Bank a priority criterion for project selection and appraisal. Loans for environmental projects, including sewage treatment, waste management, air pollution control, reafforestation, soil conservation, and improvement of the urban environment, have been rising steadily over the past few years. In 1991, these loans amounted to 1888 million ECU, corresponding to 14 per cent of the bank's total loan finance.

Finally, a Community Financial Instrument for the Environment (LIFE) was established in 1992, merging some previous small-scale financial instruments. The principal tasks of LIFE lie in defining and promoting models of production and behaviour which are in line with the principles of economic development, demonstrating the technical viability and economic efficiency of chosen models and actions, supporting specific demonstrations, pilot projects, and horizontal information, education, and training actions, and strengthening administrative structures.

5.5. FUTURE PERSPECTIVES

5.5.1. The New Scenario

Since the Fourth Environmental Action Programme was adopted in 1987, profound changes with major implications in relation to Community environment policy and to other Community policies have occurred. In the first place, the political scene in Europe and in the Community itself has experienced dramatic transformations. An agreement has been concluded to set up a European Economic Area embracing the Community and most EFTA countries. Accession negotiations were concluded with Austria, Sweden, Finland, and Norway in early 1994. Some other European states have applied to become members of the Community. Most importantly, as the socialist regimes of the countries of Central and Eastern Europe and of the former Soviet Union collapsed, the countries themselves came to look increasingly to the Community for both guidance and assistance in the ongoing process of economic reform.

Secondly, the Community has to respond to the new environmental challenges resulting from the development of the internal market, also taking into account the need to achieve greater economic and social cohesion. At the same time, the Treaty on European Union has initiated a process which should lead the Community towards closer economic and monetary integration by the end of this decade. The promotion of 'sustainable and non-inflationary growth respecting the environment' is one of the basic tasks the Community has to address as an integral part of this process.

This task constitutes a major challenge for the Community. The 1992 Report on the State of the Environment in the Community, published by the Commission in conjunction with the Fifth Action Programme, shows that, despite the efforts undertaken over the past twenty years and the progress achieved in some areas, there has been a slow but relentless deterioration of the general state of the environment of the Community and that pressure on the natural resource base is steadily growing. For example, municipal waste generation has increased by 13 per cent since the mid-1980s, and the rate of water withdrawal experienced a 35 per cent growth during the period 1970–85.

At the same time, the report indicates that the evolution of some key economic sectors, including energy, transport, tourism, and agriculture, is a major cause of concern in the Community:

- If no change in current growth rates takes place, there will be a 25 per cent increase in energy demand by 2010, which might in turn result in a 20 per cent increase in CO_2 emissions;
- a 25 per cent increase in car ownership and a 17 per cent increase in mileage is expected by the year 2000;
- tourism in the Mediterranean region might experience a 60 per cent growth in this decade alone with consequent increase in emissions;
- farming might also have a very negative impact on the environment if present trends remain unchanged, especially in view of the fact that during the period 1970–88 there has been a 63 per cent increase in fertilizer use in agriculture.

The scope and nature of today's environmental challenges has also significantly changed. While the solution of regional and transboundary environmental problems remains a priority, we are currently witnessing an accelerated process of 'globalization' of environmental issues. Problems such as climate change, the reduction of biological diversity, ozone-layer depletion, and deforestation are seriously threatening the ecological balance of our planet as a whole, and can only be effectively dealt with on a world level, by implementing a coherent and effective response by the international community.

The 1987 report of the World Commission on Environment and Development (*Our Common Future*) demonstrated that the emergence of unsustainable development patterns in both industrialized and developing countries and the unbalanced distribution of wealth and natural resources are the primary cause of such problems. The Community, along with other industrialized countries, has a special responsibility in this area. For example, per capita consumption of energy in the Community—although only half that of the United States—is over ten times greater than that of many developing countries. Similarly, a child born in the Community will consume over twenty times the amount of natural resources over its lifetime as will a child born in the majority of developing countries, although that is still only half what an American child will consume.

5.5.2. The Fifth Action Programme

At the meeting of the European Council held in Dublin in June 1990, the EC Heads of state and Government adopted a declaration on 'The Environmental Imperative', where they stated:

> We recognise our special responsibility both to our own citizens for their environment and in a wider context. We undertake to intensify our efforts to protect and enhance the natural environment of the Community itself and the world of which it is part. We intend that action by the Community and its Member States will be developed on a coordinated basis and on the principles of sustainable development and preventive and precautionary action.

The European Council called therefore for the continuation and reinforcement of Community action in the field of the environment. To this end, the Commission was invited to prepare a Fifth Environmental Action Programme and to use the objectives and the principles contained in the declaration as the basis of the new Programme.

Following the invitation made by the European Council in June 1990, the Commission published in March 1992 a new European Community Programme of Policy and Action in relation to the Environment and Sustainable Development (*Towards Sustainability*). The basic guidelines of this Programme were endorsed by the Environment Council in December

1992. The Programme was written alongside the Agenda 21 adopted at the Rio Conference, and was inspired by it. Both are founded on the principles of sustainable development, integration, and 'green' growth.

The Fifth Programme constitutes a turning point for Community environment policy. Although building on previous programmes and existing legislation, the new Programme differs considerably from the preceding four Programmes in its general approach and structure. It will mark a change of direction and provide a clear sense of purpose for future Community action in the environmental field until the end of the present decade, by drawing not just a shopping list of actions and initiatives to be undertaken within a certain time-frame, but a comprehensive strategy focused on the agents and activities which deplete natural resources and damage the environment. This strategy is aimed at achieving sustainable development. The Programme stresses, in particular, that this objective will require in some instances profound changes in consumption and production patterns and in lifestyles, with the aim of reducing wasteful practices and ensuring sustainable use of natural resources.

5.5.2.1. The Guiding Principles: Shared Responsibility, Integration, and Subsidiarity

In accordance with the European Council's Declaration on 'The Environmental Imperative', the strategy set up in the Fifth Action Programme is based on the concept of 'shared responsibility'. A more broadly based and active participation of all economic and social players is regarded as a basic precondition to achieve long-term sustainability. In order to initiate changes in current trends and practices which are unsustainable and detrimental for the environment, the Programme aims at promoting the optimum involvement of all sectors of society in a spirit of shared responsibility and partnership. Three main actors are specifically addressed: public authorities at national, local, and regional level; public and private enterprise; and the general public, as both individual citizens and consumers. Similarly, the new Programme focuses especially on five target sectors—industry, energy, transport, agriculture, and tourism—which rank among the main sources of depletion of natural resources and environmental damage. It is important to note that the approach to these target sectors is aimed not only at protecting the environment, but also at improving their performance and efficiency. Both objectives are closely interrelated, since the balanced and sustainable development of all economic sectors is highly dependent on the quality of the environment and the availability of natural resources.

The Fifth Action Programme has also recognized that the achievement of sustainable development requires a considerable change in almost all major policy areas in which the Community is involved. The integration of environmental requirements into the definition and implementation of other Community policies will therefore remain one of the guiding principles of Community action during the period covered by the Fifth Action Programme. Since the new Programme was published, the Community has adopted a number of policy initiatives aimed at promoting a higher level of policy integration. In particular, two regulations to stimulate more sustainable agricultural practices were adopted in June 1992, as part of the reform of the Common Agricultural Policy. Similarly, one of the objectives of the proposals to reform the Community's Structural Funds, published by the Commission in February 1993, is to strengthen the integration of environmental considerations and to improve the efficiency of the environmental safeguards introduced in the last reform adopted in the late 1980s.

Internal institutional mechanisms and procedures are also being established with a view to making environmental protection and sustainable development requirements a permanent and integral part of the work of all relevant Commission services. Accordingly, all Community actions will be subject to strategic environmental assessment and each Directorate General will appoint a senior official responsible for following environmental questions.

All other principles listed in Article 130r.2 of the EEC Treaty, including the new precautionary principle laid down in the Treaty on European Union, have played an important role in the definition of the strategy advanced in the Fifth Action Programme. The principle of subsidiarity is also a central element of the new Programme's strategy. With the Single European Act, the subsidiarity principle was formulated in Article 130r.4 of the EEC Treaty, according to which 'the Community shall take action relating to the environment to the extent to which the objectives referred to in paragraph 1 can be attained better at Community level than at the level of individual Member States'. In the Treaty on European Union, this principle has been included among the general principles of Community action and, as a result, its field of application will cover most Community policies and activities. As laid down in new Article 3b:

> In areas which do not fall within its exclusive competence, the Community shall take action, in accordance with the principle of subsidiarity, only if and in so far as the objectives of the proposed action cannot be sufficiently achieved by the Member States and can therefore, by reason of the scale or effects of the proposed action, be better achieved by the Community.

The subsidiarity principle has been reflected, in *inter alia*, the choice of priority issues addressed in the Fifth Programme: climate change, acidification and air quality, protection of nature and biodiversity, management of water resources, the urban environment, coastal zones, and waste management. All these issues have a Community-wide dimension, because of internal market and/or cross-boundary implications or because they have a crucial bearing on environmental quality and conditions in almost all regions in the Community.

The principles of subsidiarity and of shared responsibility are however, inextricably linked. The achievement of the goals and objectives of the Fifth Action Programme requires concerted action by, and the active involvement of, all policy actors in the Community. For this reason, the Fifth Programme is not a Programme for the Community alone. It envisages a wide range of measures and actions to be carried out not only at Community level but also by national, regional, and local administrations.

5.5.2.2. A Broader Range of Instruments

One of the most innovative elements in the Fifth Action Programme is undoubtedly the mix of instruments it relies upon to promote the necessary changes in consumption and production patterns and to achieve sustainability. Until now, Community environment policy has been largely based on a 'command and control' approach. Regulatory measures, embodied in the numerous legal acts adopted by the Community in the field of the environment, have, as a result, played a central role in the development of this policy, particularly as regards the establishment of product standards and rules applying to pollution from industrial processes. In the future, regulatory instruments will continue to be used, especially to provide Community-wide rules necessary to preserve the integrity of the internal market and to set up common standards for the protection of the environment and human health. But, at the same time, it is intended that market-based instruments, including economic and fiscal measures, will be increasingly used to internalize environmental costs, to promote the effective implementation of the 'polluter pays' principle, and to ensure that environmentally friendly goods and products are not at a market disadvantage *vis-à-vis* polluting or wasteful competitors.

The proposal to establish a combined carbon/energy tax, as one of the main elements of the Community's strategy to stabilize CO_2 emissions, as well as the recently adopted eco-audit and eco-label schemes, constitute the first examples of this new approach. Similarly, in March 1993 the Commission issued a Green Paper on 'Remedying Environmental Damage', where different options as regards the definition of environmental damage, civil liability, and the appropriate financial solutions are examined.

The Fifth Action Programme relies also on horizontal, supporting instruments, education and vocational training, environmental information, and green statistics. In this context, besides existing financial instruments, the new Cohesion Fund, already established on an interim basis, will play an important role in the implementation of the Fifth Programme, by providing financial assistance for environmental and transport infrastructure projects in four Members States (Greece, Ireland, Portugal, and Spain). Similarly, the contribution of the European Environment Agency, once effectively established, will be crucial by supplying Community institutions and Member States with reliable and comparable environmental information and data.

5.5.2.3. The International Dimension

In the declaration on 'The Environmental Imperative', the European Council stressed the special responsibility of the Community and its Member States to encourage and participate in international action to combat global environmental problems. It was stated that 'the Community must use more effectively its position of moral, economic and political authority to advance international efforts to solve global problems and to promote sustainable development and respect for the global commons'. The Fifth Action Programme has fully taken into account this requirement. Part II of the Programme addresses the Community's role in the wider international arena, recognizing that, in view of the global scope of many environmental problems, the Community's involvement in international environmental action has to be stepped up. It is also stressed that the implementation of the measures agreed at the United Nations Conference on Environment and Development (UNCED), held in Rio de Janeiro in June 1992, is today's most urgent task.

Although this Conference did not entirely meet the Community's initial expectations, UNCED was in many respects a historic event. Its outcome—Agenda 21, the Rio Declaration on Environment and Development, the Statement of Forestry Principles, and the two Conventions on Climate Change and Biodiversity—constitutes a first global commitment on sustainable development and environmental protection. The 'Earth Summit', attended by over 100 Heads of State and Government, demonstrated political will at the highest level to materialize this commitment. The Community, which took part as a full participant in the Rio Conference, intends to play an active part in the follow-up process. At the meeting of the European Council held in Lisbon in June 1992, just a few weeks after the Rio Conference, the EC Heads of State and Government welcomed the results of UNCED and announced an eight-point plan for the implementation of the measures agreed at Rio.

At Community level, the strategic environment policy framework for the follow-up to UNCED has already been established. Internally, the Fifth Action Programme itself provides a comprehensive approach to sustainable development whose implementation will make a major contribution to the follow-up to UNCED by the European Community.

The new Programme was drawn up during the preparations of UNCED and thus shares many of the principles contained in the Rio Declaration and the objectives of the Agenda 21 action programme.

Similarly, the Community is participating actively in the wide array of international activities to follow UNCED up, including taking part in the work of the Commission on Sustainable Development, the new UN body in charge of reviewing progress in the implementation of the Rio outcome. Furthermore the Community ratified the Climate Change and Biodiversity Conventions at the end of 1993.

Furthermore, the Community will intensify its efforts to ensure a sufficient flow of funds to support the implementation of Agenda 21 in developing countries. In Rio, the Community and its Member States announced that they would make available 3 billion ECU, including new and additional resources, as a contribution to the early implementation of Agenda 21. Fight against poverty, institution building, and technology transfer were listed as the main cross-sectoral priorities in the allocation of funds and the selection of projects. In 1993, the Community set aside from its development aid budget 770 million ECU for environmental projects. Besides its participation in this initiative, the Community has also launched certain actions—for example, on clean and efficient energy for development in which transfer of environmentally friendly technologies is foreseen—which address some of the key issues dealt with in Agenda 21.

5.5.2.4. Implementation of the Programme

The operational elements of the Fifth Action Programme follow a strategy sequence which comprises, for each of the main issues addressed in the Programme, long-term qualitative objectives, measurable targets up to the year 2000, and specific actions to be decided upon or carried out in order to achieve those targets within a designated time-frame. The principal actors called upon to participate in implementing the various actions are also indicated.

The Programme recognizes that, in order to achieve its targets and objectives, better preparation of measures, more effective co-ordination and follow-up, and stricter compliance checking and enforcement are required. To improve transparency, the Commission is committed to providing regular reports to the Council, the European Parliament, and the general public on the extent and quality of implementation and enforcement throughout the Community.

Similarly, with a view to promoting a greater sense of responsibility among the principal social and economic actors and ensuring effective and transparent application of measures, it has been decided to establish three *ad hoc* dialogue groups:

- A 'Consultative Forum' comprising representatives of enterprise, consumers, unions, and professional organizations, non-governmental organizations, and local and regional authorities.
- An 'Implementation Network', which is primarily aimed at achieving consistency in the practical implementation of Community policy and measures as between Member States.
- An 'Environmental Policy Review Group', comprising representatives of the Commission and of Member States at Director-General level, which should contribute to the development of mutual understanding and exchange of views on environment policy and measures.

It is also important to note that the Fifth Action Programme is designed as a 'rolling' Programme. While it has adopted the end of the decade as its horizon, it will bc reviewed and 'rolled-over' at the end of 1995 in the light of improvements in relevant data, results of current research, and forthcoming reviews of other Community policies. The 1992–5 phase is therefore regarded as a priming period to change the sense of direction. A comprehensive reappraisal of the situation will be undertaken before the end of 1995, on the basis of an updated report on the state of the environment, with a view to getting the implementation of the Programme under full steam in the 1996–2000 phase.

5.5.3. Environmental Protection and Economic Recovery

An essential feature of the Fifth Action Programme is that it is not aimed at environmental protection exclusively but rather at growth management, at striking the right balance between normal human aspirations towards economic and social improvements, and the fragility of the environment and the limitations of the natural resource base. In particular, as stated above, the approach to the target sectors listed in the Programme—industry, energy, transport, agriculture, and tourism—is designed not only for the protection of the environment as such, but also for the benefit and sustainability of the sectors themselves.

This aspect is becoming increasingly important, in view of the dramatic degradation of the economic situation which has taken place in the Community over the past two years. Slow or negative economic growth, loss of competitiveness, and continuing structural change have led to an unacceptably high level of unemployment which not only results in serious human and social problems but also represents a massive waste of human resources. At the same time, environmental awareness remains very high, as local environmental problems directly affect the quality of life of Community citizens, and concern about damage to the global environment increases. Against this background, it is essential to examine how the Community could make progress simultaneously in both areas of concern. Certainly, the policies needed to tackle each of these problems must be pursued on their own merits. However, if synergies are effectively exploited, the policies for environmental protection and sustainability, on the one hand, and those for economic recovery and employment, on the other, can be mutually reinforcing.

In a Communication on 'Industrial Competitiveness and Protection of the Environment' submitted to the Council in November 1992, the Commission stressed that:

> What is good for the environment can also be good for business. There is a competitive advantage to be gained by EC industry if the environmental dimension is integrated in a progressive, responsible and constructive manner. Over time, this will be derived from improved internal performance and increased competition, the development of a sound, progressive, technological base, more sustainably managed economic activity, leading to positive trade effects.

Accordingly, the Commission proposed that Community action in the interface between competitiveness and the environment should be based around three axes: a qualitative improvement in the degree of integration of environment and industrial policies in order to derive positive benefits for both policies; constructive dialogue with industry to improve the effectiveness of environment policy; the maintenance of the integrity of the Internal Market whilst promoting protection of the environment at a high level.

The eight-point plan for economic renewal submitted by President Delors to the Copenhagen European Council in June 1993 is based on the same philosophy and approach. One of the proposals included in the plan relates to the pursuit of a new model of development by exploiting the job-creating potential of environmental protection, shifting taxation from labour to utilization of scarce natural resources with a view to enhancing Europe's economic competitiveness, and using increases in productivity to improve the quality of life and create new jobs. Following the presentation of this plan, the European Council invited the Commission to present a White Paper on a medium-term strategy for growth, competitiveness, and employment. The Commission prepared this White Paper, where the various elements outlined in the Delors plan were developed. The White Paper was then considered and very well received by the European Council at its meeting in December 1993. Other initiatives—for example, an open seminar on sustainability and employment which was held in Brussels in November 1993, organized jointly by the Commission and the Belgian Government (holding the Presidency of the European Community)—also contributed to exploring further how best to achieve complementarity and mutual supportiveness between policies in the field of environmental protection and economic recovery.

5.6. CONCLUSIONS

The paper has addressed the general framework, legal basis, achievements and failures, and future perspectives of the EC environmental policy. Achievements in terms of quantity of legislation are remarkable. Member states, who in some cases had virtually no environmental legislation, now have all the tools of the legislative arsenal necessary to create and sustain a sound environmental policy at their disposal. However, the experience within the Community is that the creation of legislation alone is not sufficient. Implementation is not yet satisfactory and in some areas is patchy. We have also seen a period of substantial economic growth, and in particular of motor traffic, which in some cases has undone the achievements made in curbing industrial emissions. We therefore need to seek alternative solutions.

The other major trend which has influenced the European Community over the past seven years or so has been the increasing realization that just as environmental problems have to be solved at the Community level because in many cases they can not be solved at the national level (e.g. the River Rhine problem), so the European Community scale is also too small. We have become aware of the urgent and grave global environmental problems such as the global climate change which is taking place, the rapid disappearance of species and general weakening of our natural resource base, and the criminal dumping of toxic waste especially in developing countries. Such global problems require a global solution.

For these reasons the Community, together with its Member States, played a leading role in the United Nations Conference on Environment and Development which took place in 1992. The Community and its Member States there underwrote a series of important commitments, not only the signature of the global climate change and biodiversity conventions, but also the Agenda for the twenty-first century, the blueprint for national and international sustainable development policies and plans. We are now trying to put flesh on to these commitments and to carry out over the next decades the obligations we have subscribed to. The chosen vehicle for the implementation at Community level of the Agenda 21 commitments is the Fifth Action Programme. This action programme was written in parallel with the Agenda 21 and is informed by the same sustainable development philosophy and principles.

The Fifth Action Programme, like the Agenda 21, reposes on a much larger selection of instruments to achieve sound environmental policies such as economic instruments, codes of conduct, involvement of all the social factors, information, education, and training. As the Fifth Action Programme is implemented one can therefore expect that while regulation will continue it may well do so at a slower rate than before, because the legislation arsenal is already in place, and additional and sometimes alternative series of instruments such as taxes, incentives, and codes of conduct may well be used also. This more holistic approach to the environment, will it is hoped, bear fruit nationally and at the Community and international levels, by ensuring a more profound involvement of administrators, industrialists, non-governmental organizations, and the general public with the aim of achieving more widely based and sounder environmental policies.

ANNEX:

Treaties Revising the Treaties Establishing the European Communities and Acts Relating to the Communities

1. SINGLE EUROPEAN ACT, 1986

Subsection VI—Environment

Article 25

A Title VII shall be added to Part Three of the EEC Treaty reading as follows:

Article 130r

1. Action by the Community relating to the environment shall have the following objectives:
   (i) to preserve, protect and improve the quality of the environment;
   (ii) to contribute towards protecting human health;
   (iii) to ensure a prudent and rational utilisation of natural resources.
2. Action by the Community relating to the environment shall be based on the principles that preventative action should be taken, that environmental damage should as a priority be rectified at source, and that the polluter should pay. Environmental protection requirements shall be a component of the Community's other policies.
3. In preparing its action relating to the environment, the Community shall take account of:
   (i) available scientific and technical data;
   (ii) environmental conditions in the various regions of the Community;
   (iii) the potential benefits and costs of action or of lack of action;
   (iv) the economic and social development of the Community as a whole and the balanced development of its regions.
4. The Community shall take action relating to the environment to the extent to which the objectives referred to in paragraph 1 can be attained better at Community level than at the level of the individual Member States. Without

prejudice to certain measures of a Community nature, the Member States shall finance and implement the other measures.

5. Within their respective spheres of competence, the Community and the Member States shall cooperate with third countries and with the relevant international organisations. The arrangements for Community cooperation may be the subject of agreements between the Community and the third parties concerned, which shall be negotiated and concluded in accordance with Article 228.

   The previous paragraph shall be without prejudice to Member States' competence to negotiate in international bodies and to conclude international agreements.

Article 130s

The Council, acting unanimously on a proposal from the Commission and after consulting the European Parliament and the Economic and Social Committee, shall decide what action is to be taken by the Community.

The Council, shall under the conditions laid down in the preceding subparagraph, define those matters on which decisions are to be taken by a qualified majority.

Article 130t

The protective measures adopted in common pursuant to Article 130s shall not prevent any Member State from maintaining or introducing more stringent protective measures compatible with this Treaty.

The Council, acting in accordance with the procedure referred to in Article 189c and after consulting the Economic and Social Committee, shall adopt the provisions referred to in Articles 130j to l. Adoption of the supplementary programmes shall require the agreement of the Member States concerned.

Article 130p

At the beginning of each year the Commission shall send a report to the European Parliament and the Council. The report shall include information on research and technological development activities and the dissemination of results during the previous year, and the work programme for the current year.

2. TREATY ON EUROPEAN UNION, 1992

Title XVI—Environment

Article 130r

1. Community policy on the environment shall contribute to pursuit of the following objectives:
   - preserving, protecting and improving the quality of the environment;
   - protecting human health;
   - prudent and rational utilisation of natural resources;
   - promoting measures at international level to deal with regional or worldwide environmental problems.

2. Community policy on the environment shall aim at a high level of protection taking into account the diversity of situations in the various regions of the Community. It shall be based on the precautionary principle and on the principles that preventive action should be taken, that environmental damage should as a priority be rectified at source and that the polluter should pay. Environmental protection requirements must be integrated into the definition and implementation of other Community policies.

   In this context, harmonisation measures answering these requirements shall include, where appropriate, a safeguard clause allowing Member States to take provisional measures, for non-economic environmental reasons, subject to a Community inspection procedure.

3. In preparing its policy on the environment, the Community shall take account of:

   - available scientific and technical data;
   - environmental conditions in the various regions of the Community;
   - the potential benefits and costs of action or lack of action;
   - the economic and social development of the Community as a whole and the balanced development of its regions.

4. Within their respective spheres of competence, the Community and the Member States shall cooperate with third countries and with the competent international organisations. The arrangements for Community cooperation may be the subject of agreements between the Community and the third parties concerned, which shall be negotiated and concluded in accordance with Article 228.

   The previous subparagraph shall be without prejudice to Member States' competence to negotiate in international bodies and to conclude international agreements:

Article 130s

1. The Council, acting in accordance with the procedure referred to in Article 189c and after consulting the Economic and Social Committee, shall decide what action is to be taken by the Community in order to achieve the objectives referred to in Article 130r.
2. By way of derogation from the decision-making procedure provided for in paragraph 1 and without prejudice to Article 100a, the Council, acting unanimously on a proposal from the Commission and after consulting the European Parliament and the Economic and Social Committee, shall adopt:

   - provisions primarily of a fiscal nature;
   - measures concerning town and country planning, land use with the exception of waste management and measures of a general nature, and management of water resources;
   - measures significantly affecting a Member State's choice between different energy sources and the general structure of its energy supply.

   The Council, may under the conditions laid down in the preceding subparagraph, define those matters referred to in this paragraph on which decisions are to be taken by a qualified majority.

3. In other areas, general action programmes setting out priority objectives to be attained shall be adopted by the Council, acting in accordance with the procedure referred to in Article 189b and after consulting the Economic and Social Committee.

   The Council, acting under the terms of paragraph 1 or paragraph 2 according to the case, shall adopt the measures necessary for the implementation of these programmes.

4. Without prejudice to certain measures of a Community nature, the Member States shall finance and implement the environment policy.

5. Without prejudice to the principle that the polluter should pay, if a measure based on the provisions of paragraph 1 involves costs deemed disproportionate for the public authorities of a Member State, the Council shall, in the act adopting that measure, lay down appropriate provisions in the form of:

   - temporary derogations, and/or
   - financial support from the Cohesion Fund to be set up no later than 31 December 1993 pursuant to Article 130d.

Article 130t

The protective measures adopted pursuant to Article 130s shall not prevent any Member State from maintaining or introducing more stringent protective measures. Such measures must be compatible with this Treaty. They shall be notified to the Commission.

Title XVII—Development Cooperation

Article 130u

1. Community policy in the sphere of development cooperation, which shall be complementary to the policies pursued by the Member States, shall foster:

   - the sustainable economic and social development of the developing countries and more particularly the most disadvantaged among them;
   - the smooth and gradual integration of the developing countries into the world economy;
   - the campaign against poverty in the developing countries.

2. Community policy in this area shall contribute to the general objective of developing and consolidating democracy and the rule of law, and to that of respecting human rights and fundamental freedoms.

6

Looking Ahead: Environmental Regulation—A Future?

BRIAN GREENWOOD

6.1. INTRODUCTION

What has changed? Why is the 'environment'—howsoever defined—now so important when ten or even five years ago few would have been able to find time for a two-day working colloquium on the subject? Other chapters have considered environmental regulation from the point of view of the regulatory authorities, commerce and industry, and the financial institutions. A strong thread running through all these chapters, however, is the influence now being exerted by Europe, and what can best be described as the stimulus provided by the 'American experience'.

At the time of writing, the popular perception of the United Kingdom Government's green agenda is that the environment has been relegated very much to the back burner. The environment cannot, however, be ignored. Within the last year or so, a fire in a chemical warehouse in Bradford resulted in dangerous contamination of the adjacent water-courses. In Hampshire protestors continue, with what some might consider to be remarkable resilience, to oppose the extension of the M3 motorway through Twyford Down, near Winchester. The site now presents a horrific white scar through the middle of what was once a beautiful hill falling within an Area of Outstanding Natural Beauty and a Site of Special Scientific Interest on the edge of Winchester. Elsewhere, the House of Lords have decided, in the *Eastern Counties Leatherwork plc* case,[1] that a party will not be liable for the then unforeseeable consequences of a chemical spill many years ago which forced a local water company, no longer able to meet EC imposed standards on drinking water, to relocate its source of water extraction—the implication being that the consequences might be foreseeable today. All these incidents and many others, it is suggested, point to a growing concern for an increasingly damaged environment. The purpose of this chapter is to look ahead

[1] [1994] 2 WLR 53.

and to pose the question—what does the future hold? It would be impossible to draw together every thread of the environmental debate in the space available. This chapter concentrates, therefore, on what are perceived as the most brightly lit signposts—looking at the past to speculate on the future.

6.2. THE PAST

The environment is not new. 'Environmental' legislation has been on the statute book for well over a hundred years, albeit appearing piecemeal and in a haphazard fashion, and designed to cater more for an identified specific problem than for broader issues. The care and health of the citizen were then foremost because that was where the political will, or at least the political votes, lay. If the health and care of the citizens incidentally aided the health and care of the environment, then all the better, although issues such as pollution of the air and water, protection of wildlife and fauna for a world that had just extracted itself from one world war and was about to enter a second, were inevitably low on the political agenda.

After the Second World War came a gradual realization that industrial growth, although much needed by an ailing economy, too often led to unwanted and unforeseen environmental consequences. The notorious smogs of the early 1950s brought home this lesson with a vengeance and as time went by governments produced the Clean Air Acts, smokeless zones, and legislation of which the general emphasis was on environmental health. The Public Health Acts, the Town and Country Planning Act, the Control of Pollution Act 1974, all added to a growing body of 'environmental' legislation—even though few recognized it as such at the time.

It is therefore perhaps surprising that the Treaty that established the European Communities contained no environmental provisions.[2] It was not until 1986, with the advent of the Single European Act, that Chapter VII on the environment was adopted, comprising Articles 130r–t. That is not to say, however, that in the interim, the environment had been ignored. Indeed during the late 1960s and early 1970s directives were adopted dealing with issues such as the classification, packaging, and labelling of dangerous substances, noise levels, and polluting emissions of motor vehicles.[3]

The pace was nevertheless unconvincing.

In the early 1970s the European Commission suggested that the Member States should adopt a Community Action programme on the

[2] See, generally, M. Brusasco Mackenzie, *supra*, Ch. 5.

[3] OBJ 1967 86/1 Dir.70/157 OJ 1970, L42/6; Dir.70/220 OJ 1970, L76/1.

environment. The political debate that followed concentrated on whether environmental issues were best dealt with at Community level or individually by the government of each Member State, where necessary, supplemented by intergovernmental agreements. As the previous chapter shows, the 'Community' view ultimately prevailed.[4]

6.3. THE EUROPEAN LEGISLATIVE FRAMEWORK

6.3.1. The EEC Treaty

When the Community heads of state and leaders of Government came together for their summit meeting in Dublin in June 1990, they issued the following statement:

> We recognise our special responsibility for the environment both to our own citizens and to the wider world. We undertake to intensify our efforts to protect and enhance the natural environment of the Community itself and the world of which it is part. We intend that action by the Community and its Member States will be development and preventive and precautionary action . . . The objective of such action must be to guarantee citizens the right to a clean and healthy environment . . . The full achievement of this objective must be a shared responsibility.

The emphasis is on co-ordination, shared responsibility, and the principle of sustainable development. The problem, or perhaps more appropriately the challenge, is the responsibility that falls to Europe to influence trends in the rest of the world.

Martin Coleman and Margaret Brusasco Mackenzie in their chapters have already highlighted some of the problems encountered by Member States and the European Community in the interpretation of Articles 100 and 130r–t,[5] the discretion that the wording affords, and the complications of achieving environmental harmony in the face of, or perhaps despite, political need. It is necessary to recognize the breadth and scope of these Articles, and to appreciate their importance and the part they play as the legislative foundation of a European environmental regulatory framework which has now been consolidated by the 1992 Treaty on European Union.

The Treaty on European Union includes a number of provisions designed to strengthen the objective of environmental harmony, a concept which inevitably runs either slightly ahead or alongside environmental regulation. Article 2 refers to the promotion of 'a harmonious and balanced development of economic activities, sustainable and non-inflationary growth respecting the environment'.

[4] European Commission, Sixth General Report (1972), 8.
[5] Text reproduced *supra*, Ch. 5, annexe.

Article 3k provides that the activities of the Community shall include 'a policy in the sphere of the environment'. The amended Article 130r.2 provides, *inter alia*, that the policy should 'aim at a high level of protection taking into account the diversity of situations in the various regions of the Community. It shall be based on the precautionary principle and on the principles that preventive action should be taken, that environmental damage should as a priority be rectified at source and that the polluter should pay'.

An important political ingredient is provided by Article 3b which emphasizes the principle of subsidiarity while Article A states the objective that decisions should be taken 'as closely as possible to the citizens'. Whether subsidiarity is practical in the content of achieving environmental harmony throughout Europe is a question that has not yet been answered, but the new article provides as follows:

> The Community shall act within the limits of the powers conferred upon it by this Treaty and of the objectives assigned to it therein. In areas which do not fall within its exclusive competence, the Community shall take action, in accordance with the principle of subsidiarity, only if and insofar as the objectives of the proposed action cannot be sufficiently achieved by the Member States and can therefore, by reason of the scale or effects of the proposed action, be better achieved by the Community.
>
> Any action by the Community shall not go beyond what is necessary to achieve the objectives of this Treaty.

6.3.2. The Fifth Environmental Action Programme

A vital partner for this European legislative framework is the Fifth Environmental Action Programme, *Towards Sustainability*. In the introduction to the Programme it is recognized that

> over the past two decades four Community Action Programmes on the environment have given rise to about 200 pieces of legislation covering pollution of the atmosphere, water and soil, waste management, safeguards in relation to chemicals, biotechnology, product standards, environmental impact assessments and protection of nature. The Community's 4th Action Programme on the Environment has not been completed. It runs up to the end of 1992—and its impact will not be known for some years to come. While a great deal has been achieved under these programmes and measures, a combination of factors calls for a more far-reaching policy and more effective strategy at this juncture.[6]

The Action Programme refers to the *Report on the State of the Environment* published in conjunction with the programme which indicates 'a slow but relentless deterioration in the general state of the environment of the community notwithstanding the measures taken over the

[6] *Towards Sustainability: A European Programme of Policy and Action* in relation to the Environment and Sustainable Development, Com. (92) 23 final—vol. II, p. 3, para. 1.

past two decades'. It suggests that the 'present approach and existing measures are not geared to deal with the expected growth in international competition and the upward trends in community activity and development which will impose even greater burdens on natural resources, the environment, and ultimately, the quality of life'. On a global level it expresses concern about 'the climate change/deforestation/energy crisis, the seriousness and persistence of problems of under-development and the progress of political and economic change in Central and Eastern Europe [which] add to the responsibility of the European Community in the international field'.[7] The programme lays emphasis on 'the precautionary approach', effective implementation of the 'polluter pays' principle and 'full integration of environmental considerations into all aspects of policy making'.

'Sustainable development' was defined in the 1987 Brundtland Report as 'Development which meets the needs of the present without compromising the ability of future generations to meet their own needs.' As the Fifth Action Programme rather helpfully suggests, 'In more prosaic terms it has been defined by the admonition: Don't eat the seed corn which is needed to sow next year's crop.' In less prosaic language, however, sustainable development entails 'preserving the overall balance and value of the natural capital stock, redefinition of short, medium and long term cost/benefit evaluation criteria and instruments to reflect the real socio-economic effects and values of consumption and conservation, and the equitable distribution and use of resources between nations and regions over the world as a whole'.[8]

The Fifth Action Programme is very much a framework document. That is not to denigrate its value. It poses many questions and if it provides few answers, it does at least point to the way ahead. It concentrates on the agents and activities which it perceives as being responsible for damage to the environment, urging consideration of action before the environment is actually damaged. Very much akin to the dentist who offers preventive treatment rather than waiting for the decay to appear! It identifies necessary changes and acknowledges that the objectives defined in the Programme cannot be met purely by action at Community level, but require participation at all levels of society, from the government of Member States, through the local authority level, financial institutions, commerce and industry, to the individual citizen. The basic strategy, therefore, 'is to achieve full integration of environmental and other relevant policies through the active participation of all the main actors in society (administrations, enterprise, general public) through a broadening and deepening of the instruments for control and behavioural change including, in particular, greater use of market forces'.[9]

[7] Ibid. 3 para. 2.
[8] Ibid. 18.
[9] Com. (92) 23 final—vol. II, p. 3, para. 19.

Accompanying the Fifth Action Programme was an updated report on the state of the environment. This report places the Fifth Action Programme in context. It considers atmospheric pollution, aquatic pollution, soil degradation, nature conservation, the urban environment, waste management, etc. It records some disquieting trends which, 'if not satisfactorily contained, could have significant negative consequences for the quality of the environment as a whole'. For example,

- Energy: a 25 per cent increase by 2010 if there is no change in current energy demand growth rates, resulting, in turn, in a 20 per cent increase in EC carbon emissions (reference year 1987).
- Transport: a 25 per cent increase in car ownership, a 17 per cent increase in mileage by 2000 (reference year 1990).
- Agriculture: a 63 per cent increase in fertilizer use between 1970 and 1988.
- Waste: a 13 per cent increase in municipal waste over the last five years, despite increased recycling of paper, glass, plastics.
- Water: a 35 per cent increase in the Community's average water withdrawal rate between 1970 and 1985.
- Tourism: a 60 per cent increase in Mediterranean tourism projected by 2000 (reference year 1990).

It is stated in the Fifth Action Programme that the 'overall objective of the Community is the improved and continued welfare of all its citizens'. To achieve that objective it is necessary to consider various independent components, politics, monetary framework, geography, natural resources, independent economics, even national pride—all, save the last, subject to some form of regulation. The Programme points out, however, that the

> long term success of the internal market will be dependent upon the relative constitutions of the industrial, energy, regional development and agricultural policies and the ability of the transport policy, literally, to deliver the goods. All of these policies are inter-dependent; the ultimate limiting factor for continued efficiency and growth as they interface with one another is the tolerance level of the natural environment.[10]

If it is accepted that the 'natural environment' is, indeed, the common denominator, then the debate that logically follows, given that the environment must be protected, is how? Can that protection be achieved by regulation, and, if so, can adopted measures be capable of enforcement, and will they actually be enforced? Are there any viable alternatives to regulation? Finally, if the natural environment is damaged, who repairs it—and who pays?

[10] Com. (92) 23 final—vol. II, p. 3, para. 25.

Although it is accepted that the broader issues of climate change, acidification, water pollution, etc. are still central to the problem, the EC is in effect attempting to 'descend from the clouds' where it inevitably will only see the consequences of actions that have gone wrong, and tackle the problems at ground level looking at the 'players' first and then the results—not vice versa. In the words of the Programme, therefore, the strategy 'is to create a new interplay between the main groups of actors and the principal economic sectors through the use of an extended, and integrated range of instruments'.

In this context, almost anticipating the cry, 'But what of subsidiarity?' the Programme states that this

> can best be done efficiently within the Community framework. Without an overall Community framework within which all these activities can be integrated and co-ordinated, there is a danger that the actions carried out by individual Member States or regions, or by other actors will not have their full impact, or that the integrity of Community achievements or actions in other policy areas, notably the Internal Market, could be called into question'.[11]

This is probably one of the most important paragraphs in a Programme, which identifies the actors as being public authorities, public and private enterprise, and the general public. It then identifies selected target sectors worthy of special attention, namely manufacturing industry, energy, transport, agriculture, and tourism.

Having established the players and the games, it is then necessary to select the playing fields. The list is not surprising: climate change, acidification, air quality, protection of nature and biodiversity, management of water resources, the urban environment, coastal zones, and waste management. To ensure that the Programme remains at a practical level, there are within the identified media a number of intermediate goals, targets to be achieved in specified time-frames up to the year 2000. For example, in the area of *coastal zones* (the European Community has about 58,000 kilometres of coastline, excluding small islands and inland seas):

- The *objective* is sustainable development of coastal zones and their resources in accordance with the carrying capacity of coastal environments;
- the *EC targets to 2000* are higher priority to the environmental needs of coastal zones, through, *inter alia*, better co-ordination between relevant EC policies and between policies at EC, national, and regional levels;
- the *instruments* are to be a framework of integrated management plans at appropriate levels;

[11] Ibid.

- the *time-frame* is before 1998; and
- the Sectors/Actors are Member States—local authorities—European Community.

Turning to the medium of *waste*, a typical example in the context of municipal waste is as follows:

- *objectives* are the prevention of waste (closing of cycles);
- *EC targets up to 2000* are waste management plans in Member States;
- *actions* are landfill Directive operational;
- *time-frame* is before 1995; and
- *sectors/actors* are the European Community + Member States + local authorities and industry.

The broad objectives set out above clash singularly with the concept of subsidiarity. Interestingly, the Fifth Action Programme includes a relatively short chapter on this subject entitled 'Subsidiarity and Shared Responsibility'. As already noted, subsidiarity has been given prominence in the Maastricht Treaty. Bearing in mind that Article 3b of the Treaty looks to a process 'in which decisions are taken as closely as possible to the citizen' it is acknowledged that the Community will take action in accordance with the principle of subsidiarity, but 'only if and insofar as the objectives of the proposed action cannot be sufficiently achieved by the Member States and can therefore, by reason of the scale or effects of proposed action, be better achieved by the Community'.

In the context of the environment, it is suggested that there is little or no place for subsidiarity. The entire premiss of this paper is that the environment and its regulation can only be established by consensus and the lowest practical level for environmental consensus must be Europe, not the Member States. The ideal, of course, at the highest level in accordance with Agenda 21, would be an international approach. The only possible place for subsidiarity, therefore, at Member-State level must be as to the means whereby the European 'will' is given effect at the national level. Understandably, the authors of the Fifth Action Programme have been obliged to be just a little coy in dealing with the practice as opposed to the theory of subsidiarity. It should therefore be noted that the central part of the chapter dealing with subsidiarity and shared responsibility states that, since

> the objectives and targets put forward in the Programme and the ultimate goal of sustainable development can only be achieved by *concerted* action on the part of all the relevant actors working together in partnership, the Programme combines the principle of subsidiarity with the wider concept of shared responsibility. This latter concept involves not so much a choice of action at one level to the exclusion of others but, rather, a mixing of actors and instruments at the appropriate

levels, without any calling into question of the division of competence between the Community, the Member States, regional and local authorities. For any one target or problem, the emphasis (actors and instruments) could lie with the Community/national/regional government level and for another with the regional/local/sectoral level or at the level of enterprise/general public/consumers.[12]

Happy ambiguity!

6.3.3. The Ideal

It is this European legislative framework, the Fifth Action Programme, and public opinion that will signal the way ahead. The ideal has been summarized by the European Commission as:

> The achievement of the desired balance between human activity and development and protection of the environment requires a sharing of responsibilities which is both equitable and clearly defined by reference to consumption of and behaviour towards the environment and natural resources. This implies integration of environment considerations in the formulation and implementation of economic and sectoral policies, in the decisions of public authorities, in the conduct and development of production processes and in individual behaviour and choice. It also implies effective dialogue and concerted action among partners who may have differing short term priorities; such dialogue must be supported by objective and reliable information.[13]

Running parallel to this EEC legal framework, however, and sometimes crossing its path, not always with happy consequences, is national environmental law. Consideration of just two recent examples will illustrate vividly the importance and the increased effectiveness of the higher-level European framework.

6.4. THE EUROPEAN INFLUENCE

6.4.1. Packaging Waste

It is estimated that within the European Community there are more than 100 million households generating waste from consumer packaging. In addition, industry and commerce throughout the community produce packaging waste to meet their own various needs. It is believed that the amount of packaging waste produced annually by the European Community totals some 50 million tonnes, households being responsible

[12] Ibid. 73. [13] Ibid. 3, para. 4.

for the most (25 million tonnes) followed by public services (15 million tonnes), and industry (10 million tonnes).

Only 9 million tonnes of that annual total is recycled (approximately 18 per cent) and the degree of recycling varies depending on the practice of each member state and the type of material to be recycled. The packaging of goods, of course, serves an important economic and social role; for example, it permits safe transport of products, preserves packed goods, permits division of products by weight and/or volume, enables easy identification, and enables a hygienic method of handling eliminating contamination, etc. The UK packaging industry has an annual turnover of about £8.5 billion.

Over the years there have been a number of attempts to regulate surplus packaging, although these attempts have concentrated almost exclusively on containers of liquids for human consumption. The methods now available to Member States either individually or jointly, by which they may deal with the packaging waste problem comprise essentially reuse of the packaging, recycling, incineration, or disposal by landfill. A European Council Directive in 1985[14] sought to provide for the production, marketing, use, recycling, and refilling of containers of liquids for human consumption and the disposal of used containers in order to reduce the impact of the latter on the environment and to encourage a reduction in the consumption of energy and raw materials in this field. Member States were required to draw up programmes for reducing the tonnage and/or volume of containers of liquids, to develop consumer education, to facilitate refilling and recycling of containers, etc. The concept was unimpeachable. In 1990, however, 6.7 billion litres of soft drinks were consumed in the United Kingdom alone. To that should be added 785 million litres of fruit juice and 400 million litres of bottled water—and those figures do not include beer, wine, and spirits.

Implementation of the Directive by Member States has varied and has on occasions proved an obstacle to the free movement of goods. Denmark unilaterally introduced rules for containers of beers and soft drinks. Their legislation required that such drinks could only be marketed in 'returnable containers', that is, approved containers for which there was a system for collecting and refilling. Companies that wished to sell liquids in non-approved containers, including importers, were limited to 3,000 hectolitres per producer per year. The Commission, with the United Kingdom intervening in support, brought an action in the European Court on the grounds that the Danish legislation prevented the 'importation to Denmark of foreign beer and soft drinks in their original containers because of the associated administrative difficulties as well as the cost

[14] 85/339/EEC (27 June 1985) Containers of Liquids for Human Consumption.

involved for importers in establishing a collection system as prescribed'.[15] The Commission argued that the discriminatory effect meant that it was not possible for Denmark to justify the collection system as a mandatory requirement relating 'to the protection of the environment'.

The Advocate-General Sir Gordon Slynn stated that the case 'raises a difficult and sensitive issue—the compatibility of measures taken to protect the environment with the fundamental rule of the EEC Treaty that quantity restrictions and measure of equivalent effect in relation to imports into one member state from another are unlawful'.

The European Court in its judgment on 20 September 1988[16] held that:

1. the protection of the environment is a mandatory requirement which may limit the application of Article 30 of the Treaty (Article 30 prohibits quantitative restrictions on imports and all measures having equivalent effect);
2. the restriction of the quantity of beer and soft drinks which could be marketed by a single producer in non-approved containers to 3,000 hectolitres a year was a contravention of Denmark's obligations under Article 30 of the EEC Treaty;
3. as regards the requirement to establish a deposit and return system for empty containers, however, this is an indispensable element of a system intended to ensure the reuse of containers. It is therefore essential if aims pursued by the contested rules are to be achieved. That being so, the restrictions which it imposes on the free movement of goods cannot be regarded as disproportionate to the objective of protecting the environment.

In other words, a points victory to Denmark!

That was Denmark—what was happening elsewhere in Europe? In Belgium there was a voluntary agreement between Government and representative commercial and industrial associations to develop an action programme to reduce, collect, and recycle packaging waste, this also to include a programme for phasing out toxic substances used in packaging. The Netherlands had agreed a 'packaging covenant', one object of which was to reduce the annual production of packaging waste from 2 million tonnes in 1987 by 10 per cent in the year 2000 (This was in fact considered to be an ambitious target bearing in mind that on current estimated growth, with no action, packaging waste produced by the Netherlands would total 2.8 million tonnes in the year 2000).

In France a decree on the elimination of packaging waste was adopted on 1 April 1992. This required companies to establish a deposit system for packaging or arrange joint companies for separate collection. As for

[15] Case 302/86 *Commission of the European Communities* v. *Kingdom of Denmark*, 4609.
[16] Judgment of the Court, 4627.

the United Kingdom—well, probably the least said the better. *This Common Inheritance* indicates that the Government 'is encouraging industry to reduce unnecessary packaging of consumer goods'.[17]

The most dramatic example of a country adopting its own course, however, is presented by Germany. In that country the *Verpackungsverordnung* (Packaging Ordinance) of 8 May 1991 requires manufacturers and/or distributors to take back packaging with a view to reusing or recycling it. In so doing they are not allowed to make use of the public waste-disposal system. The result is to shift responsibility for packaging waste from the public to the private sector. This has led to the establishment of the *Duales System Deutschland* (*DSD*) financed by the member companies (originally 400, now over 3,000) which co-ordinates the collection of the packaging waste. Qualifying packaging is marked by a green dot and is collected either from households or communal collection points. All German companies and companies wishing to export to Germany which produce waste which qualifies under the ordnance will have to contract with DSD to ensure collection of the packaging, or make their own collection arrangements.

The system is being introduced in phases and has encountered considerable difficulties. The waste packaging mountains are, it is alleged in some quarters, growing out of control, there being insufficient recycling facilities available. There are also accusations that, as a consequence, much of the packaging waste has found its way to Eastern Europe or even further afield.

In the face of the disparate, almost unilateral action taken by Member States in the context of packaging waste, some of whom have done nothing whilst some have done a great deal—and others almost too much—there were a number of options open to the European Committee. First, they could have taken no action at all. If they adopted this course, however, there was a concern that Member States would be encouraged to enhance their own legislative measures, thereby increasing the possible obstacles to the internal market. Secondly, the EC could enlarge upon the 1985 Council Directive. The response to that directive, however, has been extremely disappointing. Although specific objectives could be added to the original directive, many of them had already been taken on board by a number of Member States. Thirdly, the EC could adopt the German approach, but doubt was expressed as to whether this would be practicable in the light of the alternative measures already adopted by other Member States. A fourth option involved voluntary agreements, but these would, of course, be dependent upon the goodwill of Member States and even more dependent on the goodwill of trade and industry. The only

[17] *This Common Inheritance* Cm. 1200, 189 para. 14.17.

option open, therefore, was an entirely new directive with the dual purpose of protection of the environment and harmonization of national policies.

Discussions on the first draft of the Directive began almost three years ago. A second informal draft was published in 1991, a third draft in July 1992. The draft continues to meet political obstacles but the Directive, when implemented, will have the twofold purpose of securing a reduction of the quantity of produced packaging waste whilst at the same time achieving the harmonization of national policies. The Directive's structure comprises:

1. targets, i.e. a defined percentage of packaging waste which should be recovered recycled over specific periods—all targets being subject to review;
2. return and management systems—systems for the return of used packaging with provisions for collection;
3. marking—agreed identification marks to facilitate reuse and recovery of packaging;
4. consumer information.

The draft directive has had a far from easy passage. It has fuelled the debate on the benefits of recycling as opposed to incineration with energy recovery or landfill. There has been considerable criticism of the percentage targets. It has been criticized by some as being unfair and too ambitious and by others as not going far enough. This dichotomy of view is nicely illustrated by comparing the view of the Danish system as stated by Sir Gordon Slynn:

> The measures taken by Denmark in relation to approved bottles are highly effective. The producer or importer supplies bottles in cases against deposits to the wholesaler or retailer, who in turn charges the retail purchaser the same deposit on the bottle. The retail purchaser can return the bottle to any retailer selling beer and soft drinks. He gets his deposit back. The retailer collects the various bottles and returns them down the chain to the producer or importer who finally refunds the deposit. Vehicles go out with cases of filled bottles and return with cases of empty bottles. The retailer, the wholesaler or the producer sorts out the different categories of bottles. In the result, it is said that 99% of such bottles are returned and may be used up to 30 times. Some bottles which are not returned by the purchaser are returned by enterprising children, the deposit repaid forming a valuable source of pocket money. The result is a cleaner countryside and a saving of raw materials.[18]

with the view of the draft directive taken by the Friends of the Earth:

> The Directive gives carte blanche to all sectors of the packaging industry to go on producing as much packaging as they want. It protects the interest of industry

[18] Opinion of Advocate-General Sir Gordon Slynn, 24 May 1988, 4623.

instead of the environment. The Commission should dump this rubbishy text and go back to the drawing board.

An interesting perspective on the contrary views expressed above is the fact that the decision on the *Danish Bottles Case* was given in September 1988. The Friends of the Earth's comment was made in July 1992. Within months, the United Kingdom Government assumed the presidency. It quickly found itself faced with European demands on the one side and pressure from the packaging industries on the other, as a consequence of which little was achieved. Much was hoped of the Danish presidency, which succeeded the United Kingdom one, particularly in view of its 'track record' on bottles! Again, however, a surprisingly lethargic presidency achieved little. It was heartening, therefore, when the new Belgian presidency raised packaging waste high on its agenda and amended proposals were presented during Autumn 1993. Under the new German presidency, however, the proposal was blocked again and has now been referred to the newly established Conciliation Committee. A single example, therefore, illustrates vividly how this unilateral action can cause serious transboundary confusion—and dissent—at the European level.

6.4.2. Urban Waste Water

The Urban Waste Water Directive[19] illustrates a problem nearer home. The Council Directive *Concerning Urban Waste Water Treatment* was adopted on 21 May 1991. The Directive deals with 'the collection, treatment and discharge of urban waste water and the treatment and discharge of waste water from certain industrial sectors'. Its objective is to protect the environment from the adverse effect of urban waste-water discharges. The Directive sets priorities for sewage treatment according to the size of the discharge and the sensitivity of the waters receiving the discharge, and requires secondary treatment as the norm. However, in 'less sensitive areas' at least primary treatment is required, and in 'sensitive areas', more comprehensive treatment is necessary.

In brief, the Directive requires water authorities (however constituted) in all Member States to ensure that before waste water is discharged it must have been treated, to standards set by each Member State, within parameters set by the EC, depending on the size of the population creating the discharge and the sensitivity or type of water into which the discharge is to be made.

The Directive was the subject of three United Kingdom consultation papers, the first setting out proposed criteria and procedures for identifying sensitive waters and less sensitive waters, and the second dealing with

[19] 91/271/EEC (21 May 1991).

the methodology for identifying sensitive areas. The third was an explanatory consultation paper issued at the same time as the draft Urban Waste Water Treatment (England and Wales) Regulations. This last was the instrument by which the United Kingdom Government converted the EC Directive into law. The draft Regulations and accompanying guidance notes were issued for public consultation on 22 April 1993. Generally, the draft Regulations closely followed the wording of the Directive, although in England we now speak of 'high natural dispersion areas' as opposed to 'less sensitive areas'.

The reader will be relieved to learn that it is not the intention of this chapter to enter into a detailed discourse on the treatment of sewage waste. This Directive and the consequent Regulations, however, illustrate another practical difficulty of environmental regulation, not so much *vis-à-vis* Member States, although it can be safely assumed that implementation of the Directive is unlikely to be universal or comprehensive, but internally within each Member State.

It would be unfair to generalize and state that no treatment works in the United Kingdom satisfy the criteria laid down in the Directive and the consequent Regulations. It would be fair to assume, however, that many fall short, and in some areas lamentably short, of the required standard. As a consequence, the water utilities are now obliged to upgrade their existing treatment works, or construct new ones, to satisfy the time-scale requirements set out in the Regulations. This requires funding, and new works will require planning permission. To secure such planning permission the water companies will have to negotiate with the planning authorities and in many instances will have to agree to provide what is officially known as planning gain, but which many would describe as planning blackmail. In other words, before a local planning authority is prepared to grant planning permission for an unsightly sewage treatment works, almost certainly near to the coast and in an attractive area, they may well require some form of 'contribution' for the community good. This may be the provision of a car park on top of the new sewage works, an extension to an existing promenade, the construction of playing fields, etc. It is certainly not the purpose of this chapter to consider the ethics of planning gain. The fact is, however, that before the public utilities can comply with the EC Directive and the UK Regulations they must secure their planning permission, which may mean contributing some form of expensive planning gain. That expense will need to be written into the budget estimates submitted by the water companies when negotiating and obtaining approval for their water charges. Such a financial obligation—and no mention has yet been made of the capital cost of carrying out the works—will rest ultimately on members of the public. All this so that the United Kingdom Government can secure compliance with a Directive which is praiseworthy but which many in the profession consider sets standards that are too high and which, no doubt to the immense irritation of government, will be (as usual?) the subject of varying degrees of compliance in the other Member States. It is, therefore, perhaps not surprising, although possibly disappointing, that the United Kingdom is now attempting, with the assistance of a number of other Member States, to lengthen the periods of compliance and reduce the prescribed standards.

The above are, admittedly, only two examples of environmental regulation through the EC. There are many others including the voluntary Eco-Audit,[20] the limitation of noise emission from civil subsonic jet aeroplanes,[21] the reduction of air pollution from existing municipal waste incineration plants,[22] the deliberate release into the environment of genetically modified organisms,[23] the assessment of the effects of certain public and private projects on the environment,[24] and so on. The list is endless—and growing daily.

The question that should be asked, however, is whether the heightened environmental awareness now being exhibited by some, but patently not all, of the Member States, is a trend for the future, or whether it is possible to perceive the beginning of a reaction which will lead to a move away from environmental regulation directed by Europe to a more nationalistic approach, or to put it in political terms, an emphasis on environmental subsidiarity? It would be foolish to suggest that neither course is possible. The premiss upon which this chapter is based, however, is that although environmental regulatory retrenchment within United Kingdom shores is possible, such retrenchment would be both a mistake and impracticable, because we cannot ignore what is happening in Europe.

Putting aside the environmental legislative framework to which reference has been made at the beginning of this chapter, and which has been discussed most authoritatively elsewhere[25] there would appear to be a number of distinct signposts for the way forward. In theory the most important of these should be the Fifth Community Action Programme which looks to the concept of sustainable development. But can such an objective be achieved by environmental regulation or would the greater use of voluntary agreements or economic instruments act as a means to circumvent over-regulation and yet secure the same end? If so, what of the 'polluter pays' principle? What liability should be imposed upon the polluter—and how should any resultant environmental damage be remedied? Further, what is happening outside Europe?

[20] EEC/1836/93 (29 June 1993).
[21] 89/629/EEC (4 Dec. 1989).
[22] 89/429/EEC (21 June 1989).
[23] 90/220/EEC (23 Apr. 1990).
[24] 85/337/EEC (27 June 1985).
[25] See Chs. 1 and 2.

6.5. ECONOMIC INSTRUMENTS

The framework for the future protection of the environment is set out at the international level in Agenda 21[26] and at the European level in the Fifth Action Programme. Can regulation, however, provide the complete solution? Indeed, is regulation the correct way forward, or is there an alternative—that provided by deregulation and economic instruments? Secretary of State for the Environment Rt. Hon. John Gummer MP has stated that 'abolition of control is always the first option, but where controls remain necessary, I have looked at ways of streamlining systems and reducing bureaucracy. Deregulation means cutting unnecessary red tape, not reducing environmental objectives or standards.'[27] To date the Government has proposed the relaxation of existing regulation under the Clean Air Act 1993, the Prescribed Processes and Substances Regulations (EPA 1990), listed buildings and conservation areas, provisions affecting the construction of buildings, water pollution, the carriage of waste, air emission controls, and water abstraction licensing systems. The acid test is whether deregulation really is necessary and more efficient or whether it is simply a reaction to the outcry from businesses when faced with what is perceived as heightened regulation. Regulation in some sectors is unavoidable. The United Kingdom has accepted this in the context of the control of certain dangerous industrial chemicals, pesticides, radioactive substances, and genetically modified organisms.

Do economic instruments, however, provide an effective substitute? 'It is generally recognised that economic instruments provide "more flexibility, efficiency and cost-effectiveness" in environmental policy' stated the OECD in its recent publication, *How to Apply Economic Instruments*.[28] The British Government, in its pursuit of a policy of deregulation, has embraced economic instruments as an alternative to regulation. The second year report, *This Common Inheritance*, asserts that 'direct regulation can be complicated, slow to devise and enforce and . . . may impose greater costs on industry than economic instruments . . . In some cases the process of regulation imposes unnecessary costs on industry and can slow the rate of improvement'. The British Government, citing as an example the success of lower-rate taxation in encouraging people to use lead-free petrol, believes that the application of economic instruments may be greatly broadened to encompass the medias of water, waste, and air.

The main categories of Economic Instruments are as follows:

[26] *Report of the UN Conference on Environment and Development* (1992), UN DOC.A/CONF.151/26/REV.1.

[27] D.o.E. News Release, 20 July 1993.

[28] OECD, Paris, 1991.

Emission Charges. These are defined as 'Charges on the discharge of pollutants into air, water or soil, based on quantity or quality'[29]—these are appropriate to stationary sources, for example, emissions into water or from chimneys.

European Energy Tax: in 1991, the European Commission proposed that all energy used should be taxed to halt the build-up of carbon dioxide in the earth's atmosphere. Following both the appointment of Ioannis Paleokrassas as the EC Environment Commissioner and President Clinton's energy tax measure directed at oil and estimated to initially raise US$20 billion, a new impetus has been given to the carbon tax debate. Britain, by imposing VAT on domestic fuel and increasing petrol and car licence taxes, is ahead of many Community members on measures to restrain carbon emissions, although, politically, the British government is opposed to taxation directly from Brussels.

Product Charges. These are defined as 'Charges levied on products that are harmful to the environment when used in production processes, consumed or disposed of'[30]—products used in large quantities and readily identifiable. For example, restrictions on sulphur in fuel in France and lead in fuel in the United Kingdom; charging non-returnable containers more than returnable containers; or charging aircraft if they produce excessive noise.

A report, *Recovery of Resources in Waste*, commissioned by the President of the Board of Trade, found that several economic instrument options to reduce waste were inappropriate, that is, changes to corporation tax, VAT differentiation, and market support schemes. Municipal waste in Britain annually is estimated at about 20 million tonnes, 13 million of which is collected from households, 3 million from commercial sources, and the balance delivered to civic amenity sites or recycling schemes. Paper accounts for one-third of this, and plastics and glass together for 18 per cent. Packaging waste accounts for 8.4 million tonnes. The Government aims to reach a target of 50 per cent recycling but is mindful and rightly wary of the mountains of unrecycled waste created by German regulation. Economic instruments could therefore be used to combat waste: charges on products or raw materials; changing responsibilities for waste; waste-collection charges; and waste-disposal charges, have all been found to be efficient solutions. By implication, economic instruments have three potential benefits: to make waste generators pay the costs of waste disposal; to raise revenues to finance collection of materials for recycling; and to provide an incentive for increased recycling levels.

[29] OECD, Paris, 1991, 100. [30] Ibid. 102.

Deposit Refund Systems. These are defined as 'Deposit levied on a potentially polluting product, to be refunded when the product is returned to storage, treatment or recycling point'[31] which induces safe disposal, reuse, or recycling of products where serious environmental problems are attached to disposal. For example, these could be applied to containers of water pollutants such as pesticides or batteries, products containing potential air pollutants such as CFCs in refrigerators, or containers which pollute the air when burned.

Marketable Permits. These are defined as 'Environmental quotas, allowances or ceilings on pollution levels that, once initially allocated by the appropriate authority, can be traded subject to a set of prescribed rules'[32]—a market solution where a number of fixed sources are involved sufficient to establish a well-functioning market, each of which has differing marginal compliance 'with environmental standards' costs.

The recent US Environmental Protection Agency auction of emission permits was a landmark in air pollution schemes aimed to reduce acid rain. Permits allow production of one tonne of sulphur dioxide gas from a fossil-fuel power station. From 1995, if any of the 110 most polluting power stations in the United States produces more pollution in a year than allowed by the permits it possesses, it will face large fines. The idea is that the market, not the regulator, is best at working out cost-effective ways of bringing down pollution. Fresh permits will be issued each year but the number of permits will decline to a level that halves sulphur dioxide emissions early in the next century. Broking firms have sprung up that specialize in permits. At the first reported trade of such permits, 10,000 tonnes sold for nearly US$3,000,000. Brokers in the auction bought 5 per cent of the total, the majority predictably being bought by utilities. Tradable rights already exist in Australian legislation regulating production of ozone-depleting substances where companies have fixed quotas but are allowed to trade these amongst themselves. Wider Australian tradable permits are envisaged. The British Government is also examining sulphur-dioxide and nitrogen-oxide emissions in the same light. Generators may be allowed during a year to alter distribution of their aggregate sulphur-dioxide and nitrogen-oxide quotas from plant to plant and perhaps to switch quotas with other operators.

The above four categories highlight the overlaps that exist in controlling pollution. A car during its lifetime may be subject to product charges upon fuel, regulations concerning catalytic converters, deposit refunds upon its battery, and eventual recycling of its glass and shell due to incentives to recycle.

Economic instruments, or rather economic disincentives, must therefore

[31] Ibid. 104. [32] Ibid. 106.

play a part in the scheme of environmental regulation—but, it is suggested, only a part. A regulatory code based on a European framework is unavoidable.

6.6. LIABILITY AND REMEDIES FOR ENVIRONMENTAL DAMAGE

6.6.1. The Convention on Civil Liability for Damage to the Environment

The difficulty with environmental regulation is that the consequences of environmental damage are so far-reaching that regulatory controls as presently framed in all Members States do not easily provide the means for remedying the damage, punishing the offender, and compensating the polluted. The Fifth Action Programme and Agenda 21, with their emphasis on the 'player', and the increasing dependence on codes of conduct and economic instruments, still fall short of the reality—remedying actual environmental damage, and ensuring that the polluter pays.

The broad principle of 'the polluter pays' raises a number of questions that no European legal code has yet been able to answer. What if the polluter cannot pay? What if the pollution occurred so many years ago that the polluter no longer exists? What of the accident that is not insured? Most importantly, perhaps—are cause and fault the proper target—or should more emphasis be placed on remedying the damage? The questions are not new, but in view of the inevitably controversial answers, not surprisingly the EC has been a little slow in coming forward with the solution. As a consequence, its deliberations have to a certain extent been overtaken by the Council of Europe (of which the United Kingdom is a member), which in March 1993 adopted the 'Convention on Civil Liability for Damage to the Environment'. The Convention is the first international legal instrument to set out the general principle of civil liability for all damage caused to the environment—damage to the environment meaning loss of life or personal injury, loss of or damage to property, loss or damage by impairment of the environment, and the cost of preventive measures. There are inevitable exceptions to the definition, and the Convention does not cover transport of dangerous products and nuclear accidents which are covered by other international Conventions. Where it does brave new territory, however, is in the area of liability in that the entire framework for the Convention is based on the concept of *strict liability*, that is, liability irrespective of fault, although this will only arise in the case of risk posed by a 'dangerous activity'. This is defined in the Convention and includes the production, handling, storage, use, or discharge of specific 'dangerous substances', the operation of a permanent waste site, the operation of an incineration site, etc. Further, the dangerous activity must be carried out in a professional capacity.

Despite these limitations, the Convention bravely considers the question of insurance and requires each party which conducts a dangerous activity to 'participate in a financial security scheme or to have and maintain a financial guarantee up to a certain limit, of such type and terms as specified by internal law, to cover the liability under this convention'. It further provides for actions for compensation subject to a limitation period of three years from the date on which the claimant knew or ought reasonably to have known of the damage. There is an overall limitation to the effect that no actions can be brought after thirty years from the date of the incident which caused the damage.

The Convention is an important first step. It sits a little uncomfortably *vis-à-vis* the EC, although to avoid the difficulties that might be encountered by the Member States ultimately adopting a framework that conflicts with or is contrary to the Convention, Article 25(2) specifically provides that 'in their mutual relations, Parties which are members of the European Economic Community shall apply Community rules and shall therefore not apply the rules arising from this Convention except insofar as there is no Community rule governing the particular subject concerned'.

Certainly there is little prospect of a similarly positive document emerging from the EC for some considerable time, and it is perhaps, therefore, a point of concern to note that in Lugano on 21 June 1993 the Convention was signed by Cyprus, Finland, Greece, Italy, Liechtenstein, Luxembourg, and the Netherlands. There are some obvious absentees and indeed the United Kingdom and Denmark, and possibly Germany and Ireland have already indicated that they are not prepared to sign.

6.6.2. EC Green Paper: Remedying Environmental Damage

It would, however, be a little unfair to suggest that the EC is doing nothing. There is a growing awareness that positive steps must be taken to achieve a community-wide framework for liability that satisfies three basic criteria, namely:

1. acceptance by all Member States so as to secure transboundary consistency;
2. compatibility with each Member State's existing regulatory framework; and
3. adherence to the principle that the polluter pays.

The first step in what is likely to be a rather long journey was the publication in May 1993 by the European Commission of a Green Paper entitled 'Remedying Environmental Damage'. The Green Paper is intended 'to provoke the wide-ranging discussion which the Commission seeks on the subject of remedying environmental damage in order better to inform its future actions in this area'. In its opening paragraph it draws attention to the fact that major environmental incidents including Seveso, Amoco, Cadiz, Sandoz, Corunna, and the Braer, by reason of their impact, steal the headlines and arouse public outrage. Such incidents, however, represent only the visible part of the iceberg floating on the polluted seas, far more remains below and is, in the words of the Green Paper, 'no less in need of remedial action'. The Green Paper seeks wide-ranging discussion on three issues with a view to directing the way forward. First, fault-based as opposed to strict liability; second, compulsory insurance; and last, joint compensation funds.

6.6.3. Strict or Fault-Based Liability

The Green Paper suggests that the use 'of different systems of civil liability for remedying environmental damage among the Member States could lead to distortions of competition and the single market'. If industries are treated differently by each Member State, the penal consequences imposed on one industrial sector for remedying environmental damage may be totally out of proportion to those imposed on the competition in a neighbouring Member State. This could result in some companies gaining a distinct competitive advantage over their neighbours, leading ultimately to the 'cleaner' Member State losing industry to those countries with the less 'enthusiastic' environmental regimes.

Every Member State, of course, has in place some measure of environmental regulation. At the higher level, the EC continues to legislate and regulate on a transboundary basis. The Fifth Action Programme and Agenda 21 recognize the dangers faced by the natural environment. They propound the education of the players which will lead to the rectification of damage and eradication of future risks. That damage has been caused, however, cannot be denied. That damage has been caused and has not yet been discovered is also unfortunately true. The Green Paper therefore wishes to stimulate discussion on what should happen once that damage has been discovered—an issue entirely separate from education, rectification, and eradication. If the polluter should pay, should he pay regardless of fault? If not, who pays?

There are two faces to the question of liability:

1. *Fault-based liability*. If a party is to be liable for environmental damage under a fault-based liability regime, it would be necessary to *prove* that that party committed a negligent or otherwise wrongful act which caused the damage. A prerequisite is that that party must have had a

duty to behave according to the legal environmental requirements. The relationship between fault-based liability and the regulatory framework is, therefore, very strong. That having been said, by the very nature of statutory regulation, exceptions (i.e. defences) will be available, and it may often be difficult for the party who has suffered the damage actually to be able to prove that the party that caused the damage has in fact acted wrongfully.

2. *Strict liability*. This is in effect liability without fault. In other words, there is no requirement to prove that, for example, the party that caused the damage has breached statutory regulations—although it would still be necessary to prove that the damage has in fact been caused by someone's actions. It has been argued that by removing this difficult hurdle, strict liability will act as an incentive to take measures to prevent damage from occurring in the first place. Although this is an outwardly simple concept, there are difficulties. For example in a strict liability case, when environmental damage occurs, the level of costs incurred in remedying it may be so out of proportion with the return on the particular commercial activity that strict liability could in fact stifle investment. At the same time, even in a strict liability regime, it would be necessary to define what degree of damage to the environment will bring strict liability into play. An agreed definition of the term 'damage to the environment' will be required.

The Green Paper, clearly in favour of some degree of strict liability, queries whether a first step would be to decide whether certain activities and processes should be subject to such a regime. It suggests that some of the factors that could be considered in deciding whether a strict liability regime would be appropriate for a particular sector or type of activity could include:

- the type of hazard posed by the activity;
- the probability that damage might occur;
- the possible extent of the damage;
- whether a strict liability regime would provide an incentive for better risk management and prevention;
- the feasibility and cost of restoring the damage that would be likely to occur;
- the potential financial burden of strict liability on the economic sector; and
- the need for and availability of insurance.[33]

A further complication is the question of multiplicity of liable parties. This will arise where more than one party is or may be liable for environmental damage. Some jurisdictions within the EC allow the

[33] *Remedying Environmental Damage*, 7.

injured party to proceed against all the parties who may be liable for the damage. This does, of course, raise difficult questions as to the standard of proof and a great deal depends on whether the jurisdiction operates a system of joint, or joint and several, liability. Under a joint liability regime each party will only be liable to pay compensation for the damage specifically caused by its actions. This will raise different questions as to apportioning liability and calculating compensation. In a joint and several liability regime each party against whom the action is taken will be liable for the whole amount and it is then left to the parties to determine among themselves their respective liability. Inevitably, this introduces a large degree of dissension amongst the parties, leading to delay, which in turn delays the remedial action required. Additional problems arise in the context of the 'deep pocket' factor, that is, commencing action against the party with the most funds—to say nothing of the transboundary disputes that would arise with Member States operating within different regulatory regimes.

A further component that will inevitably add to the delay in determining the identity of the polluter, and then drawing from that polluter funds to remedy the damage, is the difficulty of actually agreeing a definition of 'damage to the environment'. For example, the damage to the forests of Norway caused by acid rain is the result of an aggregation of airborne pollution from a number of countries. It is impossible to identify any one specific cause and, bearing in mind the length of time over which the acid rain damage has become manifest, impossible to determine the initiator.

On the other hand, however, some industrial activities are actually authorized by their national regulatory authorities, in effect, to pollute. For example, a power station in the United Kingdom receives the requisite IPC authorization from HMIP. The emissions of one power station with a legal authorization, however, will be entirely different when those emissions have merged with the emissions of twenty other power stations in Europe, possibly within a relatively short distance of each other, but in different countries. If the total emissions cause damage to the environment, should not, as the Green Paper queries, the regulatory authorities that authorized those emissions themselves be liable?

Then there is the problem of damage from the past. There will be occasions when damage identified now was caused so many years ago that the perpetrators can no longer be identified. There will be other instances when, although the polluter can be identified, the actions carried out at the time were entirely within the law. The difficulties arising in this area are well demonstrated by the *Eastern Counties Leatherwork plc*[34] case.

[34] *Cambridge Water Company* v. *Eastern Counties Leatherwork plc* [1994] 2 WLR 53.

It must of course be accepted that the problems facing the European Commission and indeed the Governments of all the Member States are so immense in an area of law and science that is as yet so uncertain, that one can understand the reluctance of many governments actually to approach the problems in a genuinely creative frame of mind. Annexe I to the Green Paper provides a list of current legislation in Member States based on liability without fault. Annexe II describes the situation in Japan and the United States of America, and Annexe III provides a schedule of extant international instruments. Clearly, no solution will please all sides and for this reason the Green Paper considers another option, namely the concept of limited liability and insurance.

6.6.4. Limited Liability and Insurance

Insurance for damage caused to the environment is somewhat difficult to obtain, to say the least. One cannot, of course, insure against criminal liability leading to damage to the environment, but civil liability and economic loss are areas where, technically, the market should be able to provide some form of insurance cover. In practice, however, the fact that liability is unlimited, the difficulty of establishing the commencement of gradual pollution, and the potential magnitude of compensation in some environmental scenarios render the risks too great for the insurance market to accept—unless, of course, the site is clean, the activity is clean, and the premiums are sufficiently high to cover all potential liability. As a result, many of the larger industrial companies self-insure, a luxury that smaller companies—usually the very companies that require the cover—cannot afford.

France, Italy, and the Netherlands have created pools of insurance to cover gradual as well as sudden pollution, and the German Environmental Liability Act lists certain industrial installations which must be covered for environmental liability. Indeed, the proposed EC Directive on *Civil Liability for Damage Caused by Waste*[35] contained a requirement that the producer and the operator of the waste's ultimate destination should also obtain sufficient cover for environmental liability—a proposed requirement that has raised considerable controversy.

In the light of this market uncertainty, the Green Paper moots the possibility of compulsory insurance. It accepts that in such a scenario insurers may well become 'licensers' of industry through their ability to withhold cover based on their judgment as to whether the coverage was a 'good' or a 'bad' risk. From a practical point of view, however, the rigorous evaluation of any site/activity carried out before insurance is obtained

[35] Com. (91) 219 final—SYN 217.

provides a useful practical check for the 'public' as well as achieving the end of reducing the insurers' risk.

The problem of the extent of liability would still remain even if insurance were available. Would it therefore be practical to introduce a cap on liability?

6.6.5. Joint Compensation Funds

Compulsory insurance and national pools for insurance are, it is suggested, but one short step away from joint compensation systems. Always bearing in mind the exhortation of Article 130r and the 'polluter pays' principle, one comes to the logical conclusion that there will still be occasions when funds to remedy environmental damage following an 'incident' are simply not available due to insolvency, unknown identity of polluter, etc. A joint compensation fund is in effect a blend of insurance, tax, and the public purse. Funds are sustained by contributions from those sectors of industry and commerce most likely to have need to call upon them. As the Green Paper indicates, the 'cost of damage linked to the aggregate impact of a sector's activities becomes apportioned among the individual enterprises, and thereby internalised'.

The concept offers distinct advantages. The readiness of available funds should technically (not it would seem in the United States) enable the regulatory authorities to act quickly in direct comparison in a system based on civil liability, which usually involves an element at least of procrastination. In addition, the collective aspect of the funds means that the responsible sectors are sharing the burden as opposed to depending on the financial ability of the individual party concerned. Conversely there are of course a number of difficulties. To what standard should the environment be restored? Which party will be responsible for monitoring the works both during their execution and after their completion?

A number of compensation funds are already in existence. For example the oil industry has set up various voluntary funds designed to facilitate remedial damage in instances of major oil spills at sea. International conventions covering the same issues also exist although their effect is weakened by the non-signature of a number of major international players. Sweden, under its Environmental Damage Act 1986, has a system that provides compensation for personal injury and damage to property in cases where either it is not possible to identify the source of the damage, or, where a cause or link can be established but the originated party is insolvent or the liability is statute barred under Swedish law. Under the Swedish Act, any party that requires an environmental permit must also contribute a fixed amount to the fund, calculated according to the size of the activity. There is, incidentally, an additional requirement of insurance cover.

Perhaps the most notorious example of a joint compensation fund is the system that has been in operation in America since 1980 known as 'Superfund'.[36] This was set up as part of the Comprehensive Environmental Response Compensation and Liability Act (CERCLA). The money is raised from a variety of sources, about half from direct taxes on industry. The average yearly income to the fund is as follows:

$550 million from petroleum excise taxes;
$275 million from chemical foodstock taxes;
$500 million from environmental income taxes; and
$440 million from cost recovery actions and fines.

Impetus for Superfund came partly as a result of the 'Love Canal' disaster of the late 1970s. Between 1942 and 1953 some 21,000 tonnes of chemical waste was dumped in a disused canal in New York State. The adjacent land was developed and a small community grew up. Some twenty years later, the ground water entering basements and cellars was found to be highly toxic, and in a number of cases it burnt upon contact. Ultimately, in 1978 the entire community had to be evacuated. A lawsuit against Oxidental Chemicals, the owner of the site, was commenced by New York State which is attempting to recover $250 million in compensation and punitive damages. Litigation is still continuing. Oxidental Chemicals were not the owners of the site at the time of the dumping and neither were they responsible for the dumping, which was in any case the result of a government contract.

Clearly the aim of any joint compensation fund is to achieve the most effective remedial action in the shortest possible time. The costs involved, however, are so huge that companies fight hard to avoid liability and Superfund is only found at the end of a very long litigious tunnel. The average cost of a clean-up has proved to be between $29 million and $35 million. In America, with more than 35,000 sites already reported to that country's environmental regulatory body, the Environmental Protection Agency (EPA), it is a practical impossibility to expect instantaneous clean-up. Although the EPA does technically have the power to apply the stringent liability provisions of CERCLA which will enable them to pass the cost of clean-up directly and immediately to the polluter, in practice liability lawsuits delay prosecution and the machinery of the Superfund has proved extremely inefficient.

In practice, the EPA identifies sites and tries to ensure clean-up at the polluter's expense where it is possible to establish liability. If this is not possible Superfund is brought into action. The EPA is also required to identify a certain number of sites where contamination is extreme and in respect of which high priority is given to immediate clean-up. Such sites

[36] See Ch. 4 *supra*.

are registered on the National Priorities List (NPL). Out of 35,000 potential Superfund sites reported, at present some 1,250 are on the list. Most Superfund capital was originally directed at these 'disaster scenario' sites.

It is noticeable, however, that the EPA's emphasis is gradually shifting, and incorporating a monitoring role in tandem with responsibility for clean-up of priority sties. The system was originally distinctly bureaucratic, but over time it has been recognized that the most efficient way to secure speedy clean-up is to bypass statutory regulation and instead rely on self-regulation. There are obvious benefits to both sides in allowing the producers of contaminants to clean up with as little regulatory monitoring as possible. Now the EPA positively encourages potentially responsible parties to clean up within their own constraints of self-regulation. Benefits to parties undertaking such work include reduced fines if they are eventually held liable for extended clean-up, and the more immediate financial advantage of expenditure on such work being generally deductible under the United States' tax code.

It is interesting to contrast the American system with the French equivalent. In the French case, industry has been far more receptive, on the surface at least, to the demands of government. The French fund, which is designed to be used to clear up some 150 sites where no responsible party has been identified—called 'orphan' sites—was created from money contributed by leading French industrial and commercial firms. The business community preferred a 'voluntary' method of environmental management to the waste disposal-tax which the Government had threatened to impose. Leading firms contribute some 40 million francs per year to the fund. In practice this sum is probably less than the envisaged waste tax. It was originally thought that the scheme would run for a finite length of time since the new legislation was designed to prevent 'orphan' sites occurring. The American experience, however, and indeed, one suspects, common sense, has indicated that this is a fallacy; there will always be more waste than people willing to clear it up. There are some quarters that believe that for this reason a waste tax would still be a useful revenue-making tool for Government. For the time being, however, the 'voluntary' system prevails in France. French business has in any case noted the complicated legislation imposed on American businesses under CERCLA and no doubt felt it prudent to co-operate with French Government.

In the broader European context, mention has already been made of the proposed Council Directive on *Civil Liability for Damage Caused by Waste*, which looked to mandatory insurance. Article 11 of the amended draft also provides that the Commission shall study the feasibility of the establishment of a 'European fund for compensation for damage and impairment of the environment caused by waste' to deal with those cases where the party liable for the environmental damage cannot be identified or is unable to provide full compensation.

Similarly, the proposed Council Directive on the *Landfill of Waste*[37] requires Member States, by Article 18, to establish 'landfill aftercare funds'. These funds are designed to finance damage to the environment after the cessation of landfill operations. The practicality is now being seriously debated—is the step too great for the EC?

6.7. LOOKING AHEAD

The Green Paper raises a number of issues and poses a number of questions. The document's importance lies not so much in the actual questions that have been asked, because they raise nothing that has not already been raised and tested elsewhere, but more in the fact that the EC has thought fit to raise them at all.

Considering environmental regulation in the broadest terms, one is faced with facts as they stand and aspirations to do better. On the side of fact, there is the Member State environmental regulatory and legislative framework, above which hover the EC Treaties and Directives. On the side of aspiration, there have been five Community action programmes, the current programme having as its objective sustainable development. The bridge between the two is the principle that the polluter should pay.

The objective of sustainable development is an environmental ideal. That is not to say that it cannot be achieved. It is common sense—and this and past generations should feel guilty that it has been necessary to give form to such common sense in the Fifth Action Programme. It is not pessimism but realism, however, to say that the objective is unlikely ever to be universally achieved. Common sense therefore requires a regulatory framework which will provide both sanction and remedy.

The United Kingdom really began to produce an environmental legislative framework with teeth only after its accession to the European Community. What changed after accession? Simply that by its very nature, the European Community has had to take a realistic transboundary view of the damage being caused to the environment by both Member States and those outside, a view that might have concerned Member States previously, but a view over which they had little or no control, and it must be conceded, little internal stimulus. The United Kingdom's Environmental Protection Act is in essence merely a reflection of the will of Europe, albeit with an element of consolidation and tidying up! The fact that the United Kingdom is only now bringing into effect

[37] Com. (93) 275.

Part II of the Act (waste), however, and has therefore placed itself outside the European timetable, demonstrates the difficulties faced by just one Member State as it struggles to satisfy the demands of Europe on the one hand and the demands of industry and commerce at home on the other. On the European level, the proposed waste-packaging directive has been drafted in the hope that it will provide an equitable European solution to the confusion that has arisen because some Member States were not prepared to wait on the Community but instead, when perceiving an environmental problem within their own boundaries, set their own standards. The Urban Waste Water Directive on the other hand is an example of how high European standards, designed to achieve an environmentally level playing-field, can be imposed upon Member States regardless of the serious national consequences that follow.

Voluntary agreements and economic instruments will always play a part in the environmental regulatory framework. One queries, however, whether such vehicles can ever constitute a deterrent or an incentive (depending on one's viewpoint) sufficient to render superfluous a formal regulatory framework.

To protect the environment from damage and to ensure that there are always sufficient funds available to remedy that environmental damage, there must be a central source of finance on which to call when all other sources fail. A joint compensation fund, tested already in the United States, France, and elsewhere, is the only practical means of securing such an end. The fact that the American regime has encountered serious difficulties does not point to a defect in the concept, but more, it is suggested, a defect in its administration. It is this chapter's contention that a tax on industry and government, possibly linked to authorizations and supplemented by the public purse, is the only way forward. It is in addition suggested that a European joint compensation fund would be too difficult to administer. Recognizing the principle of subsidiarity, each Member State should be required to legislate for its own national compensation fund sufficient to meet the environmental needs of that country.

This inevitably raises questions as to the definition of environmental damage. Certainly as an initial yardstick, the definition provided in the Convention on Civil Liability for Damage Resulting from Activities Dangerous to the Environment provides more than just a suitable starting point:

> 'Damage' means:
> (*a*) loss of life or personal injury;
> (*b*) loss of or damage to property other than to the installation itself or property held under the control of the operator, at the site of the dangerous activity;

(*c*) loss or damage by impairment of the environment insofar as this is not considered to be damage within the meaning of sub-paragraphs (*a*) or (*b*) above provided that compensation for impairment of the environment, other than for loss of profit from such impairment, shall be limited to the costs of measures of reinstatement actually undertaken or to be undertaken;

(*d*) the cost of preventive measures and any loss or damage caused by preventive measures;

to the extent that the loss or damage referred to in sub-paragraphs (*a*) to (*c*) of this paragraph arises out of or results from the hazardous properties of the dangerous substances, genetically modified organisms, or micro-organisms or arises or results from waste.

It should incidentally be noted that 'dangerous substances' are defined in the Convention as, *inter alia*, 'substances or preparations which have properties which constitute a significant risk for man, the environment or property'.

In so determining, Member States will also have to decide whether they are seeking to repair damage caused to the environment *per se*—or merely to secure remediation sufficient for future use. In the context of sustainability, the former must be the correct approach.

What of the polluter? The Green Paper considers insurance and the Convention itself has raised the question of compulsory insurance. The insurance market has already demonstrated that it is unable (or unwilling) to meet the needs of industry, and as has been pointed out, it is the smaller industrial companies that will suffer as a result. It is not within the mandate of any Member State government to require insurance companies to provide insurance. It is open for the Government of Member States, however, to require the polluters to arrange insurance cover or some form of financial security to a limit approved by the regulatory authorities at the time of authorization. It is accepted that some companies will be unable to meet such a requirement—but if they are unable to satisfy those prepared to provide the insurance or financial security that they can meet satisfactory standards, should they in fact be allowed to continue their activity?

This finally leads to the question of liability—fault-based or strict liability? Sustainability will never be achieved if current environmental legislation, albeit implicitly, acknowledges uncertainty. If parties participate in business that may at some stage in the process result in environmental damage, it surely cannot be argued that the injured innocent party, in effect the 'environment' in its broadest definition, should suffer without the certainty of ultimate recompense and/or remediation. A framework built on fault-based liability leads to uncertainty and delay. Strict liability provides certainty, for the environment if not the responsible parties. Strict liability must, therefore, be the way forward. To argue otherwise would be to strike at the very foundations of the concept of sustainability.

Not surprisingly the British Government's response to the Green Paper on Remedying Environmental Damage is not entirely in accordance with the views expressed here. That response is succinctly summarized in the following two paragraphs:

> The UK view, based on its own statutory and private, common law provisions, is that action by the Member States alone to remedy environmental damage can generally be sufficient to achieve the objects of the Community's environmental policy, including improving the quality of the environment and protecting human health, in accordance with the applicable environmental principles, in particular, the polluter pays principle and the principle that preventive action should be taken.
>
> There is no evidence that Community-level action on civil liability could lead to any additional, real benefits, nor that Member States are likely to be hindered by the absence of Community-level action in this area. Moreover, national action for remedying environmental damage is not restricted to provisions for civil liability but may also include provision for pollution control and land use planning, as well as criminal sanctions.[38]

Looking ahead, if the dual objectives of making the polluter pay and the sustainability of development are to be achieved, Member States must accept that environmental regulation will be led by Europe, and that that regulation will be based on a framework of strict liability supplemented by a system of compulsory insurance and national environmental compensation funds.

[38] See also House of Lords Select Committee on the European Communities, 14 Dec. 1993 (HL Paper, 10) on 'Remedying Environmental Damage' and the UK strategy on Sustainable Development (Cm. 2426), Jan. 1994.

7

Environmental Barriers to Trade and European Community Law

MARTIN COLEMAN

7.1. INTRODUCTION

Balancing free trade and environmental protection is a delicate exercise. Regard for the environment, particularly in richer, industrialized countries, has led to the rapid development of environmental legislation which has had the effect of restricting trade: the potential for protectionist ambition to masquerade as environmental concern—'green protectionism'—is apparent. This paper examines the problem at European Community level in its worldwide context.

One of the objectives of the Treaty of Rome was to establish at Community level the economic conditions that prevail within the market of a single state. This involves the abolition of all duties and quantitative restrictions in trade between Member States; the removal of barriers to the free movement of business, labour, and capital and the establishment of a common external customs tariff. Environmental protection measures may have an impact on the working of the internal market—because they give rise to barriers to trade and free movement between Member States. In addition, the economic strength of the Community means that measures adopted by the Community will have a greater impact on third countries than similar measures adopted by one Member State.

The significance of the Community in this regard is likely to grow as new Member States are admitted and as the impact of Community law and policy is extended to third countries through arrangements such as the European Economic Area Agreement which came into force on 1 January 1994 and extends most of the internal market rules to the EFTA countries (except Switzerland and, for the time being, Liechtenstein) and agreements with Central and Eastern European countries which provide for free movement of many goods and services across the border between the Community and other countries subject to their observing key aspects of Community internal market rules.

Under Community law, exceptions to the fundamental principle of the free movement of goods between Member States may be justified on grounds of environmental protection. But such exceptions endanger the smooth operation of the internal market. In an attempt to stem this threatened fragmentation, and in recognition of the need to safeguard the environment, the Community is developing legislation which seeks to draw a balance between environmental protection and free trade. The provisions adopted affect the conditions of trade, both between Member States, and between the Community and the rest of the world. Measures entailing the restriction of imports, exports, consumption, and production have a direct impact, whilst other instruments indirectly affect trade by influencing conditions of market access or competition. Community policy does not regard legislation as providing a complete solution for the protection of the environment. It sets store by the constructive influence of co-operation with industry and unfettered competition. However, it is arguable that this approach, with its voluntary instruments designed to harness market forces for the environment's good, is no less restrictive of trade and, perhaps, underscores the Community's tendency to the parochial.

It may be that as EC environmentalism gathers momentum, bearing an increasingly comprehensive body of trade-related measures, out of kilter with developments on a worldwide level, the Community must plead guilty to the charge of 'green imperialism'.

7.2. THE PROBLEM

Trade affects the environment. It has long been recognized that methods of production and patterns of consumption may promise protection of, or exacerbate damage to, our surroundings. This relationship has become reflected in policy and legislation at national, Community, and international levels. Early examples of measures include the multilateral conventions on flora and fauna of the 1930s and 1940s[1] and national pollution control measures introduced in the 1960s.[2] As safeguarding the environment has been assigned a higher priority, in particular by richer, developed countries, there has been a rapid proliferation of measures regulating and limiting trade in the name of environmental protection. In addition, the power of trade sanctions as a method of ensuring a State's compliance with environmental standards has been acknowledged.

But it is not only environmentalists who are interested in restricting

[1] e.g. Convention Relative to the Preservation of Fauna and Flora in their Natural State, 1933, 172 *LNTS* 241; International Convention for the Protection of Birds, 1950, 638 *UNTS* 185.

[2] See chapters by Christy and Greenwood.

trade. Protectionist motives may shelter under a mantle of environmental concern. In the *Danish Bottles Case*[3] (see below, 7.3.1) where, as an anti-pollution measure, restrictions were placed on containers for beer and soft drinks, it was noted by the European Commission that

> the sincerity of the Kingdom of Denmark's ecological concerns may be doubted if it is borne in mind that it has not considered it necessary to fix a maximum level of protection for the environment in relation to containers of products such as milk and wine, which for different reasons are not subject to competition between domestic and foreign producers.[4]

A similar example is Ontario's tax on beer cans, but not bottles, which affects mainly foreign suppliers. The use of cans for soups and juices (where local producers would have been affected) is not taxed. In addition, at the end of June last year a United States federal district court delayed completion of the North American Free Trade Agreement (NAFTA) by ruling that United States law required the filing of a statement of NAFTA's environmental impact. It has been claimed that the 'real' reason for challenging NAFTA lies with fears that the agreement will lead to a haemorrhage of jobs and prosperity over the border to Mexico.

While environmental legislation may restrict trade, it does not necessarily follow that the interests of free trade conflict with those of environmental protection. It may be that free trade is good for the environment. Increases in per capita income—which are boosted by increased market access and expanding trade—provide more resources for environmental protection.[5] As the income of a country rises, it is more likely to increase expenditure on limiting damage to the environment. The remainder of this chapter will examine the balance achieved by the European Community in its attempt to reconcile free trade and the prevention of 'green protectionism' with regard for preservation of the environment.

7.3. EUROPEAN COMMUNITY LAW AND POLICY

7.3.1. Free Movement of Goods

7.3.1.1. Articles 30–36 of the Treaty of Rome

The free movement of goods is a tenet of the Community legal order, aimed at the creation between Member States of a single market without internal trade barriers. The doctrine is set out in Articles 30–34 of the Treaty of Rome (the Treaty). Article 30 provides that quantitative

[3] *Commission* v. *Denmark*, Case 302/86 [1988] ECR 4607.
[4] Ibid. 4612.
[5] For studies demonstrating this, see GATT, *Report on International Trade* (1990–1), 30.

restrictions on imports and all measures having equivalent effect are prohibited between Member States. The European Court of Justice (ECJ) interpretation of 'measures having equivalent effect' is broad and includes 'all trading rules enacted by Member States which are capable of hindering directly or indirectly, actually or potentially, intra-Community trade'.[6]

However, the principle is not absolute. Article 36 sets out a number of limited grounds on which exceptions to the free movement of goods may be justified, including the protection of health and life of humans, animals, and plants, provided that the exceptions do not constitute a means of arbitrary discrimination or a disguised restriction on trade. Environmental protection is not identified as a ground justifying derogation from Article 30 (although some environmental measures fall under the protection of life and health ground, for example rules designed to cut the spread of animal and plant diseases).

7.3.1.2. Mandatory Requirement of Environmental Protection

Although the ECJ has stated that the exceptions in Article 36 are exhaustive,[6] its judgment in the *Cassis de Dijon*[7] case, in effect, provided further grounds upon which derogation from Article 30 may be permitted. It was held that in the absence of Community measures, restrictions on the free movement of goods resulting from disparities between national marketing laws 'must be accepted in so far as those provisions may be recognized as being necessary in order to satisfy mandatory requirements [of the Treaty]'.[8] The reasoning behind this apparent inconsistency is that, rather than extending the scope of Article 36, *Cassis de Dijon* defined the limits of Article 30. Thus the existence of a mandatory requirement means that (provided that the tests set out below are satisfied) Article 30 will not apply at all.

In *Cassis* consumer protection and the prevention of unfair competition were specially identified as 'mandatory requirements', but not to the exclusion of other objectives. Subsequently, in *Procureur de la République*,[9] the ECJ held that the protection of the environment was 'one of the Community's essential objectives' which may justify certain trade restrictions. This view was confirmed in 1987 when the Treaty was amended by the Single European Act expressly to include Title VII, Articles 130r–t concerning the environment. In the *Danish Bottles Case*, the court stated unequivocally that 'the protection of the environment is

[6] *Procureur du Roi Dasonville*, Case 8/74 [1974] ECR 837 at 852.

[7] *Rewe-Zentral AG* v. *Bundesmonopolverwaltung für Branntwein*, Case 120/78 [1979] ECR 649.

[8] Ibid. 662.

[9] *Procureur de la République* v. *Association de Défense des Brûleurs d'Huiles Usagées*, Case 240/83 [1985] ECR 531.

a mandatory requirement which may limit the application of Article 30 of the Treaty.'[10]

However, mandatory requirements may only be invoked where the tests of *proportionality* and *non-discrimination* are fulfilled.

7.3.1.3. Proportionality

In order to be lawful, a restrictive measure must be necessary to achieve the objective pursued by that measure and must represent the means which least restricts the free movement of goods.[11] In *Procureur de la République*, the court stated that trade restrictions may be allowed so long as they do not 'go beyond the inevitable restrictions which are justified by the pursuit of the objective of environmental protection'.

The *Danish Bottles* judgment closely examined the application of the principle of proportionality in relation to environmental restrictions on trade, and warrants consideration in some detail. The case concerned Danish legislation which implemented, first, a compulsory deposit and return system in respect of containers for soft drinks and beer. Secondly, it prescribed that the containers and ancillary deposit and return scheme be approved by the National Agency for the Protection of the Environment (NAPE). Approval could be refused if, in particular, the container in question was not technically suitable, the return scheme did not ensure a sufficiently high rate of reuse, or if an approved container of equal capacity was already available. The reason for the requirement of approval was so that any type of authorized container could be returned to any shop selling beer and soft drinks, thereby achieving as high a rate of return as possible. It was maintained by the Danish authorities that in order for this comprehensive system to be workable, the maximum number of containers and return schemes approved at one time had to be limited to around thirty.

Following objections to the legislation by the Commission, a derogation from the second requirement was introduced permitting the sale of a limited quantity of drink in non-approved containers (except metal ones). Sales to test the market were also allowed. Deposit and return schemes were to be set up in respect of each non-approved container, with the deposit being no less than that generally charged under approved schemes. In effect, under the derogation schemes, containers could only be returned to the shop at which they were purchased, or to another shop selling the same container, with the result that a lower proportion of containers was likely to be returned than under the approved schemes.

The court found the requirement for a deposit and return scheme to be

[10] Point 9 of the judgment, p. 4630.

[11] *Simmenthal* v. *Italian Minister of Finance*, Case 35/76 ECR 1871. See also *Ratti*, Case 148/78; *Denkavit*, Case 251/78.

proportionate to the aim of protecting the environment through the reuse of drinks containers: 'it must be observed that this requirement is an indispensable element of a system intended to ensure the re-use of containers and therefore appears to be necessary to achieve the aims pursued by the contested rules. That being so, the restrictions which it imposes on the free movement of goods cannot be regarded as disproportionate.'[12]

In relation to the requirement of NAPE approval however, the court found it to be disproportionate to the environmental aim:

> It is undoubtedly true that the existing system for returning approved containers ensures a maximum rate of re-use and therefore a very considerable degree of protection of the environment since empty containers can be returned to any retailer of beverages. Non-approved containers, on the other hand, can be returned only to the retailer who sold the beverages, since it is impossible to set up a comprehensive system for these containers as well.
>
> Nevertheless, the system for returning non-approved containers is capable of protecting the environment and, as far as imports are concerned, affects only limited quantities of beverages compared with the quantity of beverages consumed in Denmark owing to the restrictive effect which the requirement that containers should be returnable has on imports. In those circumstances, a restriction of the quantity of products which may be marketed by importers is disproportionate to the objective pursued.[13]

In other words, even though the system of returnable non-approved containers does not ensure a maximum rate of reuse, unlike the system established for approved containers, it is still capable of protecting the environment, especially as the quantity of beverages likely to be imported is limited in relation to total national consumption by reason of the restrictive effect of the requirement that containers should be returnable.

Although the court did not follow his reasoning, the Advocate-General took the proportionality test further in considering whether the environmental aim itself was disproportionate: 'There has to be a balancing of interests between the free movement of goods and environmental protection even if in achieving the balance, the high standard of the protection is reduced. The level of protection sought must be a reasonable one . . .'[14]

It may be that in a future case the court will consider the environmental mischief addressed by a trade restriction. However, such consideration would now be in the light of Article 100a.3 of the Treaty, inserted by the Single European Act, which requires environmental harmonizing legislation to take as a base a high level of environmental protection. Unfortunately, in the *Walloon Waste Import Ban Case*,[15] decided in July 1992 and discussed more fully below, the test of proportionality was not addressed in detail by either the Advocate-General or the court. The

[12] Point 13 of the judgment.

[13] Points 20 and 21 of the judgment.

[14] p. 4626.

[15] *Commission* v. *Belgium Case*, Judgment of 4 July 1992, Case 2/90.

Commission did not challenge the claim of the Belgian Government that the import ban was necessary to protect the Walloon environment with its limited capacity to deal with a sudden influx of imported waste. Unlike the *Danish Bottles Case*, alternative, less restrictive, measures were not suggested by the Commission. The court merely concluded: 'the argument that the imperative requirement of the protection of the environment justify the contested measures, must be considered well founded'.[16]

7.3.1.4. Non-Discrimination

The restrictive measure in question must apply equally to domestic and imported goods. For example, in *Commission* v. *Ireland*,[17] the ECJ held as discriminatory the requirement that imported products bear an indication of their country of origin. Consequently, it refused to entertain recourse to the mandatory requirements of consumer protection and fairness of financial transactions. Even national rules mandating marks of origin on both imported and domestic goods have been held to be in breach of Article 30, as although not discriminatory in form, they are in effect, because they allow consumers to select domestic products.[18]

With regard to environmental protection, the test of non-discrimination was recently considered in the *Walloon Waste Import Ban Case*, which resulted from Commission action in respect of a Decree issued by the Walloon Regional Executive.[19] The Decree prohibited the storage, tipping, or dumping of waste from a foreign country or from the other Belgian regions, Flanders and Brussels, subject to exceptions in favour of the Belgian regions. It was introduced in response to the discovery that the population of the Wallonian town of Mellery was suffering from toxic contamination caused by foreign waste dumped at a local site.

The Commission contended that the waste import ban infringed Article 30 of the Treaty, and recourse to the mandatory requirement of environmental protection was not possible as the measure was clearly discriminatory. The Advocate-General supported this view. However, perhaps surprisingly, the court ruled that:

> to assess the discriminatory character or otherwise of the barrier in point, it is necessary to take account of the particular nature of wastes. In effect, the principle that environmental damage should as a priority be rectified at source, a principle established for action of the Community in the area of the environment in Article 130r para 2 of the Treaty, implies that it is up to each region, com-mune or other local entity to take the appropriate measures to ensure the receipt, treatment and

[16] Point 32 of the judgment.

[17] Case 113/80 [1981] ECR 1625.

[18] *Commission* v. *United Kingdom*, Case 231/78 [1979] 1447.

[19] Articles 1 and 3, Decree of the Walloon Regional Executive concerning the disposal of certain waste products in the Region of Wallonia of 19 Mar. 1987 (*Moniteur Belge* (28 Mar. 1987), 4671) as amended by Article 130 of the Decree of 23 July 1987 (*MB* (29 Sept. 1987), 14078).

elimination of its own wastes: these must indeed be eliminated as close as possible to the place of their production, with a view of limiting their transportation as much as possible.

Moreover, the principle accords with the principles of self-sufficiency and proximity expressed in the Basel Convention of 22 March 1989 on the control of transfrontier movements of dangerous wastes and their elimination of which the Community is a signatory party.

It emerges from this that taking into account the differences between wastes produced in one place and another and their connection with the place of production, the contested measures cannot be considered as discriminatory.[20]

The judgment would appear to say that, in the light of the principles of 'self-sufficiency' and 'proximity' which promote the processing of waste as close to its source as possible, waste produced locally is essentially different to that produced in other regions or countries. The ban is not discriminatory as it applies uniformly across the distinct category of 'foreign' waste. This treatment of discrimination is difficult to reconcile with the previous jurisprudence, for example the cases concerning country of origin labelling mentioned above. It is notable that, in formulating its distinction between 'local' and 'foreign' waste, it sought to rely on the provisions of the 1989 Basel Convention. Although it came into force on 5 May 1992, the Convention was not binding on the EC at the time of the judgment as, of all the twelve member states required to ratify it, only France had done so. And even if the Convention had been ratified, it is questionable whether Member States could derive the legal rights from it to uphold import bans on waste contrary to Community law.

7.3.1.5. Other Aspects of the Walloon Waste Import Ban Case

The *Walloon Waste Case* is important in other respects: first, in its consideration of whether waste is a 'good' falling under Article 30, and secondly, in its examination of the effect of existing Community legislation. These issues are relevant in the context of developing Community legislation on waste, in particular the Regulation on Waste Shipments which is discussed in section 7.3.3.3 below.

Whilst conceding that recyclable waste is a 'good', the Belgian Government claimed that unusable and non-recoverable waste is not, because it has no intrinsic commercial value. Such waste should be covered by the Treaty provisions concerning services, it claimed. The Advocate-General's second Opinion dealt exclusively with the question. Here it was argued that the Treaty provisions relating to services cover a residual category of transactions not covered by the free movement of goods, capital, or persons. The fact that waste disposal involved a service

[20] Points 34 to 36 of the judgment.

was not, of itself, sufficient to invoke the services provisions. It could not be said that the movement of goods was incidental to the provision of the service (as in the case of transport of goods for repair, for example). The formulation of the definition of goods in *Commission* v. *Italy*[21] as 'products which can be valued in money and which are capable, as such, of forming the subject of commercial transactions'[22] was considered. The Belgian Government argued that non-recoverable waste could not fall within this definition as it did not have a positive value. On the contrary, the Advocate-General considered that things which have a negative value (i.e. where the owner will pay for them to be taken away) may be the subject of commercial transactions. He concluded that '"goods" for the purposes of the Treaty must be taken to include any moveable physical object to which property rights or obligations attach (and which can therefore be valued in monetary terms, whether positive or negative)'.[23]

Finally, the practical difficulties in differentiating between recoverable and non-recoverable waste were highlighted in the Opinion. It would be problematic to formulate a workable distinction and, in addition, consignments may contain a mixture of recyclable and non-recyclable waste.

The court itself did not elaborate on the Advocate-General's theoretical arguments, simply stating, 'it is sufficient to observe that products which are transported across frontiers to form the subject of a commercial transaction are subject to Article 30 whatever the nature of the transaction'.[24] It then went on to reiterate the practical arguments against differentiating between recyclable and non-recyclable waste set out by the Advocate-General.

In relation to the effect of existing Community legislation, the Commission had claimed primarily that the import ban was in breach of Directive 75/442[25] on waste and Directive 84/631 on the Supervision and Control within the European Community of the Transfrontier Shipment of Hazardous Waste[26] (the contention that the ban was incompatible with Articles 30 and 36 was a secondary point).

Both the Advocate-General and the court concurred in finding that, as Directive 75/442 sets out only general provisions in connection with waste disposal, it was merely a general framework of rules which was not expressly concerned with movements of waste. As such, no breach could be established. However, with regard to Directive 84/631, the court considered that it set up a comprehensive system of control of hazardous waste movements, under which Member States had the right to object to specific consignments of waste, but not to impose a general ban.

[21] Case 7/68 [1968] ECR 423.
[22] pp. 428–9.
[23] p. 18.
[24] Point 26 of the judgment.
[25] OJ 1975 L194/39.
[26] OJ 1984 L326/31, Amended by Council Directive 86/279 OJ 1986 L181/13 and Council Directive 87/112 OJ 1987 L48/31.

Consequently, the Walloon ban was held to be illegal in respect of hazardous waste. The court then progressed to the question of whether a ban on imports of non-hazardous waste (i.e. the ban not ruled to be in breach of Dir. 84/631) was compatible with Article 30 and 36, as discussed above.

7.3.1.6. The Balance Between Free Trade and Environmental Protection

Community case-law to date would appear to show the scales tipping in favour of environmental protection. The court's formulation of a distinction between 'local' and 'foreign' waste in order to satisfy the test of non-discrimination, in the *Walloon Waste Case* is particularly supportive of this view. It may be that this case was a 'one-off', the outcome of which was largely the result of the particular circumstances leading up to the imposition of the ban. However, the cases do appear to be part of a trend, affording precedence to safeguarding the environment over the principle of free movement of goods. For example, following the *Walloon* judgment, the French Government took steps to ban all imports of household waste on the discovery of illegal shipments of German hospital waste. The Commission has not attempted to challenge the restriction. Similarly, the Commission has not taken action in respect of the German packaging waste recycling scheme (the 'Green Point' scheme discussed below in section 7.3.3.4) which has been complained about by other Member States as constituting a barrier to intra-Community trade.

Enlargement of the Community may strengthen the trend. The EFTA countries, which traditionally operate higher standards of environmental protection than the EC countries, insisted during the negotiations on the EEA Agreement that a high level of protection should be enforced. The EC, willing to improve its own environmental rules, allowed the EFTA countries open-ended derogations in certain areas which will enable them to maintain their national laws in force until these are matched by the Commission's own measures. As for the free movement of goods, Article 13 of the EEA Agreement allows exceptions to this principle if justified on certain grounds including the protection of health and life of humans, animals, and plants.

7.3.2. Legal Basis of Community Legislation

In an attempt to stem fragmentation of the single market, and in recognition of the need to safeguard the environment, the Community is developing its own legislation. A contentious question in relation to EC environmental measures is the choice of legal basis upon which they are founded. Under Article 190 of the Treaty, the Council and the

Commission are required to state the reasons upon which secondary legislation is based. The duty to state reasons includes an obligation to state the legal basis.[27] Following amendment of the Treaty by the Single European Act, environmental legislation may be based on either Article 100a of the Treaty relating to the implementation of the single market, or Article 130s which is concerned solely with the environment. The selection of legal basis may affect the balance between free trade and environmental protection in the Community, although less so since the Maastricht Treaty came into force on 1 November 1993.

7.3.2.1. Article 100a versus Article 130s

Article 100a provides for adoption of 'measures for the approximation of the provisions laid down by law, regulation or administrative action in Member States which have as their object the establishment and functioning of the internal market'.

It is evident from paragraph 3 of Article 100a which refers specifically to environmental protection, that the Article was intended to include harmonization measures concerned with the environment. On the other hand, legislation may be adopted on the basis of Article 130s,[28] in order to effect the objects and principles of action by the Community in relation to the environment set out in Article 130r.

The choice of legal basis has practical significance, although, as stated above, less so now that the Maastricht Treaty is in force. Prior to the Maastricht Treaty, measures based on Article 100a could be adopted by a qualified majority decision of the Council[29] whilst Article 130s required unanimity. Also, Article 100a entailed a co-operation procedure, assigning a more active role to the Parliament, whereas Article 130s required only simple consultation with the Parliament. However, the new Article 130s inserted by the Maastricht Treaty now provides for the adoption by the Council of measures under this Article also by qualified majority (although there are still some measures which require unanimity, for example, those concerning the management of water resources). Furthermore, the role of the Parliament in the enactment of measures under Article 130s has been increased. Pursuant to the new Article 189c the Council, when adopting measures by qualified majority under Article

[27] Articles 11 and 14 of the Rules of Procedure of the Council (OJ 1979 L268/1) confirmed in Case 158/80 *Rewe-Handelsgesellschaft Nord mbH* v. *Hauptzollamt Kiel* [1987] ECR 1805.

[28] Articles 130r–s (as amended by the Maastricht Treaty): see chapter by Margaret Brusasco Mackenzie.

[29] At present, a majority consists of 54 votes out of 76. The allocation of votes is weighted very approximately in proportion to the size of the population of the Member States. Germany, France, Italy, and the UK each have 10 votes; Spain has 8 votes; Belgium, Greece, the Netherlands, and Portugal each have 5 votes; Denmark and Ireland each have 3 votes; Luxembourg has 2.

130s, must follow a lengthy consultation procedure (similar to that laid down in Article 189b applicable to Article 100a measures) involving two separate readings by Parliament.

Although both Articles provide for the possibility of more stringent national measures, the right to derogate under Article 100a is perhaps less clear than when measures have been adopted on the basis of Article 130s. Paragraph 4 of Article 100a states that:

> If after adoption of a harmonization measure by the Council acting by qualified majority, a Member State deems it necessary to apply national measures on the grounds of major needs referred to in Article 36, or relating to protection of the environment or the working environment, it shall notify the Commission of these provisions.
>
> The Commission shall confirm the provisions involved after having verified that they are not a means of arbitrary discrimination or a disguised restriction on trade between Member States.
>
> By way of derogation from the procedure laid down in Articles 169 and 170, the Commission or any Member State may bring the matter directly before the Court of Justice if it considers that another Member State is making improper use of the powers provided for in this Article.

Article 100a.4 provides an exception to the general rule, for example in relation to Article 36 and *Cassis de Dijon*-type cases, that more restrictive measures cannot be justified if harmonization legislation exists. As in Article 36 and *Cassis*, the restrictive measures must not be discriminatory. The Commission is assigned the task of ensuring compliance with the requirement of non-discrimination which necessarily involves consideration of whether the trade limiting effects of national measures are proportionate to the 'major needs' being served. Following the introduction of standardization legislation, Article 100a.4 takes up where Article 36 and the mandatory requirements cease to apply (although the grounds listed in Article 100a.4 are exhaustive, unlike the mandatory requirements in *Cassis*). However, this is subject to the fact that derogations under Article 100a are not possible where harmonization measures have been adopted unanimously by the Council. In effect, more stringent measures are permitted in the same circumstances now, as prior to the Single European Act, when harmonization measures could only be adopted by a unanimous decision.

In comparison, Article 130t states: 'The protective measures adopted in common pursuant to Article 130s shall not prevent any Member State from maintaining or introducing more stringent protective measures. Such measures must be compatible with this Treaty. They shall be notified to the Commission.'

The proviso of Treaty compatibility means that protective measures must be non-discriminatory and proportionate like derogations under Article 100a4. However, unlike Article 100a, Article 130t sets out from the premise that national measures are permissible and recognizes roles for both levels of legislation. Measures must be 'more stringent', fulfilling more nearly the objectives of Article 130r, and must also be along the lines of Community legislation on the subject, not different from it. This is important as it gives the Community and other Member States the opportunity of aligning with the more stringent State and re-establishing uniform legislation throughout the Community. For example, if the Community decided, on the basis of Article 130s, to halve production and consumption of hydrofluorocarbons, any Member State may still impose an outright ban on production and consumption. However, it could not ban, on the basis of Article 130t, the use of aerosol cans as a way of protecting the ozone layer.[30] Finally, it should be noted that Article 130t provides only for exceptions where there is Community legislation founded on Article 130s. So in the same way as Article 100a.4, Article 130t picks up where Article 36 and *Cassis de Dijon* leave off. But Article 130t permits derogations to EC legislation *unanimously* adopted, unlike Article 100a.4.

7.3.2.2. When to Use Which Base

The ECJ has laid down general principles governing the choice of legal basis: the selection must be based on objective factors which are amenable to judicial review,[31] including, in particular, the purpose and content of the measure.[32] Where analysis of the objective factors shows that authority to adopt a measure arises from two or more provisions of the Treaty, the general rule is that a dual or multiple base should be used.[33] However, legal bases must not be combined if the procedures which they entail are incompatible. The court has stated that two bases respectively providing for the co-operation procedure and simple consultation followed by unanimous vote in Council, are incompatible, as 'in such a case the cumulation of legal bases would have the effect of emptying the cooperation procedure of any substance'.[34] In such cases a choice must be made between legal bases. However, as discussed above, the procedures entailed by the two legal bases are now, since Maastricht, more compatible and as a result this problem is less likely to arise.

For Community environmental legislation, the dividing line between

[30] Example given by L. Krämer in 'EEC Treaty and Environmental Protection', 96.

[31] *Commission* v. *Council*, Case 45/86 [1987] ECR 1493, point 11.

[32] *Commission* v. *Council (Titanium Dioxide Waste)*, Case C300/89 [1991] ECR 2867.

[33] *Commission* v. *Council*, Case 165/87 [1988] ECR 5545.

[34] Case 300/89 above.

Article 100a and Article 130s has been problematic.[35] The issue was considered by the ECJ in the *Titanium Dioxide Case*[36] in which the Commission, supported by the Parliament, sought an annulment of a Council Directive based on Article 130s concerning procedures for harmonizing the programmes for the reduction and elimination of pollution caused by waste from the titanium dioxide industry.[37] Having reviewed the aim and content of the measure, the court concluded that both Articles 100a and 130s could apply. Article 100a was relevant even though the measure was designed to protect the environment against the harmful consequences of an *industrial process* rather than to remove obstructions to the free movement of goods within the single market. This follows from the fact that differing national standards require industries within the Member States to incur differing costs in compliance with their respective pollution controls, and therefore may lead to distortions of competition. Measures designed to eliminate such distortions are capable of contributing to the achievement of the single market and accordingly fall under Article 100a. It was held that the legal bases were incompatible due to the different procedures they prescribed and the court was obliged to choose between them. In the end, it decided to annul the Directive on the grounds that Article 100a, as proposed by the Commission, and not Article 130s, substituted by the Council, was the correct legal basis.

The reason for the court's choice is not clear from the judgment. It does appear to suggest that whenever a measure has internal market implications, Article 100a is the correct legal basis. Explanations offered for this include the argument that Article 100a is a specific base in relation to Article 130s, and EC legal principles prescribe that a specific base be selected in preference to a residual one.[38] Alternatively, the argument is cited that Article 100a was chosen so as to safeguard the active role of the Parliament and give better effect to democracy.[39] But, if this logic is taken to its extreme, Article 130s is rendered virtually redundant. It is marginalized such that it may only constitute the basis of measures in connection with the conservation of flora and fauna which have negligible consequences for the internal market. This would appear to be contrary to the spirit of new Title VII introduced by the Single European Act and also the Maastricht Treaty which reinforces the provisions of Title VII. Again, the new consultation procedure provided for by Article 189c

[35] Academic articles written at the time of the enactment of the SEA address concerns over the uncertain delimitation between the two bases—e.g. Krämer, 'The Single European Act and Environmental Protection' (1987) 24 *CMLR* 659, and G. Vandermeersch, 'Single European Act and Environmental Policy of the EEC', 12 *ELR* (1987), 407.

[36] Case 300/89 above.

[37] Council Directive 89/428/EEC OJ 1989 L201/6.

[38] Jonathan Robinson, 4 *JEL* (1992), 109–20.

[39] Catherine Bernard, 17 *ELR* (1992), 127–33.

applicable to measures taken under Article 130s narrows the gap between the two bases and should, in theory, make the enactment of environmental measures under Article 130s more democratic.

Some light has been cast on the problem in a recently decided case concerning the legal basis of a Directive amending the general framework Directive on waste disposal.[40] Once again the case arose from a change in legal basis by the Council from Article 100a, proposed by the Commission, to Article 130s, and this was then challenged by the Commission. However, the court upheld the choice of 130s, calling a halt to the *Titanium Dioxide* line of reasoning that would have left Article 130s as a vestigial provision. It stated that, 'contrary to what the Commission purports, the fact that the creation or operation of the internal market is concerned does not in itself justify the use of Article 100a'.[41]

Although there were certain elements in the Directive which impacted on the functioning of the single market, for example the introduction of a common definition of waste and related activities, the court found that the main aim and content of the measure related to environmental protection and therefore the legal basis chosen by the Council was correct. The focus appears to have shifted back to the 'centre of gravity' or main purpose of content of a measure. Unfortunately, no new guidance was offered on divining these factors.

In the past the use of Article 100a for legislation promoting both the free movement of goods (as opposed to legislation regulating industrial processes) and environmental protection was uncontroversial. Environmental protection measures harmonizing technical specifications of products and removing national disparities promote the free movement of such products within the internal market. Accordingly, legislation such as that concerning the control of emissions from motor vehicles[42] has been introduced on the basis of Article 100a. Following the pattern, it is arguable that the correct legal basis for the Regulation on eco-labelling,[43] discussed in 7.3.4.1 below, is also Article 100a. Uniform application of labelling criteria clearly contributes to the free trade of goods within the single market. However, it is stated in the body of the Regulation that its primary purpose is the protection of the environment by providing information to consumers about products which are environmentally less harmful. Facilitation of the free movement of goods is cited in the recitals as a subsidiary purpose. In the light of the court's waste framework deci-

[40] Council Directive 91/156 of 18 May 1991, OJ L78/32.

[41] Point 18 of the judgment.

[42] e.g. Council Directive 70/442 of 20 Mar. 1970, Council Directive 88/76 of 3 Dec. 1987, OJ 1988 L36/1; Council Directive 88/77 of 3 Dec. 1987, OJ 1988 L36/33.

[43] Council Regulation (EEC) 880/92 of 23 Mar. 1992, OJ L99 of 11 Apr. 1992.

sion emphasizing main purpose and content, it appears unlikely that the legal basis of Article 130s imposed by the Council could be successfully challenged.

Further questions remain in relation to waste. In a familiar story, the Regulation on waste shipments was proposed by the Commission on the basis of Article 100a, which basis was then changed by the Council to Article 130s. The Parliament commenced action in the European Court seeking to annul the Regulation on the ground that the incorrect base was used.[44] The Regulation may be distinguished from the waste framework Directive, in that its provisions are more precise and specific than the general principles laid down in the framework. This, taken together with the ruling in the *Walloon Waste Case* that waste is essentially a 'good', may have convinced the court to side with the Parliament. However, on 28 June 1994 the Court ruled that the Council was justified in basing the Regulation on Article 130s and upheld the view taken in the waste framework Directive case that an effect on the creation or operation of the internal market does not in itself justify the use of Article 100a.

7.3.2.3. The Balance Between Free Trade and Protection of the Environment

Although the debate over legal bases appears academic, it is relevant to the free trade/environmental protection equation. First, the debate brings out the fact that derogations are possible under both available bases. And although the exception in Article 100a.4 is perhaps more limited than under Article 130s, it is certainly viable. The right to derogate has implications for free trade and affords scope for the precedence of environmental protection over the operation of the single market and free trade with the rest of the world. However, requests for derogation under Article 100a.4 have not been without controversy. On 2 December 1992 the Commission decided to confirm the provisions of a German regulation banning the manufacture, marketing, and use of pentacholorphenol (PCP) and its compounds, thereby allowing Germany a derogation under Article 100a.4 from Directive 91/173/EC.[45] However, on 9 February 1993, France brought a case before the European Court of Justice seeking an annulment of the Commission's decision on the basis that the German derogation would create an unjustified barrier to trade.[46] The Advocate-General delivered his Opinion on 26 January 1994 and recommended that

[44] Case 187/93, OJ C147 of 27 May 1993.

[45] A Commission of Communication setting out the grounds for its Decision was published in OJ C 334 of 18 Dec. 1992. Council Directive 91/173/EEC of 21 Mar. 1991 amending Directive 76/769/EEC on dangerous substances and preparations was published in OJ L 85 of 5 Apr. 1991.

[46] Case 41/93.

the court accept the French Government's petition and overturn the Commission's decision on the basis that the Commission did not establish adequate grounds for allowing the derogation. Handing down his Opinion, Advocate-General Guiseppe Tesauro said: 'the Decision constitutes the first ever case where Article 100a.4 has been applied and (. . .) given the novelty of this disposition and the doubts surrounding its interpretation, it would seem more than ever necessary to put forward comprehensive reasoning for the Decision'. On 17 May 1994 the Court followed the Advocate General's opinion and overturned the Commission's decision for lack of sufficient reasoning.

Secondly, the question remains as to why there has been a recurring pattern of proposal by the Commission on the basis of Article 100a followed by change of basis to Article 130s by the Council. Politics provides the answer. In the case of the Regulation on waste shipments the Commission was obliged to agree to the replacement of the single-market basis in the face of mounting Member-State pressure to bring the Regulation into force as soon as possible. First, as the Regulation was a prerequisite to the ratification of the Basel Convention on waste, it was politically desirable to adopt the Regulation before the UN Conference on the Environment and Development in Rio de Janeiro on 3–14 June 1992. Secondly, the scandal arising out of the discovery of German hospital waste in French landfill sites emphasized the need for legislation. It may be that the Council wished to curb the influence of the traditionally 'green' Parliament. For example, one of the reasons why the Parliament challenged the Regulation on waste shipments was that it wished to insert a provision completely banning the export of waste to developing countries. Consequently, although the derogation under Article 130s provides for the possibility of the precedence of environmental protection over free trade, on a Community level, perhaps measures adopted on this basis until now are not as 'green' as they might be.[46a]

7.3.3. EC Environmental Legislation

7.3.3.1. Established Examples of Community Measures Affecting Free Trade

Community environmental legislation, both in force and planned, has implications for trade at EC and worldwide levels. In 1982 a Community

[46a] In a recent development since going to press, the parties to the Basel Convention have agreed to a total ban on the export of hazardous waste from OECD countries to non-OECD countries for recycling and recovery from 1988 as well as an immediate total ban on such exports for final disposal. This may necessitate an amendment to Council Regulation (EEC) No. 259/93 as well as to the Basel Convention itself. All references to the Regulation and the Convention should be read in light of this recent development.

Regulation was adopted implementing the Convention on International Trade of Endangered Species of Wild Fauna and Flora, 1973 (CITES).[47] Under the Convention, trade of species threatened with extinction, and of species which may become endangered unless their trade is strictly regulated, is controlled through the issue of export and import permits approved by the scientific authorities of the parties concerned. In order to prevent trade with non-parties, an import permit is required for the issue of an export permit. Exemptions are possible under the Convention. In addition, the Community has introduced other trade-linked measures in order to protect specific types of flora and fauna. These include import licence requirements for whales and other cetacean products,[48] a ban on import of ivory from African elephants,[49] limited bans on the import of sea-pup skins,[50] and certain types of pelts.[51]

Legislation regarding the control of emissions from motor vehicles[52] has already been mentioned in 7.3.2.2 above. The measures prescribe technical standards with which cars marketed in the Community must comply, they impact on trade as they limit access to the market. On the other hand, the legislation facilitates free movement of goods within the internal market by laying down uniform specifications for the Community. In relation to the rest of the world, the relative restrictive effect of such legislation is perhaps tempered by the fact that Community legislation in this area is no more stringent than legislation, for example, in the United States and Japan.

7.3.3.2. Substances that Deplete the Ozone Layer

The Community has adopted legislation implementing the 1987 Montreal Protocol on Substances that Deplete the Ozone Layer, to which all the Member States are party. The scope of the original Council Regulation[53] extends to the importation, exportation, production, and consumption of chlorofluorocarbons (CFCs), other fully halogenated CFCs, halons, carbon tetrachloride, and trichloroethane (the controlled substances). The main trade restricting provisions affect countries which are not party to the Protocol. For instance, the Regulation provides for prohibitions on

[47] Council Regulation 3626/82 of 3 Dec. 1982; OJ L384 of 31 Dec. 1982 amended or added to on many occasions, in particular by Commission Regulation 3418/83/EEC of 28 Nov. 1983, OJ L344 of 7 Dec. 1983, and Commission Regulation 1970/92/EEC of 30 June 1992, OJ L201 of 20 July 1992.

[48] Commission Regulation 81/348/EEC of 20 Jan. 1981, OJ L39 12 Feb. 1981. Council Regulation 3786/81 of 22 Dec. 1981 OJ L377 of 31 Dec. 1981.

[49] Commission Regulation 89/2496/EEC of 2 Aug. 1989 L240 of 17 Aug. 1989.

[50] Directive 83/129/EEC of 28 Mar. 1983, OJ L91 of 9 Apr. 1983 and L282 of 14 Oct. 1983.

[51] Council Regulation 91/3254 of 4 Nov. 1991, OJ L308 of 9 Nov. 1991.

[52] See n. 41.

[53] Council Regulation 594/91 of 4 Mar. 1991, OJ L67/1 of 14 Mar. 1991.

imports into the EC from non-parties of controlled substances and products containing controlled substances, coming into effect on specified dates between 1991 and 1996. It also anticipates the restriction of imports from non-parties of products produced using controlled substances by stating that the Council may adopt future measures by a qualified majority. In relation to Community exports to non-parties, the Regulation provides for a prohibition from 1993. These restrictions are subject to a derogation in the case of non-parties who comply with certain provisions of the Protocol. Countries which are parties to the Protocol, but not Community members are affected by the Regulation in that quantitative limits are imposed on their imports into the EC. In addition, the Regulation provides for a phase-out schedule in respect of production and supply within the Community of controlled substances, together with derogations for 'essential uses'. There is provision for the transfer of quotas between EC producers of controlled substances.

Following amendment of the Protocol at a meeting of the parties in November 1992 in Copenhagen, a second Council Regulation[54] was adopted amending the original Regulation 'in order to speed up the phasing-out of substances that deplete the ozone layer'. Under the second Regulation, CFCs, other fully halogenated CFCs and carbontetrachloride are to be totally eliminated by 1 January 1995, halons by 1 January 1994, and trichloroethane is to be totally eliminated by 1 January 1996.

The amendments to the Protocol also included the addition of 'new substances': hydrochlorofluorocarbons (HCFCs), hydrobromofluorocarbons (HBFCs), and methyl bromide. Accordingly, the Commission was instructed by the Council to formulate a proposal on the new substances to ensure that the Community was in a position to ratify all of the amendments to the Protocol no later than 30 September 1993. The progress of this proposal is instructive in that it highlights the potential for conflict between the interests of industry and environmental protection.

Initially, the Commission Directorate-General for the Environment prepared a draft proposal which was considerably more stringent than the amendments to the Montreal Protocol. It provided for the phase-out of HCFCs by 2014 (as opposed to 2030 in the Protocol), a ban on use before 2014 where non-damaging alternatives exist, and intermediate reductions. The draft proposal triggered a dispute, both within the Commission and between Member States. This is because while most manufacturers, such as ICI, Hoechst, and Akzo, have planned to run down their production of HCFCs, Atochem, part of France's state-owned Elf Aquitaine Group, has been investing heavily in HCFC production. As other manufacturers have pulled out of the market, Atochem has taken

[54] Council Regulation 3952/92 of 30Ï Dec. 1992, OJ L405/41 of 31 Dec. 1992.

up the custom. Clearly, the draft proposal would have destroyed much of Atochem's market. France rejected the proposal outright and Atochem lobbied hard for concessions. The Commissioner for Industry was also opposed to the Proposal.

On 9 June 1993, the Commission presented a revised proposal.[55] It had fewer intermediate reductions and the ban on using HCFCs where ozone-safe technology exists was removed, except in relation to small refrigerators. This was more acceptable to France and Atochem as the market battle is over large refrigerators, such as supermarket coolers. Interestingly, in July 1992, France prohibited, for 'safety reasons', refrigeration units that use ammonia as a coolant, unless they are surrounded by an uninhabited zone of a kilometre square. The measure leaves supermarkets with no option but to use HCFC coolers. But in Germany, many supermarkets are now installing ammonia-cooled refrigerators, and in Britain Sainsbury's is considering them.

The progress of the draft provisions relating to methyl bromide tells a similar story. This substance has been used since the early 1970's to fumigate soil and to clean crops for transport and quarantine purposes. It is now considered to constitute a very high risk to the ozone layer. Objections to the initial draft came from France, the sole producer of methyl bromide in the EU, and also from the users of the chemical who are mainly small farming concerns in Southern Europe. The Directorate-General for Agriculture was also concerned about its severity. Thus, whilst the proposed freeze on production and consumption as from 1 January 1995 remained intact, the initial provision which prescribed a 50 per cent reduction from 1 January 1996 was amended to provide for only a 25 per cent reduction from January 1996.

Arguments that the Regulation was too restrictive were being countered by Member States such as Denmark, the Netherlands, and Luxembourg, who considered that the proposals did not go far enough towards protecting the ozone layer. In an attempt to appease these countries, the Commission changed the legal basis of the measure from Article 100a to 130s so that more stringent national measures will be automatically permitted.[56] Agreement was reached on the proposal in December 1993 by the Council, and in February 1994 the Parliament approved the proposal with amendments to impose stricter limits on the use of the ozone-depleting substances covered and earlier target dates for an end to their use. Among the main amendments adopted were: a halt to the production of trichloroethane from 31 December 1994, instead of 1995, and a ban on the manufacture of methyl bromide from 31 December 1999, instead of a reduction of 25 per cent in January 1996. Parliament also

[55] COM(93) 202.

[56] See s. 7.3.2 above.

called for more stringent and more rapid reductions in HCFCs, specifically a ban on their production effective from 31 December 2002—the Commission's proposal mentioned only the use or sale of the substances in the EU, thus allowing manufacture for export purposes. In May 1994 the Commission tabled a revised proposal and in June 1994 the Council adopted a common position on it. The objectives agreed upon surpass those of the Protocol's amendment and are as follows: a consumption ceiling for HCFCs of 2.6% from 1 January 1995; the gradual elimination of HCFCs between 2004 and 2015; and a 25% reduction in the production and consumption of methyl bromide by 1998.

The provisions concerning the new substances will also have an effect on a worldwide level. Although the Commission's proposal does not restrict the production or export of HCFCs to third countries party to the Montreal Protocol, non-EC suppliers of methyl bromide would be particularly hurt by the proposal. In 1990, for example, the EC produced 5,000 tonnes of methyl bromide and used 14,000 tonnes. Another 11,500 tonnes of the substance were imported from the United States and Israel. Companies such as Ethyl Corporation and Great Lakes Chemicals of the United States, and Dead Sea Bromine of Israel will suffer the loss of huge markets both in the EC and in America where methyl bromide is to be completely phased out by the year 2000. Leon Brittan, Commissioner for External Relations, has already voiced his concern that going beyond the requirements of the Montreal Protocol may have GATT implications.

7.3.3.3. Waste Shipments

In February 1993 Council Regulation (EEC) 259/93 on the supervision and control of shipments of waste within, into, and out of the European Community[57] came into force. It took effect in May 1994.[57a] For the free trade versus environmental protection debate, it is perhaps the most important piece of Community legislation to date. Enshrining a ban, subject to exceptions, on exporting waste to or importing waste from non-EC countries and providing for the possibility of a general prohibition on shipments between Member States of waste for disposal, the Regulation apparently subjugates free trade to the environmental principles of 'proximity' and 'self-sufficiency' set out in the Basel Convention and now part of the waste framework Directive.[58] The only type of waste shipment subject to minimal control is of waste classified by OECD countries as harmless or 'green'.

With regard to shipments *between Member States of waste for disposal*, Article 4(3)(a)(i) of the Regulation states that: 'In order to implement the principles of proximity, priority for recovery and self sufficiency at

[57] OJ L30/1 of 6 Feb. 1993. [57a] See n. 46a [58] See n. 39.

Community and national levels . . . Member States may take measures in accordance with the Treaty to prohibit generally or partially or to object systematically to shipments of waste.' This is subject to the exception that Member States may not ban imports of hazardous waste from other EC countries which produce such small quantities of hazardous waste that it would be uneconomic for them to set up specialized disposal facilities.[59]

In relation to waste for disposal and for recovery, reasoned objections to specific shipments are permitted on grounds including the principles of proximity and self-sufficiency, implementation of waste-management plans and national laws relating to environmental protection, public order, public safety, and health protection.[60]

These provisions governing intra-Community trade, in particular those concerning waste for disposal, are controversial. They appear to give clear preference to environmental protection over the operation of the single market. The impetus for the incorporation of the principles of self-sufficiency and proximity in order to justify general or partial prohibitions on trade, was provided, at least in part, by the discovery of German hospital waste in French landfill sites (mentioned in 7.3.2 above). Following extensive media coverage of such 'waste tourism', France urged other Member States to accept the inclusion of the principles into the Regulation.

More reticent Member States were persuaded to acquiesce by the addition of the proviso that any general or specific ban must be 'in accordance with the Treaty'. This means that a ban is required to be non-discriminatory and proportionate. However, in the light of the *Walloon Waste* judgment, these words may be of little effect. As recounted in 7.3.1.4 above, the judgment distinguished between 'local' and 'foreign' waste in order to find that the import ban on waste from outside the Walloon region was not discriminatory. So it would appear that Member States may still legally ban imports of each others' waste for disposal, without providing for their own waste.

Article 4(3)(a)(i) of the Regulation was recently the subject of litigation in the European Court of Justice.[61] The action was brought by three waste companies, Buralux SA, Satrod SA and Ourry SA who import German waste to France for treatment. They stated that they were being 'totally ruined' by the provision and claimed damages totalling 32,602 million ECUs. In support of their claim, the companies claimed that the Council had infringed an essential procedural requirement as there was a contradiction between the content of the measure which recognizes the necessity for Community treatment of the problem of waste and the dis-

[59] Article 4(3)(a)(ii)

[60] Article 4(3)(b) and (c) and Article 7(4)(a) and (b).

[61] Case C145/93: *Buralux SA, Satrod SA and Ourry SA* v. *Council of EC*; OJ 142/8 of 20 May 1993. This case was transferred to the Court of First Instance—Case T475/93.

puted Article which increases the Member States powers to act independently. In addition, the companies alleged that Article 4(3)(a)(i) infringed the Treaty by breaching the principle of free movement of goods, by infringing the principle of proportionality, and by not recognizing the companies' acquired rights. Finally, it was claimed that the Council had misused its powers in seeking to serve the interests of France rather than the entire Community: 'France, which had initially been hostile to the adoption of this Regulation, changed its attitude after media publicity was given to the discovery of certain German hospital waste. It did everything it could to make sure that the measures having equivalent effect taken by its Environmental Minister would be validated *a posteriori.*'

This final section of the claim perhaps illuminates the underlying reason for the action. It is referring to the French ban of household waste mentioned in 7.3.1 above and it is *this* ban which caused the three to lose money; the damage caused by the Regulation was only potential as it did not come into effect until May 1994. However, the eventual judgment on the legality of Article 4(3)(a)(i) promised to be significant for the free movement/environmental protection debate. On 17 May 1994 the Court of First Instance dismissed the application as inadmissable and the applicants have now appealed.

The Regulation also addressed Community imports from, and exports to, non-EC countries.[62] The general pattern is for a prima-facie ban, combined with various exceptions such as for trade with EFTA or OECD countries party to the Basel Convention or countries with which the Community or Member States have concluded multilateral or bilateral agreements in accordance with the Basel Convention. The exceptions are more stringent in relation to waste for disposal than for waste for recovery, and for exports in comparison with imports. In addition, the export of any kind of waste to ACP States is prohibited, except when waste processed in a Member State is being returned to its ACP State of origin. These provisions are in line with the Basel Convention and as such they are perhaps less controversial than those provisions covering intra-Community trade.

Lastly, it is interesting to review the Regulation in the light of the *Walloon Waste Case*. Whilst the point about discrimination has already been made, two other issues warrant attention. First, in deciding that all waste, including non-recoverable waste, was a 'good', the Advocate-General and the court emphasized the practical difficulties in distinguishing between recoverable and non-recoverable waste. This is significant in that the vast majority of the Regulation depends on the distinction between 'waste for disposal' and 'waste for recovery'. Second, now that there is specific and comprehensive EC legislation in place for all waste

[62] Titles IV and V.

and not just hazardous waste, it would appear that general or partial bans of intra-Community trade in waste for recovery will not be lawful after May 1994, and Member States such as France may have to adjust their national legislation accordingly.

7.3.3.4. Planned Legislation

If they are adopted, a number of prospective environmental protection measures will impact on trade, at both Community and worldwide level. The proposed energy/CO_2 tax and directive on packaging and packaging waste are examples.

The CO_2/Energy tax plan[63] is a constituent of the Community strategy to stabilise CO_2 emissions by the year 2000 at 1990 levels. It extends to all fossil energy sources (gas, oil, coal, and their derivatives) and electricity. Excluded are renewable forms of energy (such as solar and wind), energies used as raw materials in industry and electricity produced at low-capacity hydro-electric power stations. The tax would be phased in gradually, starting at $3 (17.75 ECUs) per barrel of oil equivalent, rising by $1 a barrel each year so as to reach $10 per barrel by the year 2000. Having a split base, half the tax would apply to the energy content of the fuel or electricity and half to the carbon content.

In order to redress the effect that such a tax would have on the international competitiveness of EC industry, it is proposed that its introduction should be conditional upon other OECD countries implementing similar measures or measures with equivalent financial impact. Japan and the United States are planning to introduce energy taxes, but as yet they are not regarded as equivalent. For the same reason of safeguarding international competitiveness, the proposal envisages phased reductions for energy-intensive industries and exemptions and incentives to encourage industries to reduce their levels of CO_2 emissions and energy consumption.

The tax has met with considerable resistance both within the Community and outside. Two arguments in particular relate to its potential effect on trade. Firstly, the Gulf countries whose economies depend heavily on oil revenue, have objected strongly to the proposed plan. Essentially, they claim that the EC tax (and those of the United States and Japan) will discriminate against oil in relation to other fossil fuels. At a meeting of twenty-five oil producer countries in April 1993, a report was presented by the OPEC Secretary-General stating that the proposed taxes were designed to 'promote other sources of energy such as hard coal, which is more harmful to the environment than oil, and to shrink the budget deficits of the industrialized nations'.[64]

[63] COM(92) 226 final. [64] *Agence Europe*, 14 Apr. 1993.

More recently, in June 1993, the Saudi Arabian Foreign Minister, Prince Saud-al-Faisal accused the Community of double standards. He was quoted as saying, 'a close look at the prices and taxes of different energy sources . . . will show that the justifications of environmental protection are not true. While they impose heavy taxes on oil they provide subsidies to coal.'[65]

The debate should be viewed in the wider context of the current negotiations between the Community and the Gulf Co-operation Council (GCC) on a possible free trade agreement. To date, the EC has indicated that it is not ready to open its markets to petrochemical products from the Gulf States until European industry has had time to prepare for the competition and a solution has been found to problem of distortions of competition caused by state subsidies to Arab petrochemical industries. The Community CO_2/energy tax is regarded by the Gulf States as a part of this perceived 'protectionist' attitude.

Secondly, European industry has criticized the tax. The European confederation of industry energy users and self-generators of power (IFIEC Europe) argues that whilst the tax will be ineffective in stabilizing CO_2 emissions, it will drain resources that would have been used to research and develop more efficient energy systems. It also claims that even with a conditionality clause, the already comparatively high fossil fuel prices in Europe mean that the tax will damage the Community's industrial competitiveness. These claims are countered by the Commission in particular. For example in its study on 'The Economic Effects of the Proposed CO_2/Energy Tax',[66] it says that the likely macroeconomic effects in the European Community of the introduction of a CO_2/energy tax in terms of economic activity, employment, and inflation are small provided that the tax revenue is ploughed back into the economy and the overall amount of tax in the Community is not increased. Its effect on industry will be slight except in the case of energy-intensive operations.

In October 1993 the Commission put forward a 'burden-sharing' proposal, designed to counter the cohesion countries' opposition to the tax on the grounds that it would undermine their economic development. The proposal under consideration is based on the ratio between the amount of current per capita CO_2 emissions and the per capita GDP. Member States situated below 85 per cent of the EC average (Spain, Portugal, Ireland, and Greece) would be given more time to apply the tax. Progressive application of the tax would commence when CO_2 emissions reached 50 per cent of the increase foreseen by the national programmes containing Member States' targets for the year 2000.

In relation to packaging and packaging waste, the progress of the

[65] *Arab News*, as reported by Reuter, 10 June 1993

[66] European Economy Supplement A, 'Recent Economic Trends'.

Commission's proposed directive[67] has been slow and problematic. Due to the considerable vested economic interests involved, this is a highly controversial piece of legislation which has been the subject of much lobbying since its introduction. Since the Maastricht Treaty came into force the new codecision-making procedure must be observed which necessitates the draft making several journeys between the Parliament and Council before it can be adopted.

After its first reading of the proposed Directive the Parliament proposed a number of amendments to it, some of which were incorporated into an amended proposal presented by the Commission on 9 September 1993.[68] Following much debate a common position on the draft was adopted by the Council in March 1994. During their second reading in May 1994 the Parliament backed the common position with some amendments, but in June 1994 the Council failed to agree on the revised text and the new Conciliation Procedure was triggered, delaying adoption of the Directive even further.

The Commission's proposal seeks to approximate national packaging management measures in order to reduce their harmful impact on the environment and avoid distortions to the functioning of the internal market. It aims to reduce the production of packaging waste and promote the return, recycling, and reuse of packaging. It covers all packaging and packaging waste within the EC and requires Member States to take the necessary measures to establish return and management systems. Moreover, all packaging must be marked to indicate whether it is reusable, recoverable, or partially recyclable, as well as indicating the type of materials used in the packaging, and any packaging placed on the market must comply with certain essential requirements.

It has been said of the draft Directive that it has compromised environmental protection in the interests of the single market.[69] There is evidence to support this view. A proposed amendment to expressly permit Member States to apply stricter provisions was rejected by the European Parliament. Proposals by the Parliament for exclusion of medicine packaging and small packages from the scope of the Directive were rejected by the Commission, together with the proposals aimed at reducing the overall quantity of packaging and the prevention of unnecessary packaging. The Commission also rejected the introduction of a hierarchy of waste-management systems (from prevention down to disposal by way of landfill). Environment Commissioner, Ioannis Paleokrassas, said that such proposals could not be approved, 'because [they] change the delicate balance between environmental protection and the smooth functioning of the internal market'.[70]

[67] COM(92) 278.

[68] COM(93) 416 final—SYN 436. OJ C 285/1 of 21 Oct. 1993.

[69] e.g. Greenpeace.

[70] *Europe Environment* 413, 6 July 1993.

In the course of the debate there has been a move towards more flexibility, and the common position adopted by the Council in March 1994 does allow for some derogation by Member States from the limits laid down. They agreed that any Member States which establish or have established programmes whose recovery and recycling targets to beyond those provided for by the Directive (Germany, Denmark, and the Netherlands) should be authorized to pursue those targets. This is on the conditions that they have the appropriate capacity and that the relevant measures do not lead to a distortion of the internal market and do not prevent other Member States from complying with the Directive. The Commission would verify, together with the Member States, that the measures in question were in accordance with the internal market. However, the three 'advanced' Member States (Germany, Denmark, and the Netherlands), who actually voted against the common position, issued a joint declaration stipulating that they reserve the right to cite Article 100a.4 of the Treaty giving them a right to derogate from the Directive's provisions (in which case the Commission alone—without the participation of the Member States—would decide whether the national provisions were acceptable).

However, the initial targets envisaged by the proposal have been lowered to 50 per cent as a minimum and 65 per cent as a maximum for recovery and 25 per cent as a minimum and 45 per cent as a maximum for recycling (in both cases by weight), with a minimum of 15 per cent of each category of material (the original proposal called for 90 per cent of packaging to be recovered within ten years with 60 per cent recycled). Furthermore, it is proposed that transitional derogations would be granted on certain conditions to Greece, Ireland, and Portugal, owing to their geographic situation and low level of packaging consumption.

It is significant that the Council has not changed the legal basis of Article 100a proposed by the Commission to Article 130s. Although, since Maastricht, there is less difference between the two legal bases in the legislative procedures involved, in this case it is arguable that all the institutions wanted the measure to be seen to be preserving the internal market. This may be due to the present serious fragmentation of the packaging and packaging waste market in the Community caused by the implementation of a number of national programmes, most notably the German *Grüne Punkt*, or 'Green Point', scheme.

It is instructive to examine the impact of the German scheme, as a model to illustrate the potential trade effects of legislation requiring labelling and recycling of packaging waste on States not included in the scheme. In 1991 the German government passed a packaging ordinance that imposes an obligation on manufacturers to take back the packaging in which goods are transported and sold. In response, companies arranged to collect transport packaging from retailers and established a waste-collection scheme—the *Duales System Deutschland* (*DSD*)—in order to collect recyclable waste from households and return it to the manufacturers responsible for processing it. The programme is reinforced by increasingly stringent quotas, both for the type of packaging to be taken back and for the amount to be recycled. In order to pay for the huge costs involved, the companies involved in the scheme pay to *DSD* a levy on each package and in return the package is given a green spot which is a guarantee that the maker has undertaken to recycle the wrapping and that *DSD* will collect and transport it. However, a 'green spot' will not be awarded unless *DSD* certifies the product as being recyclable (the equivalent of meeting EC 'basic requirements').

The scheme has now been described as 'a victim of its own success'. It has led to huge amounts of packaging waste being recovered, far in excess of Germany's reprocessing capacity. As a result, German waste for recycling has flooded into the markets of other Member States and third countries. This has led to a massive fall in the value of recyclable packaging waste in the Community, to such an extent that *DSD* now offers money to processors to recycle certain of its waste. The bottom has fallen out of the Community recycling market. French waste-paper collectors have blocked Parisian roads in protest and the United Kingdom has accused Germany of 'environmental dumping'.

Moreover, it has been argued that the scheme has interfered with the free movement of goods into Germany.[71] Signing on to the *DSD* scheme constitutes one more barrier in the way of foreign firms wanting to sell in Germany. In particular, foreign firms may have great difficulty in establishing that their products are recyclable. Materials traditionally regarded as recyclable in Germany may not be available in other countries and importers may be obliged to prove from scratch that their products are recyclable or made from recyclable constituents. Views of what is recyclable differ from country to country. For example, Germany does not consider the use of heat from incineration to be recycling, whereas the United States does, and arranging for recycling at the point of manufacture may be very expensive or not possible at all. Absence of a 'green spot' puts a product at a competitive disadvantage as consumers become increasingly 'environmentally aware'. In addition, retailers may refuse to stock items which are not part of the *DSD* scheme as they themselves must then deal with the transport wrappings (which are likely to be increased if goods have travelled a long way).

The results of the Community-wide packaging waste Directive may be similar. It may constitute an additional barrier to Community markets

[71] e.g. by the British Industry Council for Packaging and the Environment (Incpen).

for third countries. Indeed, the rapporteur on the draft Directive for the European Parliament's environmental committee has already noted: 'Of course there are going to be problems with trade, not only with the United States . . . [the Directive] will probably come under the GATT in the future.'[72]

7.3.4. Industry and the Environment

7.3.4.1. 'What is Good for Industry can be Good for the Environment'

The nexus between industry and environmental protection is recognized in Community policy. The Fifth Action Programme for the environment[73] promulgates an integrated approach in which environmental concerns are to be taken into account in all Community policy areas, including industry, the internal market, and competition. There is a shift in focus from purely 'compliance' legislation to emphasis on voluntary measures and 'shared responsibility' with industry, consumers, and public authorities. Great store is set by the use of market-mechanisms, economic instruments, and consumer pressure in order to benefit the environment. The voluntary eco-labelling and eco-audit schemes are examples of this approach.

Eco-labelling attempts to harness market forces in order to serve the interests of environmental protection. The theory underlying any scheme is threefold: first, consumers are made increasingly 'environmentally aware' and consequently change their purchasing habits; second, manufacturers modify their products and production methods in order to meet the demand for 'environmentally friendly' goods; and third follows a benefit to the environment.

The Council Regulation on a Community eco-label award scheme[74] was formally adopted in March 1993. At present the system is limited to consumer goods other than food, drink, and pharmaceuticals. It provides for a single label for all products covered by the scheme which is designed to signify to consumers that a product is relatively less harmful to the environment than other products of the same type.

Implementation of the award scheme occurs in three stages. Initially, a classification system of 'product groups' is established such that each group encompasses 'all competing products which serve similar purposes and which have equivalence of use'.[75] Product groups have been established for washing machines, detergents, and hairspray, for example. Following this, criteria are to be formulated against which a product's 'greenness' can be measured. Certain basic criteria apply to all products,

[72] Reuter, 23 June 1993.

[73] COM(92) 23 of 18 Mar. 1992.

[74] See n. 43.

[75] Article 5.3.

for example compliance with EC health, safety, and environment requirements. More specific criteria are to be established for each product group by conducting an analysis of its environmental impact throughout its existence—a so-called 'life-cycle analysis'. Impact on the environment is to be determined by reference to a matrix set out in the annexe to the Regulation which takes into account factors such as waste, soil pollution, water and air contamination throughout the different stages of pre-production, distribution, utilization, and disposal of the product. Finally, an application for a label may be made to a designated national body which then refers the application to a Commission jury.

On 25 November 1993 the first eco-labels were awarded to three types of washing machines manufactured by Hoover. Other requests for eco-labels have been made in the United Kingdom and other Member States and are being appraised.

In practice, implementation of the scheme has proved to be problematic. Despite the enthusiasm of the Fifth Action Programme for a spirit of co-operation and shared responsibility with industry, there have been distinct signs of resistance. For example, manufacturers of light bulbs have reacted strongly to the product group criteria arrived at by environmental consultants sponsored by the British Government. The consultants have recommended that only the most energy-efficient compact fluorescent bulbs (CFLs), which account for less than 10 per cent of the market share across Europe, should qualify for eco-labels. The European lighting Council, dominated by the four main producers—Phillips, GE Thorn, Osram, and GTE, have now informed the Commission that they will not participate in the scheme. It has been suggested that the industry does not wish to see CFLs promoted at the expense of other bulbs as investments in new production facilities may be required to meet the increased demand for CFLs, whilst other facilities making traditional bulbs would be obliged to operate below capacity. In addition, although CFLs cost more they last longer, so fewer bulbs would be purchased. Similar disputes have also arisen between paper and detergent manufacturers and the Danish and German authorities. Not surprisingly, industry weighs the acceptability of voluntary environmental protection measures against the degree of financial pain involved.

Eco-labelling schemes raise problems for free trade. In relation to the single market, the preamble to the Regulation states that 'the aim of this Regulation is to create conditions for ultimately establishing an effective single environmental label in the Community', and the Explanation Statement provides that, 'It also seeks to avoid a plethora of national award schemes for eco-labels which would run the risk of creating distortions of competition in the Community'.

The Regulation follows a number of national schemes, such as the

German 'Blue Angel' and the French 'NF Environment' labels which were threatening to create barriers to trade within the Community. EC manufacturers were obliged to make separate applications and comply with different standards in each Member State in order to obtain 'green' badges. The Regulation does not outlaw national schemes as yet, but this is subject to review five years after the Regulation takes effect. Surprisingly, as noted in 7.3.2.2 above, the legal basis of the Regulation is Article 130s.

On a worldwide level, the Community scheme may prove to be as effective in guiding consumers away from non-EC goods as it is at steering them towards 'environmentally friendly' products. There is an argument that the Regulation contains an inbuilt bias which will be enhanced by its implementation. In relation to the 'criteria' on which products are assessed, it has been noted that products must conform to Community health, safety, and environmental requirements. Even if non-EC products conform to other health, safety, and environmental standards which are as stringent as, but different from EC requirements, they will not be eligible for an award. In connection with the 'specific criteria', these are to be formulated against a matrix of the kinds of environmental damage that are important in the Community. Taking into account the geographical and climatic variations around the world, European environmental concerns may not be the same as elsewhere. The matrix may be inappropriate to developing countries, for example.

In addition, establishment of the criteria is not a precise science. The United Kingdom and France have taken very different approaches in establishing the criteria for their allocated product groups. Whilst the United Kingdom has opted for a pragmatic treatment, France has chosen to undertake extremely detailed analyses. For a specific example, when Proctor & Gamble commissioned two studies to compare the environmental impact of disposable and reusable nappies, both concluded that there was no environmental difference. In response, the Women's Environmental Network sponsored a survey of Proctor & Gamble's studies which produced a conclusion that disposable nappies were, in fact, more harmful. Although both sides used the same method of assessment—a 'life-cycle analysis'—they differed on such issues as frequency of washing and length of time spent folding reusable nappies! Clearly, establishing criteria based on the environmental impact of types of products involves an element of value judgement which could, conceivably, result in decisions bearing an affinity to the organizations paying for the report.

In order to resolve the problems of determining allocation criteria and product life-cycle evaluation methods, the Commission has now set up a new working group to devise a joint product life-cycle evaluation methodology.

What is harmful to the environment may also be at issue. One of the main problems in formulating specific criteria for washing detergents is that Member States do not agree on whether phosphates have a detrimental effect on the environment. Germany, the Netherlands, Denmark, and Italy have all banned phosphate detergents, whereas they are allowed in the United Kingdom, France, and Spain. In the United Kingdom studies have even been produced showing that phosphates may be of benefit to the environment. If Member States cannot agree on what harms the environment, the prospects for consensus with non-European countries are not promising. The testing of laundry detergents raises another point, that the location in which a product is used may influence its 'greenness'. The environmental impact of detergents depends to an extent on how much the product must be used in order to achieve acceptable results. This depends on the hardness of the water, which of course varies from region to region, let alone from country to country.

The practical implementation of the Regulation may also result in greater difficulties for non-EC producers in obtaining access to a label. First, the initiative to apply for the label must come from the Community importer, rather than the third-country producer. This lack of control may place such producers at a disadvantage as the interests of importer and producer are not always identical. Second, assessing non-EC products against the criteria may prove to be more problematic. For example, UNICE (Union of Industrial and Employers' Confederations of Europe) pointed out in their opinion on the Regulation that 'it may be more difficult to measure the environmental impact resulting from the use of some raw materials, in particular those that originate from non-Community Countries'.[76]

Similarly, where manufacturing occurs abroad, authorities may be reticent to consider applications since it will be hard for them to regulate the manufacturing process. Also, if factory inspections are required (as in the Canadian labelling scheme) an additional hurdle would result. However, the argument cuts both ways. German companies complained bitterly that their foreign counterparts were receiving preferential treatment as foreign factories were less vigorously vetted prior to the award of a 'Blue Angel' label.

Just how important will it be to obtain a Community eco-label? The scheme is of course voluntary. However, it is conceivable that once the scheme is well established, major supermarkets and stores may decide to purchase only products with a 'green' badge. Then, in effect, the scheme will become mandatory and its possible discriminatory effects will be underscored.

[76] Opinion of 14 May 1991.

Similar arguments may be applied to the Community eco-Audit programme.[77] Eco-auditing appeals to a company's corporate image and, like eco-labelling, attempts to steer companies towards 'greener' methods through consumer pressure. The scheme is designed to measure the complete environmental performance of a business, the results of which measurements are then made public, perhaps through the use of a symbol or badge in certain circumstances. However, assessment may be biased against non-EC countries for the reasons detailed in connection with eco-labels above, relating to value judgements, differences in situation, variations in environmental concerns, and the practical difficulties raised by a distant location.

Particular importance is assigned by the Community to the relation between industrial competitiveness and safeguarding the environment. The Commission's Communication on Industrial Competitiveness and Environmental Protection,[78] adopted by the EC Industry Ministers on 24 November 1992, stresses that the interests of industry and the environment need not necessarily conflict. The competitive advantage gained by the swift implementation of high environmental standards and 'clean' technologies is emphasized. For example, an industry which installs energy-efficient equipment as soon as it becomes available will have a competitive advantage in the long term. The potential for growth in the environmental protection and 'green' products industries is also highlighted. The Communication notes that the EC environmental protection market had a turnover of around $50 billion (39 billion ECUs) in 1990 and is expected to grow by 50 to 100 per cent to the end of the century. However, the Communication warns that environmental protection will only become a source of increased competitiveness if all parties concerned meet their responsibilities. Industry must incorporate environmental protection into its growth strategy, provide information to consumers, and develop and maintain a dialogue with government authorities; consumers must put their environmental concerns into practice through their purchasing decisions; government authorities should set realistic standards and ensure predictability and transparency whilst the Community should play a strategic role without creating unnecessary bureaucracy.

So much for the theory. In practice, there are numerous examples of businesses attempting to sharpen their competitive edge by 'going green'. Large numbers of Dutch companies have set up special management teams to assess the environmental impact of their activities. KPMG management consultants have said that managers view the greening of business as a way to increase market share in hard economic times. Having

[77] Council Regulation (EEC) 1836/93 of 29 June 1993, OJ L168/1 of 10 July 1993.
[78] SEC(92) 1986.

set up a non-governmental process to award certificates to firms establishing such teams, KPMG says that a certificate will 'give companies a competitive advantage because everyone knows who are the good guys and who are the bad guys'.[79]

Companies, especially major concerns, are also developing environmentally aware purchasing policies. IBM UK vet their contract office cleaners for their ability to clean without using chemicals that damage the environment. Similarly, the German Post Office has phased out battery calculators in favour of solar-powered models because batteries contain toxic chemicals. The London-based Environment Council, a charity that promotes good environmental practice in business, has said that companies which espouse green goods cannot afford to be tainted by their supplier's environmental transgressions.

Green purchasing policies have led to increased demand for environmentally friendly products and a consequent growth in the market. For instance, Inkwell, a small company in Bristol, saw an opportunity to recycle printer cartridges. In the United Kingdom an estimated 14 million cartridges, used in typewriters and some computer printers, are discarded every year. However, Inkwell invented the machinery to re-ink the ribbons. Customers can now post their spent cartridges to the company and it returns them, re-inked, a few days later.

But the relationship between industry and environmental protection is not without problems. Adoption of the highest environmental standards may not always lead to a competitive advantage. Last year, the three German chemical giants BASF, Bayer, and Hoechst, protested to the Government that the cost of domestic environmental legislation threatened to cripple the industry by reducing their competitiveness. The companies pointed to their falling profits and the fact that they are obliged to spend between 7 and 12 per cent of their turnover on environmental costs whereas comparable firms such as ICI and Rhône-Poulenc invest below 3 per cent of turnover. The three warned that if environmental cost continue to rise, they would be forced to switch more investment abroad where regulations are less stringent.

7.3.4.2. Competition Policy and the Environment

As previously mentioned, current Community policy predicates that environmental concerns are to be integrated into other sectors, including competition. In this spirit, an environmental section was added as a new feature to the Commission's Report on competition policy for 1992. On 7 June 1992 Karel van Miert, formerly Commissioner for the Environment and now responsible for competition, addressed the Institut d'Études Européennes of the Université Libre de Bruxelles on

[79] *Wall Street Journal*, 14 Apr. 1993.

'Environmental protection and competition policy: two complementary activities'.

The message from the Commission appears to be that whilst environmental concerns are to be taken into account, Articles 85 and 86 of the Treaty and the Merger Regulation continue to apply as usual. Companies may not excuse anti-competitive practices on environmental grounds. The Competition Report provides an example in the *VOTOB Case*[80] in which a Dutch association of companies in the chemicals storage business (VOTOB) decided to impose a fixed uniform 'environmental charge' on their customers. The charge was partly to cover the costs of reducing vapour emissions from members' storage tanks. The Commission objected to the charge as incompatible with Article 85 on the grounds that, as it was fixed and uniform, customers could not shop around and so encourage efficiency. Also the charge did not reflect costs as some members had nearly reached set emission objectives while others had not. In addition, the members of VOTOB employed different techniques, costing differing amounts, to reduce emissions. The Commission also objected to the fact that the charge was invoiced separately suggesting that it was government imposed. Prior to the Commission reaching a decision, VOTOB agreed to withdraw the charge and proceedings were suspended whilst the Commission reviewed VOTOB's undertakings.

The Report also notes that: 'Another problem arises where measures are taken by public authorities which might compromise the effect of the competition rules, for example by requiring firms to engage in behaviour which restricted competition . . . in such cases the Court has held that Article 85 may apply in conjunction with Articles 5 and 3(f) of the Treaty.'[81]

In addition, the Commission points out the contribution which the competition rules make to environmental protection. By safeguarding the operation of the price mechanism, the rules facilitate the 'polluter pays' principle, set out in the Fifth Action Programme, whereby the environmental costs are reflected in actual prices charged.

In relation to state aid, the Commission's scrutiny in aid proposals for environmental protection measures has until recently been based on the criteria laid down in the Communication on the Community Approach to State Aids in Environmental Matters of 1974, as amended by a Commission memorandum of 1980.[82]

Originally, the framework was intended to be a transitional measure aimed at 'catching up' on a backlog of urgently required investment. (The framework initially ran from 1974–80 and was then extended to 1986.)

[80] Point 177 of the Report. [81] Ibid.

[82] See 15th Competition Report, point 259.

However it has now been recognized that 'improvement in the environment and the need to avoid distortions of competition caused by national measures in this field will remain a major task for an indefinite period'. In view of this change, the Commission commenced a review of the framework, taking into account the 'polluter pays' principle and the concept of sustained development also set out in the Fifth Action Programme.

In December 1993 the Commission adopted new guidelines redefining allowable state aid for environmental action. Under the new Code state aid is to be considered admissible for environmental purposes for the following:

1. Investment—up to 15 per cent of the gross costs of the investment, with an incentive ceiling of 30 per cent for companies which exceed environmental protection requirements (or introduce protection measures where no norms have been set). SMEs would be allowed an additional 10 per cent. This allowable aid is only in respect of the portion of the investment devoted to environmental pursuits, not the total investment.
2. Information, training, and advisory services—this aid may be authorized for SMEs up to a rate of 50 per cent, or in assisted regions subject to the ceilings applied to regional investment aid.
3. Purchase of environmentally-friendly products—this aid is allowed provided it falls within the scope of Article 92 of the Treaty of Rome, i.e. aid of a social character; aid to make good damage caused by natural disasters or exceptional occurrences; aid destined for specific regions; aid to promote important projects of common European interest. However, this aid must not provide any unfair disadvantage to the beneficiary companies; it must not discriminate between suppliers; and it must not infringe other Treaty rules, particularly concerning the free movement of goods.
4. Operating costs—this type of aid is generally prohibited but may be allowed on a case-by-case basis if it is for a limited period of time; is digressive; is necessary for the introduction of new and more expensive policies; and preserves the international competitiveness of EC companies.

Karel van Miert, who proposed the new guidelines, stressed that they are not intended to encourage the granting of aids but to ensure that when they are granted it is for good reasons and it will not distort competition.

The Report on Competition Policy notes that a number of environment-related aid measures were approved in 1992. Cases mentioned include exemptions from taxes on carbon dioxide emissions for energy intensive industries in Denmark and the Netherlands. However, the report states that aid will be approved 'only if it does not distort competition unduly'.[83]

[83] See n. 80.

7.4. CONCLUSION: THE WORLDWIDE CONTEXT

European Community environment protection policy has a world context. A number of instruments have been introduced in order to implement multilateral environmental agreements entered into by Member States and the Community, for example CITES, the Montreal Protocol on Substances that Deplete the Ozone Layer, and the Basel Convention of Hazardous Waste mentioned above. Other Community environmental measures, including those on eco-labelling, eco-audit, packaging waste, and a CO_2/energy tax, have implications for worldwide commerce.

However, the EC programme for environmental protection would appear to be on a faster track than the development of similar global objectives. In some areas the Community has opted to take an innovative role. For example, in the recitals to both Regulations on Substances that Deplete the Ozone Layer, the 'leading role' played by the EC is noted, together with the Community's decision to adopt measures stricter than those agreed by the parties to the Protocol. At the Rio Conference the Community pushed for more stringent agreements than were actually concluded. Jacques Delors declared the agreed Convention on Climate Change and the rejection of a proposal for a Convention of Forests to be 'disappointing'. The Community criticized the Convention on Biodiversity for being 'too limp'.

In attempting to preserve the single market, the Community is adopting a policy which is leading to increased and more comprehensive environmental standards than those anticipated on a worldwide level. In order to prevent barriers to trade between Member States caused by national environmental protection requirements, Community harmonization measures are being introduced. For instance, the German 'Green Point' scheme interfered with the functioning of the internal market. Now there are proposals for a similar Community package and packaging waste regime. However, harmonization is not the only way to achieve the smooth functioning of the internal market. Member States may be prevented from implementing their national restrictions as infringements of the principle of free movement of goods. But it would appear that this is not the favoured Community option. Whilst United States courts have repeatedly ruled that discrimination against waste from other states violates the interstate commerce clause of the American Constitution, the European Court of Justice has ruled that the Walloonian Waste import ban was lawful. Now we have a Community Regulation which permits the general prohibition of trade between Member States of waste for disposal. Thus the trade barrier is raised from national to Community level. Arguably there is a danger that, through its growing network of trade-linked environmental measures the Community may become increasingly isolated.

The discriminatory effect of Community environmental measures is perhaps exacerbated by the fact that they presuppose Western European values, interests, and perceptions of what environmental protection is. The discussion of eco-labelling at 7.3.3.4 above demonstrated how legislation may have an inbuilt bias. An excerpt from a press release of the Malaysian Timber Industry Development Council (MTIDC) illustrates the differing interests of Western industrialized nations and developing countries such as Malaysia. The press release was in response to the imposition by Austria of eco-labelling requirements and the introduction of a voluntary 'sustainable quality label', which measures were eventually abandoned:

> This law only singles out tropical timber products as though they are toxic, radioactive or hazardous. It does not cover temperate softwood which accounts for more than 75% of the world's total trade in timber . . .
>
> MTIDC feels the action by the Austrian Government discriminates negatively and unfairly against developing countries who rely on timber export for a legitimate income. Malaysia is one of the few developing countries which has been able to overcome absolute rural poverty so that our forests will no longer be cleared by shifting cultivators for agriculture or fuel. We are therefore harvesting our forests commercially and effectively and still seeking improvement in our forestry policies and implementation. We recognise that deforestation of tropical rainforests (quoted at a rate of 17 million ha per year) is a serious global problem but that the main cause as highlighted by international organisations such as FAO and the GATT Secretariat, is *poverty*, not selective logging. If the action by the Austrian Government is successful and it spreads to other importing countries, tropical forests may further lose their economic value resulting in even greater pressure to clear these forests for other land uses. Therefore such action by the Austrian Government is counter-productive as it may lead to the destruction of more tropical forests . . .
>
> In addition, any importer who wishes to use a 'sustainable quality label' must secure a licence from the Austrian Government who will then vet the sources of the timber supply to see if they fit into *their* definition of 'sustainable' or 'effective exploitation'. Although the use of this quality label is optional, it will put tremendous pressure on both importers and exporters to comply as consumers in Austria will be encouraged to buy only tropical timber products with this quality label.
>
> As for the quality label, it is almost impossible to implement without infringing on the sovereignty of the tropical timber producing countries as these countries will have to subject themselves to scrutiny, supervision and checks from the Austrian side. The timber industry in Malaysia supports and subscribes to the International Tropical Timber Organisation's (ITTO) definition, guidelines and criteria of sustainable management of tropical forests. We also in principle, support the ITTO's aim of achieving trade in timber from sustainable sources by the year 2000 based on a fair and realistic international framework.

Tropical timber producing countries such as Malaysia have not imposed our own environmental standards on goods produced in Austria even though their methods of production may be polluting or non-sustainable. If every country in the world starts imposing their own environmental standards on others in trade, there will be complete chaos as the GATT Secretariat rightly pointed out in its report in February this year.

The effect of such Community isolation and discrimination may be magnified by enlargement of the Community and the Maastricht Treaty. As Eastern European and EFTA countries join up and Maastricht strengthens the bonds between Member States, the political and economic weight of the EC will increase. For example, in GATT and bilateral negotiations the Community may be able to achieve more 'stringent' Western-oriented agreements favoured by the Member States than at present. In addition, the Maastricht Treaty places environmental protection on a par with the principle of free movement of goods.

Developing countries may suffer the worst of all words. As European (and other richer industrialized) nations raise standards, 'dirty' industries may continue to migrate to poorer less restricted areas, while such poorer states became excluded from Community markets by environmental protection requirements. Under Community legislation governing substances that deplete the ozone layer, the restrictions relating to imports from non-parties into the EC are more comprehensive than those concerned with exports. With regard to the addition of 'new substances' to the regime, the draft legislation does not prevent exports to third countries. Mr Paleokrassas, Commissioner for the Environment, has said that the planned measures would not cause problems for EC Industries since an enormous market exists in third countries where HCFCs and methyl bromide may be exported under the Montreal protocol. He has commented, 'the Community cannot legislate for the rest of the world'.

So although producers in third countries such as Israel will lose their market in the EC, Community producers, such as Atochem, will not lose their overseas opportunities.

In relation to waste shipments, it will be recalled that the Member States chose to reject an outright ban on waste exports to ACP countries. In addition, to avoid restricting the scrap industry, OECD countries agreed, before the Basel Convention was signed, to permit recyclable waste including metal, plastics, and tyres to be traded amongst OECD members with minimal controls. However, when Community members addressed the issue of ratification of the Convention, they decided to extend this principle to trade between Member States and non-OECD countries.[83a] Environmentalists argue that scrap is often contaminated

[83a] See n.46a.

with heavy metals and that much waste classified as recyclable will go to poor importers who have no intention or means of recycling it. This is supported by the facts that German 'Green Point' waste has been found in Indonesian landfill sites and the Swiss have been reprimanded for dumping their waste in Somalia. At the same time, German *DSD* is now checking a list of recycling plants in South-East Asia. Scavenging has traditionally been a source of income to the very poor in South-East Asia. A flood of German recyclables on to the Asian market, depressing the value of such scrap as it has done on the Community market, will destroy a valuable source of income in this area.

The proposed packaging waste Directive raises other questions. Whilst third countries must produce packaging which meets EC recycling standards and must arrange for recycling infrastructure if they wish to gain access to Community markets, the draft Directive does not extend to exports of packaging to third countries. The message seems to be that it does not matter what we wrap our goods in or what happens to waste outside the Community. Eco-labelling schemes may be similarly exclusive and yet fail to take into account environmental concerns in third countries.

Finally, with regard to controls on industry, it will be recalled that BASF, Hoechst, and Bayer have claimed that rising environmental standards may force them to relocate. Malaysia has become the world's largest exporter of semi-conductors over the past decade, largely due to investment from Japanese and United States firms. Companies can produce electronic goods much more cheaply in Malaysia because of its lower environmental standards.

But is the answer to be found in further restrictions on trade with developing countries? Poor countries rely on methyl bromide in order to grow crops. Waste trade provides a badly needed source of revenue, as does playing host to the factories of developed countries. Recent reports have indicated that the European Community is falling under increasing pressure from environmentalists, unions, and politicians to ban imports of Asian goods that do not meet with Western environmental standards. Supporters of the ban claim that it would help to ensure uniform global environmental standards. Again, it may be that the poor countries would lose out as they are deprived of revenue and the measure would be ineffective as the States affected could not afford to improve their environmental standards. The motives behind such a ban must also be questioned as it would have the effect of disposing of cheap competition in Community markets.

It may be that richer countries, including the Member States, should acknowledge in full the implication of the 'polluter pays' principle. For example, perhaps we should pay developing countries at European rates for taking our waste and provide technological assistance for the establishment of plant for recycling and disposal. Perhaps we should consider compensating the countries who maintain their tropical forests, in recognition of the CO_2 absorption service which they are providing to the industrialized nations (which produce most of the world's CO_2).

The signs are not promising. For instance, the Member States have decided that they do not have a role to play in the area of aid to developing countries for the use of 'ozone-friendly' substitutes. Therefore, they will not participate in the chapter of the Montreal Protocol concerning financing. Similarly, prior to the Rio Summit, EC Ministers failed to agree on the pre-conference proposal to devote 0.7 per cent of their GNP to official development aid by the year 2000 and finally had to concur on a vaguer form of wording—'as soon as possible'.

In the end, it may be that trade restricting, Community environmental measures, such as those discussed in this chapter, are brought under the GATT enforcement mechanism. In the long term it will be for the GATT Trade and Environment Group to explore the wider issues of how the interests of trade and environmental protection may be reconciled.

8

Economic Growth and Protection of the Environment: The Impact of International Law and Policy

ALAN BOYLE

8.1. INTRODUCTION: UNCED AND ENVIRONMENTAL LAW

The United Nations Conference on Environment and Development (UNCED) held at Rio in 1992 focused international attention on the adoption of global policies whose explicit purpose was to reconcile economic development with environmental protection. In the Rio Declaration on Environment and Development, and in a programme of action known as Agenda 21, the Conference endorsed principles and policies with important implications for the future development of international and national environmental law.[1] These include the notions that development must be sustainable, that the polluter should bear the cost of pollution, that individuals should have access to effective redress, that environmental measures should not arbitrarily or unjustifiably restrict international trade, and that environmental measures addressing transboundary or global environmental problems should as far as possible be based on an international consensus.[2]

The Rio Conference had a very wide-ranging mandate. One of its most important objectives was:

> to promote the further development of international environmental law, taking into account the Declaration of the UN Conference on the Human Environment, as well as the special needs and concerns of developing countries, and to examine in this context the feasibility of elaborating general rights and obligations of states, as appropriate, in the field of the environment, and taking into account relevant existing legal instruments.[3]

[1] See *Report of the UN Conference on Environment and Development*, UN Doc/A/CONF. 151/26/Rev.1 (Vol. 1) (1992) for conference documents, and see generally P. W. Birnie and A. E. Boyle, *International Law and the Environment* (Oxford, 1992), and A. Hurrell and B. Kingsbury, *The International Politics of the Environment* (Oxford, 1992), esp. ch. 1.

[2] Declaration on Environment and Development, Principles 4, 7, 8, 10, 12.

[3] UNGA Resolution 44/228.

The Rio Declaration and Agenda 21, together with the Conventions on Climate Change and Biological Diversity,[4] are thus part of a subject which has evolved with remarkable rapidity over the past twenty-odd years: international environmental law. While debate continues on the long-term significance of the Rio Conference, its conclusions and the agenda it has established for further action are bound to have a world-wide impact on law, policy, and practices adopted by many governments.

This chapter attempts first to explore in general terms the key concepts of 'sustainable development' and the 'polluter pays' principle to see what implications they have for environmental regulation and its impact on economic development. It argues that both concepts are inherently uncertain and open to widely divergent interpretations, which simply mask the continuing need to make value judgements on questions of policy and priorities governments will face when trying to implement them. For this reason effective international action to control and alleviate global environmental problems, such as ozone depletion or climate change, requires co-operation and agreement on the elaboration of more detailed rules, policies and standards. This process of co-operative regulation thus leads inevitably to greater harmonization of national environmental laws and practices, and contributes, at least in part, to reducing the inhibiting effects which conflicting regulatory regimes may have on trade and development.

The second part of the chapter will therefore explore the role of multilateral regulatory treaties in providing a framework for co-ordinated national action to regulate specific environmental problems. It will seek to identify the problems for trade and economic growth which this international approach to environmental protection may entail and to consider how best these might be overcome, while recognizing that this will not always be possible. For a variety of reasons, as we shall see, complete harmonization of national environmental law is neither feasible nor desirable.

8.2. SUSTAINABLE DEVELOPMENT

'Sustainable development' has become the central objective of international environmental policy since the IUCN and UNEP published their World Conservation Strategy in 1980.[5] It has subsequently been endorsed in the 1987 Brundtland Report of the World Commission on

[4] 31 *ILM* (1992), 851 and 822.

[5] See the same organization's new programme *Caring for the Earth: A Strategy for Sustainable Living* (Gland, 1991).

Environment and Development,[6] by the Group of Seven industrialized countries at the Toronto Summit in 1988 and in the Rio Declaration of the 1992 UN Conference on Environment and Development. Agenda 21, the programme of action adopted by the UNCED Conference, talks in its preamble of the need for a 'global partnership for sustainable development', and most of its provisions are intended to promote implementation of the concept. The defining role of sustainable development in the evolution of law and policy on protection of the environment has thus secured near-universal endorsement.

But, as one author has asked, 'Can a term which commands such support actually mean anything?'[7] Does this crucial concept have a solid core of meaning, or does its content lie mainly in the eye of the beholder? Certain interpretations can be discarded immediately. First, sustainable development is not to be confused with zero growth. Economists readily accept that in some cases even zero growth may not be sustainable: zero growth in the output of CFCs will not save the ozone layer. Conversely, growth, if defined in terms of GNP, is not inevitably unsustainable, since GNP is not *per se* a measure of natural resource consumption or of pollution. The environmental economist Michael Jacobs has put this point succinctly: 'As a mere monetary aggregate, GNP does not distinguish between different types of economic activity: it simply records the overall total. It is quite possible for GNP to go up with fewer resources being used, and less pollution being generated, if the *content* of growth tends away from environmentally-degrading activities.'[8] He points to the switch from coal- to gas-fired power stations as an example of environmentally friendly growth of this kind. Whatever else it means therefore, sustainable development need not imply a policy of no growth.

A more plausible interpretation is that sustainable development entails a compromise between the natural environment and economic growth. Some element of compromise is undoubtedly part of the concept. The integration of environmental protection and economic development was for that reason an important objective of the UNCED Conference, expressed in Principle 4 of the Rio Declaration. Much of Agenda 21, and of international environmental law, has been concerned with attaining this integration; clearly, a policy of economic growth which disregards environmental considerations will not meet the criterion of sustainable development. But to view sustainable development as amounting to nothing more than a compromise between equally desirable ends is fundamentally inadequate. It fails to explain either the nature of sustainability or of development, and gives us no criteria for determining the ultimate

[6] *Our Common Future*, World Commission on Environment and Development (Oxford, 1987).

[7] M. Jacobs, *The Green Economy* (London, 1991), 59.

[8] Ibid. 54.

objective of this integration of development and environment. This is why UNCED's definition of 'sustainable development' makes no reference to a compromise but instead defines the term by reference to objectives: 'development that meets the needs of the present without compromising the ability of future generations to meet their own needs'.[9]

It is in this context that the idea of sustainable development as the conservation of *natural* capital becomes important. Pearce argues that it is not enough to define sustainable development in terms simply of constant wealth inheritance from one generation to the next, because the substitution of man-made for natural assets is only possible up to a point. There are, for example, no obvious man-made substitutes for the ozone layer or the oceans. From this perspective it is essential to ensure that the resilience and diversity of nature are protected from irreversible change so that natural capital assets do not decline over time: if this is permitted it will represent a real impoverishment of future generations. Even if Pearce's concern for the conservation of natural capital is rejected in favour of a broader mix of natural and man-made capital, it is still necessary, he reminds us, to value the environment properly: 'As long as the services of natural and other environments are treated as if they are "free goods", the wrong mix—from the standpoint of economic efficiency—of natural and man-made capital will emerge.'[10]

Moreover, on this view, sustainable development implies not merely limits on economic activity in the interests of preserving or protecting the environment, but an approach to development which emphasizes the fundamental importance of equity within the economic system. This equity is both intragenerational, in that it seeks to redress the imbalance in wealth and economic development between the developed and developing worlds by giving priority to the needs of the poor,[11] and intergenerational, in seeking a fair allocation of costs and benefits across succeeding generations.[12] Put simply, development will only be 'sustainable' if it benefits the disadvantaged, without disadvantaging the needs of the future. These points are well observed in Principles 3–7 of the Rio Declaration, and in the Conventions on Climate Change and Biodiversity. What is characteristic of these instruments is their commitment to protecting the interests of future generations, and of developing countries. The latter benefit in particular, from access to funding through the Global Environmental Facility and other sources,[13] from access to the benefits derived from

[9] *Our Common Future*, 43.

[10] D. Pearce, A. Markandya, E. Barbier, *Blueprint for a Green Economy* (London, 1989), 28–50 at 48.

[11] Ibid. 44–5; Rio Declaration, Principle 5.

[12] Rio Declaration, Principle 3, and see E. Brown-Weiss, *In Fairness to Future Generations* (Dobs Ferry, NY, 1989).

[13] The GEF is administered by the World Bank in conjunction with UNEP and

exploitation of their own genetic resources and transfer of technology,[14] and from a recognition that in a system of 'common but differentiated responsibilities' developed countries bear a larger responsibility for ensuring sustainable development 'in view of the pressures their societies place on the global environment and of the technologies and financial resources they command'.[15] Thus 'sustainable development' is intended to serve not simply the needs of the environment, but entails a much more far-reaching reorientation of the world's economic system in which the burdens of environmental protection will fall more heavily on the developed northern states and the economic benefits will accrue more significantly to the underdeveloped south.

A further element of sustainable development, however, is 'a notion of economic welfare which acknowledges non-financial components',[16] in particular the quality of the environment, health, and the preservation of culture and community. We can see some of these concerns in Principle 1 of the Rio Declaration, but more especially in such international agreements as the 1972 Convention for the Protection of World Cultural and Natural Heritage.[17] This protects areas like Stonehenge and the Great Barrier Reef. Similarly, the 1991 Protocol to the Antarctic Treaty on Environmental Protection[18] designates Antarctica a Special Conservation Area, and acknowledges its 'intrinsic value', including its 'wilderness and aesthetic values'. Another example of this approach is the 1989 ILO Convention Concerning Indigenous and Tribal Peoples,[19] which seeks to regulate the relationship between their needs and those of environmental protection.

Sustainable development is thus not exclusively concerned with narrow economic needs, but encompasses a broader environmental perspective which makes it genuinely ecocentric rather than merely anthropocentric in character. Defined in these terms, it has not been the objective of industrialized or developing countries until now, and its implementation will require a considerable departure from present global economic policy. This is most obviously true of developing countries, whose control over their own natural resources and environmental policies may be significantly limited by their dependence on short-term resource exploitation dictated by patterns of international trade within the GATT system and their external indebtedness. It is in this context that the failure of the

UNDP. See World Bank, 'Establishment of the GEF', 30 *ILM* (1991), 1739; id. Resolution 91–5 (1991), ibid. 1758; Convention on Biological Diversity, Arts. 20, 21; Convention on Climate Change, Art. 11.

[14] Convention on Biological Diversity, Arts. 12, 15, 16, 19; Convention on Climate Change, Arts. 4(2) and (3).

[15] Rio Declaration, Principle 7, and see generally the Convention on Climate Change.

[16] M. Jacobs, *The Green Economy*, 60.

[17] UKTS 2 (1985) Cmnd. 9424.

[18] 30 *ILM* (1961). Not yet in force.

[19] 28 *ILM* (1989), 1382. Not yet in force.

present GATT system to take serious account of environmental concerns or of the interests of developing states becomes a very significant structural inhibition on implementation of the policies adopted at Rio in 1992.[20] But there are also reasons why it may be just as difficult for developed economies to respond to an ethos of sustainability.

Some of the impediments to sustainability are technological and scientific. We should not assume the capability of scientists to identify all the environmental consequences of economic and industrial activity, or to provide technical solutions to problems such as the safety of nuclear power plants or the impact of chemicals on the environment. Rather, a concept of sustainability must take full account of the limitations of scientific prediction in the evaluation of environmental risks. It is in this context that the 'precautionary principle' has become a significant new principle of emerging international environmental law.[21]

Another set of limits are those of social organization and social theory. Sustainable development requires political action if it is to be implemented, and it may be easier to deliver in certain systems than in others. While on the one hand a measure of authoritarian *dirigisme* may appear superficially attractive if Draconian environmental controls are required, in reality closed totalitarian societies such as the former Soviet Union, China, or the former communist regimes in Eastern Europe have proved far less successful than participatory democracies in managing their environment and in avoiding environmental disasters. It is no coincidence that both the Soviet and Hungarian democratic revolutions of the period 1989–91 can be related directly to the environmental consequences of the Chernobyl accident and the Nagymoros dam controversy, nor is it surprising that the Bhopal disaster has greatly strengthened the emphasis which Indian courts now place on human rights and public-interest litigation in environmental matters.[22]

The notion of sustainable development is thus inherently complex and its implementation requires governments to think in very different terms from those to which they have become accustomed. Social, political, and economic choices abound. This may result in wide diversities of policy and interpretation, as different governments pursue their own priorities. A few governments have legislated specifically for sustainable development, as in New Zealand's Resources Management Act of 1991. But many others will approach the matter piecemeal, with inevitable incoherence. The problem with such an open-textured concept is that 'without

[20] See chapter by B. Kingsbury.

[21] See Principle 15 of the Rio Declaration which provides that 'where there are threats of serious or irreversible damage, lack of full scientific certainty shall not be used as a reason for postponing cost-effective measures to prevent environmental degradation'.

[22] On Indian legal developments see Birnie and Boyle, *International Law and the Environment*, 195.

authoritative third-party decision-making, conflicting claims about the concept's specific normative implications will abound and disputes over application will be exceedingly difficult to resolve'.[23]

While it is one of the roles of international environmental law to give the concept more concrete content, chiefly through multilateral environmental treaties, and now also through the Commission on Sustainable Development, this process is still very far from complete. In any event, international law cannot define 'sustainable development' as such; it can only facilitate its implementation in specific situations, such as conservation of high seas fish resources, or trade in elephant ivory. Sustainable development offers us at best a unifying concept for the exploitation of natural resources and the integration of environment and development, but it does not offer us much of a unified vision of environmental law.

8.3. THE 'POLLUTER PAYS' PRINCIPLE

8.3.1. The Meaning and Scope of the Principle

The 'polluter pays' principle is essentially an economic policy for allocating the costs of pollution or environmental damage, but it has implications for the development of international and national law as regards liability for damage and more generally in regard to environmental costs borne by public authorities.

As defined by OECD, the principle entails that the polluter should bear the expense of carrying out measures decided by public authorities to ensure that the environment is in an 'acceptable state', or 'in other words the cost of these measures should be reflected in the cost of goods and services which cause pollution in production and or in consumption'.[24] The purpose of OECD policy and recommendations on the subject is thus to internalize the true economic costs of pollution prevention and environmental damage and to ensure that governments do not distort international trade and investment by subsidizing these environmental costs.

The 'polluter pays' principle has been endorsed by OECD in a series of recommendations adopted in the 1970s, and more recently by the CSCE. It is also part of EEC environmental law under Article 130r, which provides that Community policy relating to the environment shall be based 'on the principles that preventive action should be taken, that

[23] G. Handl, 'Environmental Security and Global Change: The Challenge to International Law', 1 *Yb. IEL* (1990), 25.

[24] OECD, Recommendations C(72) 128 and C(74) 223, repr. in OECD, *OECD and the Environment* (Paris, 1986); C(89) 88, repr. in 28 ILM (1989), 1320, and C(90)177. See generally T. Swanson, in O. Lomas, *Frontiers of Environmental Law* (London, 1992).

environmental damage should as a priority be rectified at source, and that the polluter should pay'. Moreover, at the UNCED conference the principle for the first time secured international support as an environmental policy. Principle 16 of the Rio Declaration provides, in somewhat qualified terms, that: 'National authorities should endeavour to promote the internalisation of environmental costs and the use of economic instruments, taking into account the approach that the polluter should, in principle, bear the cost of pollution, with due regard to the public interest and without distorting international trade and investment.' This international support is reflected particularly in a number of treaties dealing with marine pollution,[25] but in other contexts its implementation has largely been left to national rather than international action. As a result, both the choice of methods—taxation, charges, liability laws—and the degree of implementation have been very variable, and few states have been fully consistent in their policy, including the United Kingdom.[26]

This diversity also reflects continuing evolution in the scope and definition of the principle which differing formulations in OECD recommendations and later instruments have not entirely clarified. The problematic issue is the extent to which the full internalization of the external effects of pollution is required. OECD practice has generally taken a relatively conservative view of the categories of costs to be internalized, and it has also permitted a relatively liberal range of exceptions. Thus its recommendations are mainly concerned with the cost of preventive measures, the cost of control measures, such as monitoring, and clean-up and restoration costs following accidents. The latter was the subject of recommendation C(89)88 in 1989.

OECD has allowed governmental assistance to be treated as an exception to the principle in cases where transitional arrangements leading to a more stringent control regime are needed, or where steps to protect the environment would 'jeopardize the social and economic policy objectives of a country or region', for example in holding back regional development, or research and development.[27] The broad and somewhat subjective character of these exceptions is reflected in Principle 16 of the Rio Declaration, which allows national authorities to apply the 'polluter pays' principle 'with due regard to the public interest and without distorting international trade and investment'. On the other hand some treaty formulations contain no such qualifications.

[25] 1990 Convention on Oil Pollution Preparedness, Response and Co-operation, Preamble, 30 *ILM* (1991), 735 (not in force); 1992 Convention for the Protection of the Marine Environment of the NE Atlantic, Art. 2(2)(b); 1992 Convention on the Protection of the Marine Environment of the Baltic Sea Area, Art. 3(4).

[26] For a survey of OECD practice see OECD, *Economic Instruments for Environmental Protection* (Paris, 1989).

[27] See OECD, *The Polluter Pays Principle*, OECD/GD(92)81 (Paris, 1992), 5, 26–7, 37.

Principle 16 of the Rio Declaration differs significantly from earlier OECD definitions, however, in referring to the 'internalization of environmental costs' and the polluter 'bearing the cost of pollution'. This wording shifts the focus to the environmental *impact* of pollution, in terms of the cost of damage which it causes, and not simply the cost of preventing it. OECD has itself begun to move in the same direction, in its 1991 Recommendation C(90)177 on The Use of Economic Instruments in Environmental Policy, which for the first time includes the cost of compensating for damage to the environment.[28] Rio Principle 16 in effect endorses the full internalization of environmental costs, although as we have seen, qualified by reference to the public interest, and by its own deliberately 'soft' wording which leaves much to the discretion of each state.

The inclusion of compensation for the costs of environmental damage is a sensible and inevitable development if the economic logic of the 'polluter pays' principle is to be followed through. This discussion emphasizes the point, however, that it is a principle which cannot be used by lawyers without further clarification of its precise content in the context in which it is employed. As one commentator observes, 'The main difficulty with the full internalisation policy is that it cannot be implemented in practice unless some agreement is reached on the respective rights of the polluters and the victims'.[29]

How then should the 'polluter pays' principle be used and developed? This is a more difficult question than it might appear. Taxation is a relatively crude way to recoup the external costs of environmentally harmful activities. Putting up taxes on petrol may reduce demand for petrol in some sectors of the economy, but not necessarily overall, and the income goes to the exchequer, not to those who suffer the damage. In any event to have much impact on demand taxation would tend to have to be at levels that are likely to be politically difficult. Charges to meet the cost of reducing or restoring environmental damage can be more accurately targeted, but only marginally so, and their impact in deterring environmentally harmful activities will always be unpredictable. As experience with charging for disposal of oily residues from ships shows, charges can be counter-productive if they make the polluter more likely to evade environmental protection measures in order to cut costs. The US practice of attempting to internalize environmental costs by making the polluter rather than public agencies directly responsible for conducting the clean-up and restoration after accidents such as the *Exxon Valdez* may also be counter-productive if the result is a dilatory and inadequate response. In

[28] Ibid. 6–7.

[29] H. Smets, in L. Campiglio *et al.* (eds.), *The Environment after Rio: International Law and Economics* (London, 1994), and see also OECD, *Polluter Pays Principle*, 39–44.

this sort of case there may be no practical alternative to state-organized action, with the taxpayer recovering the costs through liability laws and compensation schemes.

Thus full implementation of a 'polluter pays' approach requires consideration of the question of civil liability. The extent to which civil liability makes the polluter pay for environmental damage depends on a variety of variable factors. If liability is based on negligence, not only does this have to be proved, which may be problematic, but harm which is neither reasonably foreseeable nor reasonably avoidable will not be compensated and the victim or the taxpayer, not the polluter, will bear the loss. Strict liability is a better approximation of the 'polluter pays' principle, but not if it is limited in amount, as in internationally agreed schemes involving oil tankers or nuclear installations.[30] Moreover, a narrow definition of damage may exclude environmental losses which cannot easily be quantified in monetary terms, such as wildlife, or which affect the quality of the environment without causing actual physical damage. An illustration of this problem is the case of *Merlin* v. *BNFL*[31] where a house was rendered radioactive but the operator of the installation responsible was absolved from liability because there had been no damage to property within the terms of the statute, despite the building's loss of market value. A significant amount of environmental injury is likely to remain uncompensated under civil liability in English law, and the same is true of some other legal systems, though not uniformly.[32] To this extent the polluter remains free to offload certain environmental costs even under a strict liability regime.

8.3.2. Defining the Polluter

Another problem with the 'polluter pays' principle is that it is not always clear who the polluter is. If an oil tanker sinks, in one sense the operator is the polluter and should be responsible. But it can equally be said that the cargo causes the damage and the cargo owner is in that sense the pol-

[30] 1960 Convention on Third Party Liability in the Field of Nuclear Energy, UKTS 69 (1968) Cmnd. 3755; 1963 Convention on Civil Liability for Nuclear Damage, 2 ILM (1963), 727. See also OECD, *Polluter Pays Principle*, 41, which concludes that the extra cost involved in applying strict liability instead of fault liability counts for very little in industry and the insurance sector, and is offset by lower legal fees and less litigation.

[31] [1990] 2 QB 557.

[32] See also s.1 of the German Environmental Liability Act, 1990 which confines liability to cases of 'death, personal injury or property damage'. Cf. the more generous approach to environmental compensation under the 1990 US Oil Pollution Act, s.1006(d)(1) and, under US tort law, *Commonwealth of Puerto Rico* v. *S.S. Zoe Colocotroni* 628 F 2d. 652 (1980). See also 1992 Protocol to the 1969 Convention on Civil Liability for Oil Pollution Damage and the 1993 Convention on Civil Liability for Damage Resulting from Activities Dangerous to the Environment, Arts. 2(7), (8), and (10), which both allow a measure of recovery for environmental restoration costs.

luter. Sensibly, the present internationally agreed scheme of liability and compensation for oil pollution treats both the ship's owner and the cargo owner as sharing responsibility, while excluding the liability of any other potential defendant in order to facilitate easy recovery by plaintiffs.[33] In this sort of case what matters is how the responsibility is shared, and how the compensation is funded. But in more complex situations, such as the carriage of hazardous wastes, the question of who is the polluter is not so easy to answer, and the allocation of shared responsibility is comparatively harder to engineer.[34]

An altogether different problem arises in the case of nuclear accidents. Here it is reasonably clear that the polluter is the operator of the nuclear installation, but the adoption of a strict 'polluter pays' approach to liability is simply not economically feasible. In the event of a serious accident, the scale of absolute and unlimited liability would be uninsurable and quickly bankrupt even the largest utility company. Unless the losses are to fall mainly on the innocent victims, some other approach to allocating them must be found, almost certainly by involving other states which use nuclear power. Thus in Western Europe the uninsured risks are borne first by the state in which the installation is located and then, above a certain level, by a compensation fund to which participating governments contribute in proportion to their installed nuclear capacity and GNP.[35] Here the basic concept is not one of making the polluter pay but of an equitable sharing of the risk. An even more extensive departure from the 'polluter pays' principle is emerging with regard to Eastern European nuclear installations. Here the costs of remedial measures are so high, and the local economies so weak, that some Western European governments, who represent one large group of potential victims of any accident, have proposed funding the work needed to improve safety standards. The same approach has reluctantly been adopted by the Dutch and other riparians on the Rhine in order to persuade the French to reduce pollution from their potassium mines.[36]

Thus the 'polluter pays' principle and the general policy of internalizing environmental costs cannot be treated as a rigid rule of universal

[33] 1969 Convention on Civil Liability for Oil Pollution Damage, UKTS 106 (1975), Cmnd. 6183; 1971 Convention on the Establishment of an International Fund for Compensation for Oil Pollution Damage, UKTS 95 (1978), Cmnd. 7383.

[34] See proposals under discussion in IMO for a convention on liability for carriage of dangerous goods at sea, IMO Doc. LEG64/4 and 65/3 (1991) and OECD, *Polluter Pays Principle*, 8.

[35] 1960 Convention on Third Party Liability in the Field of Nuclear Energy; 1963 Supplementary Agreement, UKTS 44 (1975), Cmnd. 5948.

[36] 1976 Convention for the Protection of the Rhine from Pollution by Chlorides, 16 *ILM* (1977), 265. For a general survey of this approach to the funding of environmental measures see OECD Environment Committee, *The Use of International Financial Transfers in Resolving Transfrontier and Global Pollution Problems*, ENV/EC (90)25 (1990).

application, nor are the means used to implement it going to be the same in all cases. A great deal of flexibility will be inevitable, taking full account of differences in the nature of the risk and the economic feasibility of full internalization of environmental costs in industries whose capacity to bear them will vary. It is no doubt considerations of this kind which account for the heavily qualified nature of Principle 16 of the Rio Declaration. Once again a basic concept of international policy cannot supply clear guidance on the content either of national or international environmental law.

8.4. INTERNATIONAL REGULATION AND THE HARMONIZATION OF ENVIRONMENTAL LAW

Modern international environmental law and policy are now much more concerned with the prevention and abatement of environmental harm through regulation and international co-operation than with liability for harm. In this sense international environmental law mirrors developments in national environmental law, where extensive administrative regulation has come to supplant tort liability as the core of the subject. Internationally, this system of regulation is supplied primarily by a large number of global and regional treaties which deal with matters such as dumping at sea, transboundary air pollution, ozone depletion, conservation of wetlands and migratory species, or trade in hazardous wastes and endangered species.[37] The Conventions on Biological Diversity and Climate Change negotiated at Rio in 1992 represent the two most recent global examples of this genre.

By contrast, EEC environmental law has an additional, quite separate objective. One of the assumptions on which the Community's competence to regulate environmental matters is based is that harmonization of national environmental laws is necessary to ensure a 'level playing-field' for trade and industry to move freely within the Community. By and large this has been achieved through directives establishing common emission and quality standards for air, water, and marine discharges, by setting common standards for compliance with treaties such as the Ozone Convention, and through regulations and directives on the control of environmental risks, such as the 'Seveso' directive. A proposed directive on liability for waste has not come into force, but a new Green Paper proposes harmonization of environmental liability laws in the Community.[38] Clearly, from a business point of view there are undoubted advantages in harmonization of this kind, although to be fully effective it

[37] See generally, Birnie and Boyle, *International Law and the Environment*.

[38] EC Commission COM (93) 47, *Remedying Environmental Damage*.

must also be accompanied by comparable levels of enforcement in each member state, which have not always been achieved.

Assuming then that harmonization is in principle beneficial to trade and industry, and thus to economic growth, how far does international regulation of the environment either promote or hinder this objective? As we have already seen, global and regional treaties are the primary means by which international regulation is effected. But the mere fact that a group of states have become parties to a treaty committing them to take measures to deal with some environmental problem does not *per se* ensure, or even necessarily promote, harmonization of national law. In some legal systems certain treaties may be regarded as self-executing and therefore will form part of national law; in others, such as the United Kingdom, this is not the case unless legislation has been adopted. But in either case, whatever the domestic legal status of treaties generally, most environmental treaties are typically of the type which is not self-executing; they will almost always require further legislation or administrative action to ensure implementation. This has two important consequences.

First, the degree and form of national implementation will largely determine how successful the treaty is as an instrument of change, assuming its objectives and techniques are themselves realistic, and that the parties intend to make more than symbolic gestures, which is not always the case. This is why so much attention has been paid both at UNCED and elsewhere to the methods and institutions which can be used to supervise compliance with environmental treaties, and ensure through international inspection and reporting procedures that they are adequately implemented.[39] Secondly, states will often have considerable discretion in the methods of implementation they use, and possibly also in the standards and timetables they set. It is in this respect that regulatory conflicts can arise, since the result will often be a lack of uniformity in what individual governments actually do. They may all be working to the same goal, but doing so in very different ways.

A good example of this problem was the 1974 Paris Convention for the Prevention of Marine Pollution from Land-Based Sources.[40] The innocuous title of this agreement conceals the fact that it dealt, *inter alia*, with the very important subject of industrial waste emissions to the air, to watercourses, and from coastal outfalls, wherever these may result in marine pollution of the North Sea or North Atlantic. The Convention did not so much set detailed rules as a series of objectives. The more dangerous blacklisted substances were to be 'progressively eliminated',

[39] See in particular, UNCED, *The Effectiveness of International Agreements* (Cambridge, 1992).

[40] UKTS 64 (1978), Cmnd. 7251. This agreement was superseded in 1992 by the Paris Convention for the Protection of the Marine Environment of the North-East Atlantic.

but no timetable was set, and in the meantime it was left to the parties to agree on discharge standards and eventual elimination. If they could not agree then compliance with this obligation was left to each government. Grey-listed substances had only to be controlled so that their amount and location of discharge were compatible with protection of the marine environment. It was left entirely to each government to regulate these discharges through licensing procedures and to set their own standards for what was acceptable.

Not surprisingly, a treaty such as this proved very difficult to implement in a co-ordinated, consistent way.[41] The possibility of the parties adopting the same standards did exist if they were able to reach further agreement, but in practice there was little to stop each government pursuing its own particular priorities. This was largely what happened: some states were simply more willing to go further than others in controlling this form of pollution. Moreover, enforcement even of agreed standards remained the responsibility of national authorities; since there was no provision for independent inspection, or prior approval of permits by intergovernmental bodies, and no formal non-compliance procedure, it was unlikely that there would be common standards of enforcement.

Not all environmental treaties are like this. Some, such as the protocol to the Ozone Convention, lay down very specific standards which leave very little room for national discretion in their implementation, though developing states do not have the same obligations as developed state parties.[42] Similarly, the 1973/8 Convention for the Prevention of Pollution by Ships[43] (MARPOL) lays down precise standards on construction and pollution prevention which leave little or no latitude in implementation. But even these conventions may well be enforced to very different degrees by individual states; the MARPOL Convention is more honoured in the breach by a number of flag and port states.

Should international environmental agreements therefore aim to lay down more detailed and precise rules and try to ensure greater harmonization? The problem is that this is unlikely to be either possible or desirable in many cases. It may not be possible because a certain flexibility is often the price which has to be paid to secure international agreement. Much will then depend on how far the parties are prepared

[41] See S. Saetevik, *Environmental Co-operation Among North Sea States* (London, 1986); Wettestad and Andressen, *The Effectiveness of International Resource Co-operation* (Lysaker, 1991).

[42] 1985 Vienna Convention for the Protection of the Ozone Layer, UKTS 1 (1990) Cm. 910; 1987 Protocol on Substances that Deplete the Ozone layer, UKTS 19 (1990) Cm. 977, as amended 1990 and 1992. See further Birnie and Boyle, *International Law and the Environment*, ch. 10.

[43] UKTS 101 (1976), Cmnd. 6647; 1978 Protocol, 17 *ILM* (1978), 546. See further Birnie and Boyle, *International Law and the Environment*, ch. 7.

subsequently to adopt more specific rules. This has certainly been true of agreements regarding land-based sources of marine pollution and dumping at sea. But greater harmonization may also be undesirable. Environmental problems tend to require flexible solutions to allow for changing scientific evidence, new control technologies, new political priorities, and the differing circumstances of various states. A treaty which casts precise rules in stone may be hard to renegotiate and thus too inflexible to respond to changing conditions. Most environmental treaties therefore tend to lay down only general principles, relegating the detailed standards to annexes which can be easily amended by the parties, or easily supplemented by new annexes provided the parties can agree. This is essentially the core of the problem: whereas the EEC now has the competence to legislate on environmental matters by qualified majority for all its Member States,[44] more orthodox treaty-based institutions do not have such power, and can proceed only with the support of all parties.[45] Harmonization of national law based on rules adopted within such a treaty is perfectly possible, but since the rules may themselves be controversial, it is no easy task to bring this about. Inevitably therefore, a lot of discretion is often left to governments as the only way to achieve agreement on something. This is one reason why harmonization can be a much more prominent objective of EEC environmental policy than of international environmental policy.

One possible but unorthodox solution if the lack of harmonized environmental standards is perceived as a significant problem is to encourage industries to play a greater role in co-ordinating their own standards. Multinational corporations in particular do not have to take advantage of lower environmental standards in, say, Mexico: they could agree to follow certain global minimum standards wherever their plants are located. What this will not do, however, is to deal with the state which insists on significantly higher standards, such as Sweden, but it may be wise to leave such states to make their own judgement about where their priorities should lie. As an objective of international environmental policy, however, harmonization of environmental laws is not a realistic objective in general and the impediments this conclusion may present to international trade must be addressed in some other way.

8.5. CONCLUSIONS

International environmental law and policy have become major influences on the content and direction of much national and EEC environmental

[44] 1986 Single European Act, Arts. 100a, 130s.

[45] See further Birnie and Boyle, *International Law and the Environment*, ch. 4.

law. Given the interdependent nature of much of the global environment, and the increasing globalization of the world economy, this is both inevitable and desirable. It allows the negotiation and development of rules and principles which reflect some degree of international consensus.

But it is clear that this consensus exists only at the level of very general principles, or in regard to a few very specific issues such as pollution from ships. The endorsement of sustainable development and the 'polluter pays' principle does not give clear guidance on the direction which national law must take, and does not necessarily serve as a vehicle for international harmonization of environmental law. Nor do multilateral regulatory treaties necessarily serve that purpose either. The consensual nature of the negotiating process and the need to promote widespread participation mean that international commitments on environmental matters will often conceal wide differences in policy and priorities and thus in the implementing legislation, if any. The harmonizing influence of international environmental law should not be overrated.

9

Environment and Trade: The GATT/WTO Regime in the International Legal System

BENEDICT KINGSBURY

9.1. INTRODUCTION

Connections between environmental protection and international trade have been recognized for many decades. In recent years the political rise of environmentalism has focused acute attention on possible conflicts between environment and trade values and rules. National environmental law has become more comprehensive and more central in most polities, and present or proposed measures of environmental protection often touch matters addressed by international trade rules. International environmental law has also developed rapidly, with little systematic consideration of its relation to existing or evolving rules of the international trading system. The ability of institutions engaged with the law and policy of international trade to take account of environmental law and policy has varied sharply. The principal global trade institution of the period since the Second World War has been the General Agreement on Tariffs and Trade (GATT), which has evolved considerably through practice and through formal agreements reached in eight negotiating rounds culminating in 1994 in the Uruguay Round agreements folding GATT into the newly established World Trade Organization (WTO). The inability of the GATT/WTO regime to adapt trade rules to take fuller account of emerging environmental concerns has led to present and potential conflicts, not only of policy but also of legal obligation. GATT and the WTO, which at last provides a regularized institutional structure to encompass the improvised arrangements crafted after the failure of the Havana Charter for an International Trade Organization to come into effect in 1948, face the challenge of developing agreement on accommodation of environmental objectives within the structure of the

Thanks to Daniel Bethlehem, Dan Esty, Tad Ferris, Arvind Subramanian, and Durwood Zaelke for help with sources, and to Jonathan Gluck of Duke Law School for excellent research assistance.

GATT/WTO trade rules, and of responding effectively to concerns about the adequacy of GATT/WTO institutions and procedures for dealing with trade–environment issues. Failure to find adequate means of reconciling the GATT/WTO trade regime with heightened environmental interests threatens both to obstruct the attainment of environmental and trade objectives and to add the sustained weight of the environmentalist lobby to the existing pressures on liberal international trade. This chapter examines the extent to which GATT/WTO law may conflict with environmental objectives, and considers possible strategies for reconciling such conflicts within existing institutional constraints.

The 1947 General Agreement on Tariffs and Trade, while raising no obstacle to many environmental initiatives states choose to take, contains no express reference to environmental objectives, and was crafted to accommodate only a limited range of trade–environment intersections. Supplemental agreements and other documents concluded over the following four decades made important contributions to the GATT system but for the most part treated environmental issues as peripheral. The Uruguay Round was already far advanced by 1991 when NGOs in the United States and elsewhere were galvanized by the report of the Dispute Settlement Panel upholding Mexico's complaint against a United States embargo on imports of tuna caught by vessels of countries with a high rate (measured by reference to United States practice) of incidental dolphin mortality.[1] Recognizing the serious political controversies and technical complexities of integrating environmental objectives into the trade package, as well as the risk of the Round collapsing under the weight of new issues, negotiators elected to postpone most of the difficult environmental issues. The Uruguay Round agreements concluded in April 1994 take only very limited account of environmental concerns, although their adoption was accompanied by proposals for the establishment of a Trade and Environment Committee in the WTO in which environmental issues could be further addressed.

It is not surprising that the GATT/WTO regime has had more diffi-

[1] *United States Restrictions on Imports of Tuna* (*Mexico* v. *USA*), GATT doc. DS 21/R, 30 *ILM* (1991), 1598. This panel report does not have direct legal effect, as it was not adopted by the GATT Council, principally because of US resistance combined with Mexico's political interest in finding other means to settle the dispute with the USA. However, discussions in the GATT Council indicated general support for the approaches taken in the report. The 1992 International Dolphin Conservation Act opened a means in US law for the executive branch to cease enforcing the US court-ordered but GATT-illegal embargo on Mexican tuna imposed under the Marine Mammal Protection Act, but the conditions set in the 1992 Act were onerous for Mexico or indeed for any of the harvesting nations affected by the MMPA embargo (Colombia, Mexico, Panama, and Venezuela). An operable agreement on reduction and monitoring of dolphin mortality was reached under the auspices of the Inter-American Tropical Tuna Commission in June 1992, but US law was not amended to reflect its terms. See generally S. Charnovitz, 'Environmentalism Confronts GATT Rules: Recent Developments and New Opportunities' (1993) 27 *JWT* 37–53.

culty in addressing trade–environment issues than regional institutions with much smaller and less diverse memberships. The greening of the European Community began with the adoption of the first environmental Action Plan in the aftermath of the 1972 Stockholm Conference, and has been implemented through amendments to the Treaty of Rome as well as numerous directives and other instruments in the environment field.[2] It has thus been possible for the EU simultaneously to address environment and trade issues with a degree of coherence, although this has by no means eliminated all conflicts between the different objectives. In the case of the North American Free Trade Agreement (NAFTA), the initial unwillingness of the parties to include provisions on environmental protection was overborne by an NGO-led political outcry in the United States. The 1992 NAFTA together with the 1993 North American Agreement on Environmental Co-operation do not themselves establish significant environmental standards, but they provide means to address several of the most contentious environment–trade problems,[3] and the 1993 Agreement provides for the establishment of a North American Commission for Environmental Co-operation with reasonably extensive powers to supervise enforcement of national environmental laws and to initiate and promote environmental co-operation.[4] The GATT/WTO regime has no authoritative source of substantive environmental standards to weigh alongside trade standards, only a politically limited and arduous process for making new rules, and a system of dispute settlement and supervision that has not hitherto been environment-oriented or as open as many environmentalists wish.

[2] See e.g. N. Haigh, 'The European Community and International Policy', in A. Hurrell and B. Kingsbury (eds.), *The International Politics of the Environment* (Oxford, 1992), 228–49; and the chapter by M. Brusasco Mackenzie in this volume.

[3] See C. Thomas and G. A. Tereposky, 'The NAFTA and the Side Agreement on Environmental Co-operation' (1993) 27 *JWT* 5–34. On NAFTA see R. B. Ludwiszewski, '"Green" Language in the NAFTA: Reconciling Free Trade and Environmental Protection' (1993) 27 *IL* 697–706.

[4] For the purposes of provisions requiring states parties to enforce effectively their environmental law, the 1993 North American Agreement on Environmental Co-operation (Article 45) stipulates: '"environmental law" means any statute or regulation of a Party, or provision thereof, the primary purpose of which is the protection of the environment, or the prevention of a danger to human life or health, through

(i) the prevention, abatement or control of the release, discharge, or emission of pollutants or environmental contaminants,

(ii) the control of environmentally hazardous or toxic chemicals, substances, materials and wastes, and the dissemination of information related thereto, or

(iii) the protection of wild flora or fauna, including endangered species, their habitat, and specially protected natural areas

in the Party's territory . . .' (Provisions directly related to worker safety or health, and certain provisions concerning natural resources, are expressly excluded.)

9.2. FRAMING THE ISSUES

The trade–environment debate spans a range of issues which at the operational level can only be analysed separately, although protagonists of particular positions often present a unified analysis in terms of compatibility with a free trade regime, economic efficiency, or the advancement of environmental goals. Trade–environment issues were canvassed extensively in the early 1970s,[5] and again at the end of the 1970s,[6] but the distinct and vociferous debate concerning GATT in the early 1990s was characterized by an initial absence of shared frames of reference, so that the formulation of the matters at issue was highly contentious. A series of broad policy questions underlies the debate: ought a state to be permitted to impose unilateral trade restrictions to promote that state's environmental objectives in the state's own territory or environment, in foreign states, in areas beyond national jurisdiction? Ought trade sanctions to be used to further the objectives of multilateral environmental agreements? Is differing willingness to suffer environmental degradation simply another aspect of comparative advantage, and even if not, is it susceptible to regulation? Ought states to be able to establish domestic environmental standards going beyond internationally agreed standards? Can conflicts between trade and environment objectives be addressed adequately within trade-oriented bodies such as GATT, or are new or reformed forums needed? Is 'environment' a discrete area in which special rules ought to apply, or will any environmental exceptions to free trade rules be a pretext and an inspiration for a disastrous cycle of protectionism? To what extent do the practicalities and limited capacities of any likely trade and environment law system necessitate use of environmentally or economically 'second-best' rules, and how much is lost by accepting these?

9.2.1. GATT/WTO Economic and Policy Approaches

For some diehard fundamentalists in each camp the conflict between environment and trade is at core one of irreducible basic values. The unreconstructed free trade view is that trade promotes economic growth and specialization and is either causally unrelated to environmental quality or is instrumental in environmental improvement through a positive

[5] See e.g. GATT, *Industrial Pollution Control and International Trade* (Geneva: GATT Studies in International Trade No. 1, 1971); W. J. Baumol, *Environmental Protection, International Spillovers and Trade* (Stockholm, 1971); OECD, Guiding Principles Concerning the International Economic Aspects of Environmental Policies (1972); and F. Kirgis, 'Effective Pollution Control in Industrialized Countries: International Economic Disincentives, Policy Responses, and the GATT' (1972) 70 *Mich. LR* 859.

[6] See e.g. S. Rubin (ed.), *Environment and Trade* (Totowa, NJ, 1982).

correlation between prosperity and environmental protection.[7] 'Environmental protection' is thus another problem of protectionism or subsidy. In its major 1992 report on the topic, the GATT Secretariat argued that sustainable development is not intrinsically linked to international trade, and that trade is simply a magnifier, enabling countries with adequate sustainable development policies to pursue these better.

> [I]f such policies are lacking, the country's international trade may contribute to a skewing of the country's development in an environmentally damaging direction, but then so will most of the other economic activities in the country. Clearly the correct action in such cases is to work for the adoption of an appropriate overall domestic environment policy, rather than focusing attention on problems that are allegedly trade-related.

Likewise 'unilateral restrictions on trade would never be the most efficient instrument for dealing with an environmental problem'.[8] Seeking to hold the purist line, the Secretariat blithely avoided the stark real-world problem of what is to be done where a government shows no interest in improving its environmental policy, or where more efficient instruments for dealing with environmental problems are not available.

While the position defended by the GATT Secretariat is extreme, it utilizes two distinct sets of arguments which are widely accepted among international trade practitioners: arguments drawn from standard economic and trade theory, and a set of arguments—or at least assumptions—about the international political and legal system and the nature of the GATT/WTO regime.

Standard economic theory analyses most environmental problems as cases of market failure,[9] or of erroneous government policy (e.g. tax

[7] The argument that the demand for environmental protection, and eventually the standard of national environmental protection in any particular country, rises with income, is often presented as a truism, with little discussion of the evidence as to conditions under which it does or does not apply. See e.g. G. Feketekuty, 'The Link Between Trade and Environmental Policy' (1993) 2 *Minn. JGT* 171 at 179. The few research papers on the subject, of which the most discussed is G. M. Grossman and A. B. Krueger, *Environmental Impacts of a North American Free Trade Agreement* (Princeton, NJ: Working Paper, 1991), deal only with particular types of environmental degradation in particular settings. While the effective demand for, or at least delivery of, certain forms of environmental protection is highest in the richest countries, the process of attaining such levels of prosperity may have massive environmental effects. The essential problem of sustainable development is how to attain and maintain acceptable levels of prosperity worldwide without disastrous environmental degradation. As Jagdish Bhagwati points out, growth is not *tightly linked* to either the improvement of the environment or its degradation. 'Trade and the Environment: The False Conflict?', in D. Zaelke, P. Orbuch, and R. F. Housman (eds.), *Trade and the Environment: Law, Economics, and Policy* (Washington, DC, 1993), 159 at 163.

[8] GATT Secretariat, *Trade and the Environment* (Geneva: GATT, 1992, advance copy), 3, 4.

[9] See e.g. W. J. Baumol and W. E. Oates, *The Theory of Environmental Policy*, 3rd edn. (Cambridge, 1988); and K. Anderson, 'The Standard Welfare Economics of Policies Affecting Trade and the Environment', in K. Anderson and R. Blackhurst (eds.), *The Greening of World Trade Issues* (London, 1992), 25.

subsidies for deforestation to establish unproductive cattle ranches).[10] A major contribution of economics has been the elaboration and comparative appraisal of means to overcome market failure, including establishment of property rights, Pigouvian taxes and subsidies, user charges, tradable permits, consumer information schemes, and incentives for reuse or recycling.[11] Economic criteria point to the advantages, in some situations, of: market measures over command-and-control regulation;[12] performance standards over technology standards;[13] and intervention to internalize externalities as close as possible to the source of the externality.[14] These criteria show many proposed trade interventions to be inefficient compared to other strategies.

The principle of gains from trade arising from comparative advantage is at the heart of trade theory. Trade restrictions or obligatory harmonization measures designed to eliminate environmental comparative advantage are thus suspect *per se* and because of their likely failure to take account of relevant differences in such matters as environmental conditions, absorptive capacities, and social time preferences. A related political concern is that if societal environmental choices are not treated as an aspect of legitimate comparative advantage, pressure will mount to allow trade restrictions to compensate for differences in such matters as labour rights, wage levels, social policies, and population policy, and

[10] H. Binswanger, 'Brazilian Policies that Encourage Deforestation in the Amazon' (1991) 19 *WD* 821–9.

[11] See e.g. A. Carlin, *The United States Experience with Economic Incentives to Control Environmental Pollution* (1992); R. Hahn and R. Stavins, 'Incentive-Based Environmental Regulation: A New Era from an Old Idea?' (1991) 18 *ELQ* 1; T. R. Muzando, K. M. Miranda, and A. L. Bovenberg, *Public Policy and the Environment: A Survey of the Literature* (Washington, DC: IMF Fiscal Affairs Department Working Paper 90/56, 1990); P. Kågeson, *Economic Instruments in European Environmental Policy* (Stockholm: European Environmental Bureau, 1993); and U. Steger *et al.*, *Economic Instruments in EC Environment Policy* (Brussels: Centre for European Policy Studies Working Party Report No. 8, 1993).

[12] The actual use of market-based interventions has been limited, and has often been weakened by preferences for revenue collection over efficiency. State authorities have incentives to prefer command-and-control mechanisms, which preserve greater roles and discretion for agencies, are more saleable to the public as effective state action, may be more precise in their effects, and may create barriers to market entry or otherwise advantage certain subjects of the regulations. Commenting on this experience, World Bank economists Patrick Low and Raed Safadi acknowledge that a 'preponderance of nonmarket approaches in the domestic context does raise the question of how successfully efficient solutions to environmental problems with international dimensions can be promoted.' 'Trade Policy and Pollution', in P. Low (ed.), *International Trade and the Environment* (Washington, DC: 1992), 29–53 at 34.

[13] Uruguay Round Agreement on Technical Barriers to Trade, Art. 2.8.

[14] A. Subramanian, 'Trade Measures for Environment: A Nearly Empty Box?' (1992) 15 *WE* 135 at 144.

comparative advantage as a basis for trade will be severely eroded.[15] This slippery slope argument is inevitably a matter of impression.[16]

A view strongly pressed by GATT officials and some trade economists is that a sharp distinction must be drawn between environmental problems that are intrinsically international because their effects spill over borders, and environmental problems that are intrinsically domestic.[17] This distinction is in some cases a proxy for economic efficiency, but it appears to be based on a prudential view about the desirability of national autonomy and the hazards for trade of interfering with it rather than on considerations of economic efficiency. Proponents of such a distinction argue that international trade measures should never be employed in response to purely domestic environmental policies of another country. Use of the domestic/transborder distinction is illustrated by the following taxonomy of environment-related trade measures developed by Arvind Subramanian, a former GATT economist.[18] This taxonomy posits a tripartite division of trade measures: trade measures intended to have a direct impact on the perceived environmental problem; trade measures taken in direct support of a different measure directed at the environmental problem; and trade measures (sanctions or incentives)

[15] The strongest pressure is for trade restrictions intended to compensate for alleged inadequacies in labour rights in other states. See generally S. Charnowitz, 'Environmental and Labour Standards in Trade' (1992) 15 *WE* 335–56. The Havana Charter included a provision on labour rights, and the issue was addressed in relation to NAFTA in the 1993 North American Agreement on Labour Co-operation. President Clinton suggested in 1994 that labour rights ought to be addressed in post-Uruguay Round GATT/WTO negotiations, and received some guarded support from the European Union. On US unilateral trade measures in connection with labour rights, and the discrepancies between the standards applied by the US and international standards established by the ILO and other bodies, see P. Alston, 'Labour Rights Provisions in US Trade Law: "Aggressive Unilateralism"?' (1993) 15 *HRQ* 1–35. An early GATT Dispute Settlement Panel found that a Belgian tax levied only on products of countries which lacked a system of family allowances similar to Belgium's involved breach of the most-favoured-nation rule; however, the finding against Belgium was influenced by Belgium's egregious inconsistency in the actual application of the tax. *Belgium: Family Allowances* (*Norway and Denmark* v. *Belgium*), BISD 1 Supp., 59 (1953).

[16] Many argue that the GATT/WTO system is fully capable of drawing necessary lines if these are warranted. Some environmentalists point to the absence of slippery-slope consequences from the GATT exception for restrictions on products produced by prisoners, while also relying on this exception as a precedent for an environmental exception.

[17] Bhagwati, 'Trade and the Environment: The False Conflict?', 164; Subramanian, 'Trade Measures for Environment: A Nearly Empty Box?'; P. Sorsa, 'GATT and Environment: Basic Issues and Some Developing Country Concerns', in P. Low (ed.), *International Trade and the Environment*, 325 at 326.

[18] The following classification and examples are based upon Subramanian, 'Trade Measures for Environment: A Nearly Empty Box?', 136 ff. This is set forth as 'an exhaustive taxonomy of the interactions between trade policy and environmental problems' from a GATT viewpoint. Another trade-oriented taxonomy is in T. J. Schoenbaum, 'Free International Trade and Protection of the Environment: Irreconcilable Conflict?' (1992) 86 *AJIL* 700–27.

intended to change environmental behaviour which is essentially unrelated to the trade measure.

9.2.1.1. Trade Measures which Directly Affect the Perceived Environmental Problem

1. Examples of trade measures intended directly to affect transboundary environmental issues include the United States' ban on import of tuna caught with a high incidental impact on dolphins, the EC's ban (from 1 January 1995) on fur imports from countries which do not prohibit leg-hold traps, the Basle Convention ban on unauthorized trade in hazardous wastes, and possibly the multilateral ban on trade in products from endangered species, e.g. ivory.

2. Examples of such measures intended to protect the domestic environment are proposals to levy countervailing duties on products benefiting from production in countries with low environmental standards (thus levelling the playing-field for domestic producers complying with high standards), and proposals to permit domestic subsidies of pollution abatement as non-countervailable.

9.2.1.2. Trade Measures which Support and Make Effective Related Environmental Actions

The most prominent multilateral examples are the provisions of the Montreal Protocol banning trade in ozone-depleting substances with non-parties. One purpose of these is to ensure that restrictions on consumption and production among parties are not circumvented. However, certain Montreal Protocol provisions shade into category 9.2.1.3 below as they involve some restrictions not directly related to consumption or production volumes which are to some extent intended to pressure (or encourage) non-party states to become parties in order to preserve competitiveness and prevent free-riding. Other supporting provisions include Danish requirements that foreign beverage exporters participate in Danish recycling schemes, and Ontario's levy on beer cans to support recycling and encourage use of refillable containers.

9.2.1.3. Trade Sanctions or Incentives used Instrumentally to Promote Acceptance of Non-Directly-Related Environmental Policies

1. Sanctions or incentives in essentially unrelated areas used to affect the policies of others on transboundary environmental issues include: the United States Pelly and Packwood-Magnuson Amendments used to limit fish imports from countries undermining other ocean-life regimes (e.g. concerning whales, sea turtles, driftnet bans, etc.); United States' threats of trade retaliation against the EC if the EC did not change its rules and

accept beef containing artificial hormones; the possibility of Montreal Protocol parties banning imports of products made by the use of CFCs from non-parties (e.g. consideration in Japan of restrictions on South Korean semiconductors before South Korea became a party to the Protocol in 1992); and the mixture of incentives (market access) and sanctions (fines/loss of privileges) for establishing and complying with environmental standards under NAFTA and the 1993 environmental side agreement.

2. Sanctions or incentives relating to domestic environmental issues overlap with category (1): e.g. trade sanctions to force another country to raise, lower, or harmonize its environmental standards may in effect level the playing-field for domestic producers in the domestic market, in the market of the target country, and in third markets.

This taxonomy exemplifies the problems of categorization in trade–environment issues. The transboundary/domestic distinction is problematic: many of the measures categorized as dealing with transboundary effects will simultaneously have major domestic environmental implications, and vice versa, and some of the transboundary effects of controversial environmental policies are non-physical and difficult to locate spatially. The threefold division based on the nature of the measures is also problematic in assuming away difficult questions of characterization: does the context of a trade measure affect its categorization? Is a measure to be classified by reference to the intent of the state, and if not, what objective criteria apply and who is to apply them? The taxonomy is presented with a mixture of efficiency, equity, and policy arguments: different environmentalist opponents would challenge individual elements, the mixture of arguments, and the whole analytical framework. However, Subramanian's conclusions are widely held among trade economists: that the only types of trade intervention which may be justified are a limited group of measures in category 9.2.1.2 above, namely multilateral measures to promote participation in and compliance with agreements addressing transborder environmental issues; unilateral trade sanctions are inequitable and adverse to low-income countries; trade measures intended to protect the domestic environment are flawed because they are directed at negating comparative advantage; trade measures to address transborder environmental problems are generally inefficient instruments for correcting the underlying market failure.[19] A variant is offered by Jagdish Bhagwati, who shares the view of most economists that trade restrictions imposed on products produced by processes creating cross-border physical spillovers affected the imported state (e.g. air pollution) are inefficient compared to such measures as taxes on the

[19] Subramanian, 'Trade Measures for Environment: A Nearly Empty Box?', 151.

producers, but argues that such restrictions must be accepted as a second-best alternative provided the restrictions are scientifically supportable, imposed for legitimate environmental reasons, and the least damaging to trade of the available options.[20]

As the analyses of Subramanian and Bhagwati illustrate, classical economic theory is only a part of the provenance of the GATT/WTO position on trade and environment. A number of assumptions about the international political and legal system are also embedded in the rules and practice of the GATT/WTO regime.

First, the GATT/WTO system treats territory as the basis for jurisdiction regardless of the transboundary or extra-jurisdictional dimension of many environmental and economic interests. Analyses by GATT staff try to distinguish between actions taken by a state to protect its own domestic environment from domestic production or the consumption of domestically produced or imported products, which are broadly permitted under GATT, and trade actions intended to shape the environmental policies of other countries, which in many cases are not permitted under GATT.[21]

Second, the GATT/WTO regime assumes that political processes within each state will determine the best combination of environmental and other policies for that state. This preference for national sovereignty over foreign or international interference is unsurprising in an intergovernmental institution, but there are a number of arguments in support of such an approach. Adherence to the GATT/WTO regime would be weakened if sovereign competence were routinely displaced in the environmental area. Trade pressure to take environmental measures may create domestic distortions, conflicts of external conditions, and half-hearted commitments, especially where internationally agreed standards do not exist or are not widely observed. State sovereignty and political autonomy are popular aspirations in many countries, and have intrinsic moral value and instrumental utility which is often neglected in interventionist declamations.[22] On the other hand, national sovereignty frequently excludes from the decision process people who suffer the effects of transborder spillovers, and the range of people claiming to be affected by such spillovers is becoming very wide, especially where it is argued that non-physical spillovers create a legitimate interest. Even apart from spillovers, standard human rights arguments and increasingly popular versions of

[20] J. Bhagwati, 'Trade and the Environment: The False Conflict?', 183–8.

[21] Tuna–Dolphin Panel Report, DS21 (1991), paras 6.2–6.3; GATT Secretariat, *Trade and the Environment*, 8–12. There are a number of exceptions and limitations to these propositions, some of which are discussed below.

[22] See A. Hurrell and B. Kingsbury, 'The International Politics of the Environment: An Introduction', in Hurrell and Kingsbury (eds.), *The International Politics of the Environment*, 1–50 at 7–8.

environmental ethics favour recognition of some foreign interest in how a state manages its own domestic environment. With or without spillovers, a rule of abstinence in favour of sovereign decision-making does nothing to address the 'political failures' which may be just as damaging as 'market failures'.

Third, the practice and rhetoric of the GATT/WTO system are predicated on the general undesirability of using trade restrictions not permitted under existing GATT rules to pursue environmental objectives. In many cases there are sound economic reasons to reject trade restrictions employed in pursuit of environmental aims. The GATT/WTO system does not weigh environmental and trade objectives case by case on a neutral scale, however. As indicated in the section on GATT law below, in some situations environmental justifications count for less than the application of trade rules. Yet, as Robert Repetto argues:

> From an economic perspective, neither trade liberalization nor environmental protection are inherently or inevitably more important. The measurable efficiency gains from trade liberalization have usually been estimated to be in the range of 1 to 2 per cent of GDP. Similarly, the costs of environmental controls and the residual economic losses from environmental damages are both typically 1 to 2 per cent of GDP in countries with strong environmental policies, and 3 to 5 per cent in countries with weaker policies. Therefore, there is no strong economic case that trade policy should take precedence over environmental policy, or vice versa.[23]

The result of economic analysis, assumptions made in the GATT/WTO system, and the institutional commitment to uphold the present international trade rules, is that the trade community tends to frame trade–environment issues as those situations in which environmental arguments are adduced to support a restriction on free trade.

9.2.2. Environmental Critiques

Some radical ecological views hold that in so far as the liberal trade system promotes economic growth, specialization, and integration of local economies into global markets, it runs counter to the ecologically preferred objectives of autarky and decentralization.[24] Thus tinkering with liberal trade rules may effect mild improvements but will not reach any of the fundamental ecological issues. The utter conflict between this view and that of state trade representatives is illustrated by the artful preamble of the 1994 Agreement Establishing the World Trade Organization, in which the parties recognize that

[23] See R. Repetto, 'Complementarities between Trade and Environment Policies', in Zaelke *et al.* (eds.), *Trade and the Environment*, 237–46 at 238.

[24] Cf. C. Hines, *The New Protectionism* (London, 1993).

their relations in the field of trade and economic endeavour should be conducted with a view to raising standards of living, ensuring full employment and a large and steadily growing volume of real income and effective demand, and expanding the production and trade in goods and services, while allowing for the optimal use of the world's resources in accordance with the objective of sustainable development, seeking both to protect and preserve the environment and enhance the means for doing so in a manner consistent with their respective needs and concerns at different levels of development.

Many environmentalists do not adopt the radical ecological antipathy to the pursuit of economic growth and global market integration, but are nevertheless critical of the absence of real linkage between the trade regime and such values as sustainable development, elimination of environmental externalities, environmentally conscious pricing, and recognition of the interests of future generations.[25] Environmental critiques of the GATT Secretariat's *Trade and the Environment* report criticize the promotion of freer trade without concomitant measures to promote full internalization of environmental costs, and emphasize that trade liberalization without internalization of environmental and resource costs exacerbates adverse environmental impacts and to that extent is not intrinsically desirable.[26] A more fundamental critique of neo-classical economics by Herman Daly argues that growth models have depended upon constantly increasing throughput, but that this cannot be sustained in a 'full world' where natural capital is limited and is not fully substitutable by human capital.[27] While trade can increase resource efficiency through specialization,

trade does postpone the day when countries must face up to the discipline of living within natural regenerative and absorptive capacities, and by doing that probably serves on balance to increase throughput growth and environmental degradation. Free trade also introduces greater spatial separation between the production benefits and the environmental costs of throughput growth, making it more difficult for the latter to temper the growth of the former.[28]

There are thus wide variations in the way self-identified environmentalists frame environment–trade issues. The central concern is that the

[25] See e.g. World Bank, *World Development Report 1992: Development and the Environment* (Oxford, 1992); and a critical review by L. Taylor, 'The World Bank and the Environment: The World Development Report 1992' (1993) 21 *WD* 869–81.

[26] C. Arden-Clarke, *The General Agreement on Tariffs and Trade, Environmental Protection and Sustainable Development* (Gland: WWF, 1991), 10–11. See also P. L. Lallas, D C. Esty, and D. J. van Hoogstraten, 'Environmental Protection and International Trade: Toward Mutually Supportive Rules and Policies' (1992) 16 *Harv. ELR* 271 at 318–23.

[27] See Daly's contribution to R. Goodland, H. Daly, S. el Serafy, and B. von Droste (eds.), *Environmentally Sustainable Development: Building on Brundtland* (Paris, 1992).

[28] H. Daly, 'Problems With Free Trade: Neoclassical and Steady-State Perspectives', in Zaelke, Orbuch, and Housman (eds.), *Trade and the Environment*, 147 at 156.

adverse consequences of inadequacies of environmental protection are intensified by trade. More specific concerns are that the GATT/WTO regime, through its direct rules or through its promotion of competition for markets, exacerbates pressure on countries to lower their own environmental standards, and that the regime obstructs the use of trade sanctions or incentives to achieve environmental goals. Proposals span the spectrum from rethinking the entire economic and political basis of international trade to modest post-Uruguay Round amendments to GATT.

9.2.3. Developing-Country Critiques

A different set of concerns has been raised by a number of developing countries, which suspect that environmental exceptions to liberal trade rules will in many cases inhibit economic development of the South, and may further legitimize Northern involvement in matters of Southern sovereignty. The practical experience of many developing countries has included actual or threatened reductions of trade gains because of environmental trade measures taken by developed countries. Developing countries have strong environmental interests, and in some cases wish themselves to take environmental measures affecting trade. Many have benefited from improved environmental technology or other advances made in the North. Nevertheless, they rightly perceive the current proposals to alter trade rules to have been raised and structured primarily in OECD countries and to express particular Northern environmental concerns. Sorsa articulates a view widely held in developing countries:

> GATT rules can protect them from new forms of protectionism under the guise of environmental policy, reinforce the respect of sovereignty in trade relations and shift emphasis from the use of trade sanctions to negotiations and creation of incentives in promoting the adoption of environmental policies worldwide. The rule-based multilateral system protects the interests of small countries against power-based unilateral policing by large countries.[29]

These misgivings about legalization of more restrictive environment-related trade measures parallel concerns developing countries have had about international environmental standard-setting since before the Stockholm Conference, with an intensified contemporary concern about Northern unilateralism in environmental policymaking and enforcement. The problems of promoting and achieving 'sustainable development' are much wider than those of accommodating trade and environmental

[29] Sorsa, 'GATT and Environment: Basic Issues and Developing Country Concerns', 326. For the illustrative views of a Thai government official, see K. Kittichaisaree, 'Using Trade Sanctions and Subsidies to Achieve Environmental Objectives in the Pacific Rim' (1993) 4 *Col. JIELP* 296.

agendas, and are likely to prove more intractable and more serious.[30] The extent to which a functional consensus can be hammered out on the meaning and implications of 'sustainable development' will have a considerable bearing on global trade–environment negotiations. The historical pattern is that developing countries, and NGOs from such countries, are able to secure hortatory provisions and rhetorical recognition of their positions, but that the substantive outcomes are heavily influenced by the North. The GATT/WTO trade–environment debate may have a slightly different dynamic, however, as the developing countries collectively have some commonality of interest and in many cases take positions close to the status quo, whereas Northern states have a revisionist agenda and complex interests influenced by competing pressures in domestic politics.

9.2.4. Legal Perspectives

Within the mainstream of the debate as presently constituted, there is reasonably wide acceptance that trade may have positive or negative environmental implications, that environmental policies may affect trade, that effective means to address and minimize conflicts are necessary, and that complementarities ought to be utilized and developed where possible.[31] Beyond this useful but limited core of agreement, however, the differences remain pronounced. In significant part these are differences of outlook and values between the newly connecting trade and environment commu-

[30] These fundamental issues are addressed in Alan Boyle's chapter in this volume, and for that reason will not be discussed here.

[31] A useful attempt to build dialogue and develop procedural and substantive guidelines is taking place in the OECD. Procedural issues were addressed first. In June 1993 an OECD Ministerial Meeting endorsed a joint report of the Trade and Environment Committees in which four procedural guidelines were enunciated: (1) *Transparency and Consultation*; governments should provide for transparency and for consultation with interested parties in the development of trade and environmental policies with potentially significant effects on each other. (2) *Trade and Environmental Examinations, Reviews, and Follow-Up*; governments should examine or review trade and environmental policies and agreements with potentially significant effects on the other policy area early in their development to assess the implication for the other policy area and to identify alternative policy options for addressing concerns. Governments may co-operate in undertaking such examinations and reviews. Governments should follow up as appropriate to implement policy options; to re-examine the policies, agreements, and any measures in place; and to address any concerns identified in the conclusion of such re-examinations. (3) *International Environmental Co-operation;* governments should co-operate to address transboundary, regional, and global environmental concerns, in particular through the negotiation and implementation of environmental policies and agreements among the countries concerned, with a view to enhancing the effectiveness of environmental action and avoiding undue effects on trade. (4) *Dispute Settlement*; when, pursuant to an agreement between countries, a country is a party to a trade dispute which has an environmental dimension, the government, in developing the national approach, should recognize the importance of taking into account as appropriate, environmental, trade, scientific, and other relevant expertise and should therefore work further to develop, as necessary, appropriate means to assure transparency.

nities. A widely held view among trade professionals is that many environmentalist objections to trade rules are misconceived or pernicious, and that such genuine problems as remain can be dealt with by modest changes in GATT/WTO rules, interpretations, and procedures.[32] At the legal level some of the conflicts are more serious than this analysis suggests, although the conflicts would be more severe if international environmental rules and institutions were not still fragmentary in comparison to the unified and broad structure of GATT/WTO rules and institutions. At the policy level the environmental pressure on trade rules and institutions is likely to be much greater than some in the trade community are willing to recognize; this will have significant legal implications in the future.

The functions of law in the trade–environment area are nuanced and complex. One ideal of law is as the effectual embodiment of policy decisions. In reality, however, the lack of co-ordination between trade and environmental policy-making has prevented the development of a structured legal relationship between these fields. One practical function of law is therefore to contribute to an accommodation, however *ad hoc* and unstable, between the different normative and institutional systems in order to minimize the disruptive effects of conflicts. GATT has the deeper historical entrenchment, even if doubts have periodically been voiced about the adequacy of its adaptation to the increased globalization of markets, the mobility of capital, and changes in the roles and concerns of governments.[33] The GATT/WTO institutional structure, while unsatisfactory from the viewpoint of many environmentalists, does have the capability to address these normative conflicts and to take dispositive decisions. International environmental rules have not been made in an integrated manner comparable to those of the GATT/WTO regime, and many important environmental policy principles are not directly implemented by international legal rules of general application. International environmental institutions are for the most part not in a position to address trade–environment conflicts in a quasi-adjudicative manner. Although the International Court of Justice in 1993 established a chamber to deal with environmental disputes, dispute settlement bodies of general international competence (i.e. excepting the European Court of Justice, and US–Canada Free Trade Agreement or NAFTA panels) have not yet addressed environment-trade conflicts. Policy problems concerning trade and the environment are now being examined in many forums, but the principal practical forum for legal conflicts in this field remains

[32] See e.g. D. Palmeter, 'Environment and Trade: Much Ado About Little?' (1993) 27 *JWT* 55–70.

[33] See e.g. H. Daly and J. Cobb, *For the Common Good: Redirecting the Economy Toward Community, the Environment and a Sustainable Future* (Boston, 1989).

the GATT/WTO system. The substantive rules applied by that system, and the institutional problems of the system in dealing with trade–environment conflicts, are considered in the following sections.

9.3. GATT/WTO OBLIGATIONS AND THE ENVIRONMENT

The legal structure of the GATT/WTO regime, and the nature of its institutional dynamics, shape and channel the broader policy issues. Within the structure of GATT/WTO law, trade–environment problems have been translated and re-expressed as a series of specific issues, including: interpretation of the exceptions to GATT obligations contained in Article XX, which must be undertaken in conjunction with interpretation of the core GATT rules concerning most-favoured-nation and national treatment; the compatibility with the Agreement on Technical Barriers to Trade (the Standards Code), and with the Agreement on the Application of Sanitary and Phyto-Sanitary Measures, of national product standards used to give effect to environmental or health concerns; the possibility of treating environmental externalities as subsidies to which countervailing duties might be applied by the importing state; interpretive means of resolving conflicts between GATT obligations and the obligations of states under environmental treaties and customary international law; the desirability of the GATT Council waiving GATT obligations under Article XXV where there might be a conflict between GATT and a multilateral environmental treaty; the desirability and feasibility of amending GATT to take account of certain environmental concerns; and the desirability of improving the transparency, openness, and environmental sensitivity of the GATT rule-making and dispute settlement process.

This section will examine the points of collision between trade and environment in the light of the specific rules of the GATT/WTO regime. Subsequent sections will consider whether GATT/WTO institutions are a necessary or appropriate forum in which to address these issues.

9.3.1. History of GATT and WTO

The use of trade restrictions to achieve environmental objectives, and the use of environmental arguments to justify protectionist measures, were common in the period of international institutional development from about the 1870s.[34] For example, the problem of occupational disease arising in the *production* (not consumption) of white phosphorus matches was addressed by a treaty in 1906 banning the production and importation of

[34] See generally S. Charnovitz, 'Exploring the Environmental Exceptions in GATT Article XX' (1991) 25 *JWT* 37–55.

such matches, in order to level the playing-field for manufacturers to switch to producing more costly matches which posed less risk to workers.[35] Conservation of fur seals was promoted by a 1911 treaty banning pelagic sealing (a wasteful method which reduced the proportion of females), together with a commitment not to import furs taken contrary to the treaty.[36] Unilateral measures were also taken against imports with a view to securing environmental objectives, including United States and British legislation prohibiting the importation of plumes and feathers of certain wild birds threatened by the demands of milliners.[37] An unsuccessful precursor to GATT was the 1927 International Convention for the Abolition of Import and Export Prohibitions and Restrictions; this was one of several multilateral and bilateral treaties used as a source of textual formulations in the negotiations leading to the adoption of GATT, including Article XX.

GATT was agreed in 1947, and was brought into force by a protocol of provisional application ahead of the anticipated establishment of an International Trade Organization (ITO). The Charter for the ITO was adopted at the 1948 Havana conference, but the charter did not enter into force, principally because of United States congressional opposition. The GATT 1947 thus operates as an international treaty, with a limited institutional structure (e.g. the GATT Council, in which most but not all of the 117 GATT member states have chosen to participate) established as an overlay. Further instruments adopted within the GATT framework (including the Standards Code adopted in the Tokyo Round) depended on voluntary adhesion by member states, and were in fact accepted by only limited numbers of member states (the problem of GATT à la carte). One of the problems of this patchwork of rules has been that states voluntarily accepting further legal restrictions on their trade policies may be forced by the GATT most-favoured-nation rule to confer the benefits of such restrictions on other states which have not themselves accepted such restrictions.

The Uruguay Round agreements regularized the institutional arrangements by creating the WTO, which operates through a biennial Ministerial Conference and a standing General Council. The General Council superintends the Dispute Settlement Body and numerous specialized

[35] Level playing-field issues, including concern that industries would migrate to sources of cheap labour in Asia, were frequently raised in the early twentieth century by European governments as arguments against proposals for international minimum wage or working hours and conditions standards. Another principal objection was that intergovernmental discussion of such issues intruded upon national sovereignty.

[36] See M. J. Peterson, 'International Fisheries Management', in P. Haas, M. Levy, and R. Keohane (eds.), *Institutions for the Earth: Sources of Effective International Protection* (Cambridge, Mass., 1993), 249–305.

[37] Charnovitz, 'Exploring the Environmental Exceptions in GATT Article XX', 40, cites the US Underwood Tariff Act 1913, 38 Stat. 114, as an example.

councils and committees, including the Trade and Environment Committee established with an initial two-year work programme. The Uruguay Round agreements took a strong position against free-riding by integrating most of the major agreements into a single package binding on all members, and broadly confining rights under the non-package plurilateral agreements to those states becoming parties to them.[38] The agreements rest on acceptance by states in the standard manner rather than any system of provisional application. GATT 1994, which is an annexe to the WTO Agreement, is the same in its substantive provisions as GATT 1947, but most of the other agreements annexed to the WTO Agreement are new or differ from their precursors.

9.3.2. Interpretation of Article XX Exceptions to GATT Obligations

GATT establishes a number of fundamental rules including: most-favoured-nation treatment; the obligation to treat imported products in the same way as like domestic products, and not to apply internal rules concerning products so as to afford protection to domestic production; and a general prohibition on quantitative restrictions on imports. Each of these rules is subject to certain limits on its range of application, and some are subject to specific exceptions stated along with the rule. GATT also includes general exceptions to the obligations established by the agreement, including Article XX, which has received considerable scrutiny in the trade and environment debates.

Article XX provides:

> Subject to the requirement that such measures are not applied in a manner which would constitute a means of arbitrary or unjustifiable discrimination between countries where the same conditions prevail, or a disguised restriction on international trade, nothing in this Agreement shall be construed to prevent the adoption or enforcement by any contracting party of measures:
>
> (a) necessary to protect public morals;
> (b) necessary to protect human, animal or plant life or health;
> (d) necessary to secure compliance with laws or regulations which are not inconsistent with the provisions of this Agreement, including those relating to customs enforcement, the enforcement of monopolies operated under paragraph 4 of Article II and Article XVII, the protection of patents, trade marks and copyrights, and the prevention of deceptive practices;
> (e) relating to the products of prison labour;
> (f) imposed for the protection of national treasures of artistic, historic or archaeological value;

[38] 1994 Agreement Establishing the World Trade Organization, Art. II.

(g) relating to the conservation of exhaustible natural resources if such measures are made effective in conjunction with restrictions on domestic production or consumption;
(h) undertaken in pursuance of obligations under any intergovernmental commodity agreement which conforms . . .

Formally reports of Dispute Settlement Panels do not create binding precedents, but references by panels to earlier reports have become increasingly frequent as the quality of legal reasoning in panel reports has risen. The principal issues which have arisen with respect to interpretation of the text of Article XX include the following:[39]

'arbitrary or unjustifiable discrimination': This clause preserves the general GATT commitment to non-discrimination, and is a potential restraint on attempts to combine environmental restrictions on trade with other political or economic objectives. Questions as to whether the same conditions exist and, if so, what forms of discrimination would be arbitrary or unjustified, are potentially problematic, particularly as in some cases the onus of demonstrating that a measure is justified under Article XX appears to rest on the party relying on it. However, these issues have not yet been central to the reasoning of any Dispute Settlement Panel. It is well established that facially neutral provisions may still be discriminatory.

'disguised restriction on international trade': This clause might have provided an important check on abusive use of Article XX, although the substantive criteria which a panel might use in determining that a measure was a disguised restriction would admittedly be difficult to formulate and apply fairly. Panels have avoided these difficulties by interpreting the requirement simply as a formal one of public proclamation of the relevant restrictions.[40] This narrow interpretation is now well established, although there are strong arguments for a broader interpretation in the future.

'measures': There has been some confusion in Panel reports as to whether the 'measures' requiring justification under Article XX are the specific restrictions on trade or the broader national legislation employed by a state as the basis for such restrictions. It now appears that both the underlying legislation and the specific application of it must be

[39] See generally Charnovitz, 'Exploring the Environmental Exceptions in GATT Article XX', at 47–55; J. Klabbers, 'Jurisprudence in International Trade Law: Article XX of GATT' (1992) 26 *JWT* 63–94; P. L. Lallas, D. C. Esty, and D. J. van Hoogstraten, 'Environmental Protection and International Trade: Toward Mutually Supportive Rules and Policies', 275–95; P. Sorsa, 'GATT and Environment' (1992) 15 *WE* 115–33; Sorsa, 'GATT and Environment: Basic Issues and Some Developing Country Concerns', in Low (ed.), *International Trade and the Environment*.

[40] United States: *Prohibition on Imports of Tuna and Tuna Products from Canada* (*Canada* v. *USA*), BISD 29 Supp., 91 (1982); United States: *Imports of Certain Automotive Spring Assemblies* (*Canada* v. *USA*), BISD 30 Supp., 107.

considered.[41] The measures in question are those restricting trade, not the policy objectives set forth in the lettered clauses of Article XX.

'necessary': The necessity requirement applies to clauses (a), (b), and (d) although not to clauses (e)–(h). Case-law indicates that it is up to the state concerned to determine what level of protection is required for, for example, plant health. Panels are apparently unwilling to second-guess states on such issues.[42] Panels are, however, willing to consider whether the particular measure was necessary to attain the level of protection sought by the state.[43] They have indicated that the necessity requirement precludes infringement of GATT obligations where a non-infringing means of attaining the same object would also have been available. This has been extended to holdings that Article XX permits adoption only of the least GATT-infringing measure where a choice of GATT-infringing means of attaining the objective was open.[44] Very little guidance has yet been offered as to how to compare, for instance, a violation of Article XI with a violation of Article III, and there are strong arguments that the familiar GATT 'least trade-restrictive' principle ought to operate in these Article XX cases.[45] The GATT case-law does not yet formally apply a principle of proportionality to the question of what is 'necessary'. In this respect it differs from the jurisprudence of the European Court of Justice on comparable issues under the Treaty of Rome. In the *Danish Bottles Case* the ECJ appeared to accept that it was up to Denmark to determine what level of reutilization of bottles the society required, and applied a proportionality test in evaluating the Danish deposit-and-return scheme against the Danish objective. The Danish rules about approval of containers, however, were evaluated for proportionality with environmental protection in general, rather than simply with the Danish reutilization objective.[46] In

[41] *United States: Section 337 of the Tariff Act 1930* (*Akzo*), BISD 36 Supp., 345 (1989). This report differs on significant points from an earlier and much-criticized report on Section 337: *United States: Imports of Certain Automotive Spring Assemblies*, BISD 30 Supp., 107 (1983).

[42] See esp. *United States: Restrictions on Imports of Tuna*, DS 21/R (1991), para. 5.27.

[43] See e.g. *United States: Section 337 of the Tariff Act 1930* (*Akzo*), BISD 36 Supp., 345 at 392 (1989).

[44] *USA: Section 337 of the Tariff Act 1930* (*EC* v. *USA*), BISD 36 Supp., 345; *Thailand: Restrictions on Importation of and Internal Taxes on Cigarettes* (*USA* v. *Thailand*), BISD 37 Supp., 200.

[45] Cf. *Landing Requirements for Pacific Salmon and Herring*, US–Canada Free Trade Agreement Panel Report, 19 Oct. 1989, interpreting Article XX(g) (which applied by virtue of the FTA) as establishing a least-trade-restrictive test.

[46] *Commission* v. *Denmark* (1988) ECR 4607. See L. Kramer, 'Environmental Protection and Article 30', *CMLR* (1993), 111 at 123; and more generally J. Cameron and J. Robinson 'The Use of Trade Provisions in International Environmental Agreements and their Compatibility with the GATT' (1992) 2 *Yb. IEL* 3–30 at 25–9. The ECJ did not treat the case as turning on the apparently discriminatory effect of the deposit-and-return requirement on exporters to Denmark. See D. Gerardin, 'Free Trade and Environmental Protection in an Integrated Market: A Survey of the Case Law of the United States Supreme Court and the European Court of Justice' (1993) 2 *Fla. SUJTLP*.

the *Walloon Waste Case* the ECJ did not concern itself with the proportionality of the Walloon region's ban on imported waste.[47] The actual use of the proportionality standard by the ECJ in this area has thus proved more problematic than the superficial attractiveness of the concept might suggest.

Relating to the conservation of exhaustible natural resources: This phrase has been interpreted to require that a primary purpose of the measure be conservation.[48] Article XX(g) applies only if the restriction on international trade is primarily intended to render effective restrictions on domestic production or consumption,[49] and the *Tuna-Dolphin* panel added that the reference to restrictions is to restrictions on production or consumption within the jurisdiction of the state imposing them.[50] This panel seemed to import aspects of the 'necessity' test into Article XX(g) by holding that a United States law linking import restrictions to a maximum incidental dolphin-taking rate for foreign vessels determined after the fact by reference to actual rates achieved by United States vessels during the same period was so unpredictable as not to be a measure primarily aimed at conservation.[51] The cases establish that exhaustible natural resources include fish stocks.

The *Tuna-Dolphin* panel rejected what it described as '*extrajurisdictional*' applications of Articles XX(b) and XX(g), suggesting that the exceptions apply only to protection of animal or plant life or health within the jurisdiction of the state, and to conservation of natural resources within the jurisdiction of the state. The policy reason given was that if the exceptions were interpreted more broadly, states could unilaterally determine 'policies from which other contracting parties could not deviate without jeopardizing their rights under the General Agreement'.[52] Two distinct issues are covered by this reasoning: the view that extrajurisdictional policies are not within the GATT exceptions, and the concern that sovereign GATT trade rights ought not to be subject any more than necessary to unilateral policies of other states. The notion of 'extrajurisdictional' application of policies is apparently an invention of the panel:[53] it does not presuppose any excess of jurisdiction under international law, as the United States border

[47] Case C-2/90, *Commission* v. *Belgium*, 9 July 1992.

[48] In *Canada: Restrictions on Export of Unprocessed Herring and Salmon*, BISD 35 Supp., 98 (1988), a GATT Panel indicated that a GATT-infringing measure could be defended under Article XX(g) only if it had conservation as a 'primary aim'.

[49] *Canada: Restrictions on Export of Unprocessed Herring and Salmon*, BISD 35 Supp., 98 (1988), para. 4.6.

[50] *United States: Restrictions on Imports of Tuna*, DS 21/R (1991), para. 5.31.

[51] This interpretation is advanced by R. Housman and D. Zaelke, 'Trade, Environment, and Sustainable Development: A Primer' (1992) 15 *HICLR* 535.

[52] *United States: Restrictions on Imports of Tuna*, DS 21/R (1991), paras. 5.27 and 5.32.

[53] S. Charnovitz, 'The Environment vs. Trade Rules: Defogging the Debate' (1993) 23 *EL*, 475–517 at 497.

trade measures impugned were clearly within the ordinary range of jurisdiction under international law. Given the legal and political difficulties the international community has had in dealing adequately with global commons problems, and the apparent involvement of the United States where its market demand may have spurred tuna fishing, environmentalists are concerned that effective management will be impeded if GATT/WTO rules prevent states from taking even 'necessary' actions to apply policies extrajurisdictionally.[54] As a policy matter, the scope of the holding on 'extrajurisdictional' policies may be excessively wide.

A major motivating concern of the panel seems to have been to address the related but distinct problem of *unilateralism*. The debate here is not simply about what powers of action are required for effective environmental management, but whether, as a political and economic matter, co-operation to address problems may in some cases be spurred by a state threatening or taking unilateral action, and if so whether the positive results achieved by unilateralism are outweighed by the costs of abuses and the broader disadvantages of interventionism. Unilateralism in this context is not subject to effective international supervision, and the risk of mixed motives or the appearance of self-serving behaviour is high. In the *Tuna-Dolphin Case* Mexico pointed out that the United States tuna boat industry had largely left the region where incidental catches of dolphins posed problems, and noted that it had been subject to earlier tuna embargoes for quite different reasons.[55] There is also a likelihood of subjectivity in cases where the unilateral action is not designed to give effect to an international standard: without an international agreement, it is difficult to see any basis for accepting United States GATT-illegal enforcement short of accepting that any state might determine and enforce its own 'wildlife' or 'environmental' policies. Less powerful states do not have as many options for environmental unilateralism, a point illustrated by Austria's 1992 law requiring eco-labelling of all tropical timber (but not softwoods, which Austria exported), which was repealed in 1993 under pressure from Austrian exporters threatened with trade retaliation by Malaysia and other tropical timber states. While the *Tuna-Dolphin*

[54] A superficially comparable result was reached by the European Court of Justice in the *Scottish Red Grouse Case*, in which a provision in the EC Council Directive on the Conservation of Wild Birds allowing Member States to take stricter measures than those required in the Directive could not be interpreted as allowing the Netherlands to prohibit importation of a species not found in the territory of the Netherlands, where the species was not migratory or endangered. A significant difference from the *Tuna-Dolphin Case* is that here the Netherlands was acting in an area already carefully regulated by supranational standards. Case C/169–89 (1990), ECR 2143. This case is discussed by E.-U. Petersmann, 'The Settlement of International Environmental Disputes in GATT and the EEC', in J. Cameron and P. Demaret (eds.), *Trade, Treaties and the Environment* (London, 1994).

[55] Para. 3.58. Indonesia commented that this was the twenty-third time the US had embargoed imports of tuna since 1975. Para. 4.15.

Panel's views on unilateralism were not welcomed in the United States, they are shared by the vast majority of states. The 1992 Rio Declaration provided in Principle 12: 'Unilateral actions to deal with environmental challenges outside the jurisdiction of the importing country should be avoided.'[56]

Protection of the domestic environment: The result of the interplay of GATT obligations and the Article XX exceptions is that many trade-restricting measures related to protection of the domestic environment are compatible with GATT. Nevertheless, the failure to mention environment among the public policy reasons for trade restrictions in Article XX does mean that some such measures are not permitted. There are some unresolved questions of interpretation: for example, the ambit of the term 'like products' in defining the national treatment and MFN obligations is not totally clear,[57] although it is established that in most cases differences of processes and production methods (PPMs) are not grounds for drawing distinctions between otherwise like products. Some trade–environment conflicts may be addressed through interpretation, perhaps including more expansive use of Article XX(d) and conceivably even Articles XX(a) and (h). If future GATT/WTO panels are willing to move away from previous panel reports there is scope to strike a new balance within Article XX, possibly through more generous use of the lettered exceptions, including application of a principle of proportionality, combined with an expanded interpretation of the 'disguised restriction on trade' limitation.

Protection of foreign state environments and protection of environments beyond national jurisdiction: As to this, GATT does pose obstacles to policy options favoured by some states. Thus while GATT allows certain trade restrictions based on products, it does not allow restrictions based on PPMs except in the context of technical standards related to products or sanitary and phyto-sanitary measures.[58] The sound rationale is that restrictions on PPMs would undermine the fundamental commitment to comparative advantage: but this does not solve the problem that some foreign PPMs may be domestically or internationally dangerous and politically unconscionable. They may indeed have direct transborder

[56] See also Kittichaisaree, 'Using Trade Sanctions and Subsidies to Achieve Environmental Objectives in the Pacific Rim'.

[57] Some of the relevant panel decisions are noted in Schoenbaum, 'Free International Trade and Protection of the Environment: Irreconcilable Conflict?', 722. See also *United States: State Laws on the Regulation and Taxation of Alcoholic Beverages*, GATT doc. DS 23/R (1992).

[58] The 1994 Agreement on Technical Barriers to Trade covers PPMs related to product characteristics. The 1994 Agreement on Sanitary and Phyto-Sanitary Measures extends to PPMs in general, and in para. 8 establishes a presumption that measures conforming to this agreement are in accordance with GATT obligations, including Art. XX(b). This presumption must be interpreted as being rebuttable, in contrast to the deeming provision in para. 10.

effects on the state contemplating restrictions. The argument of the GATT secretariat that trade-restrictive measures are not optimal means of intervention carries only limited political weight where other effective means of addressing environmental problems are not available.

Apart from the special problem of trade measures taken pursuant to multilateral environmental treaties (discussed below), the strongest pressures for modification of GATT are to allow states to take account of PPMs in their treatment of products, and to include an environmental exception in Article XX. Such an exception would presumably be subject to the conditions of the chapeau and to a necessity requirement. It could be effected by amendment or by an authoritative interpretative instrument adopted by consensus. There is wide acceptance that measures genuinely necessary to protect the domestic environment ought to be permitted. However, many states are reluctant to see modifications that will permit their own environmental policies to be a focus of trade measures by other states, and fear that if distinctions among products based on PPMs are accepted these will become widespread obstacles to liberal trade, and will be especially disruptive for non-OECD states.

A different point of concern is that GATT's rules as currently interpreted encourage economically inefficient means of environmental protection, such as indirect taxes which under GATT are permissibly imposed on imports as border tax adjustments to match local product taxes, but which do not pay for environmental clean-up in the country of production and may double-tax the producer.[59] Reform of the border tax adjustment rules would be a major political undertaking after the effort expended to complete the Uruguay Round, but would probably not require formal amendment of GATT.

9.3.3. Product Regulations and Standards

Further controversy arises from the developing GATT law on product standards. The Tokyo Round Agreement on Technical Barriers to Trade (the Standards Code) was an important contribution, although fewer than half of GATT's contracting parties formally accepted it.[60] The Uruguay Round Standards Code provides that product standards must be no more

[59] Report of the Working Party on Border Tax Adjustments, 2 Dec. 1970, BISD 18 Supp., 97. In the Superfund case, *United States: Taxes on Petroleum and Certain Imported Substances* (*Mexico, Canada and EC* v. *USA*), BISD 34 Supp., 136 (1987), a panel held that the reasons for imposing a border tax adjustment were irrelevant: any such tax on products was acceptable provided it was equivalent to that imposed on domestic products and did not otherwise infringe GATT. The EC argument that the US tax on US products was to make the polluter pay and that foreign products caused no or less pollution in the US was held to be irrelevant.

[60] See generally E. Patterson, 'International Efforts to Minimize the Adverse Trade Effects of National Sanitary and Phytosanitary Regulations' (1990) 24 *JWT* 91.

trade-restrictive than is necessary to achieve a legitimate objective, including protection of human, animal, or plant life or health, and protection of the environment. Member states are required to justify standards by reference to these legitimate objectives and to standard GATT obligations including the prohibition of unnecessary obstacles to trade. The Code favours international harmonization of standards, and establishes a rebuttable presumption that standards in accordance with international standards are not unnecessary obstacles to trade. In the form finally adopted the Code does not expressly require that states wishing to adopt standards differing from internationally agreed standards (e.g. higher environmental standards) must be able to produce scientific reasons for doing so. However, pressure to produce convincing justifications may become intense through the procedures for notification, explanation, consultation, dispute settlement, and oversight by the Committee on Technical Barriers to Trade. This has been criticized by environmentalists as promoting downward harmonization and conflicting with the much-acclaimed if ill-defined precautionary principle.[61] In different versions the precautionary principle has begun to be included in international environmental treaties,[62] and a commitment to it appears in the 1992 Rio Declaration, but it is not incorporated as a guiding principle in any of the GATT/WTO materials. A further concern of environmentalists is that while the GATT/WTO rules attach great weight to standard-setting by such bodies as the International Standards Organization and the Codex Alimentarius Commission, some of these bodies are dominated by industry professionals and their allies, and are not sufficiently open or accountable to NGO or public concerns.[63]

[61] See e.g. P. A. Goldman, 'Resolving the Trade and Environment Debate: In Search of a Neutral Forum and Neutral Principles', (1992) 49 *WLLR* 1279 at 1295–6. There is also concern that performance rather than product or design standards are favoured, and that there are indications that the GATT rules may require least trade-restrictive approaches and the use of risk-benefit analysis, e.g. health warning labels for at-risk groups rather than outright bans. Some argue that these features too tend to lead to excessive risk-taking and inadequate standards. See generally Lallas, Esty, and van Hoogstraten, 'Environmental Protection and International Trade: Toward Mutually Supportive Rules and Policies', 285–9.

[62] See e.g. Convention for the Protection of the Marine Environment of the North-East Atlantic, 32 (1993) *ILM*, 1072. This stipulates in Article 2(2) that the Contracting Parties shall apply 'the precautionary principle, by virtue of which preventive measures are to be taken when there are reasonable grounds for concern that substances or energy introduced, directly or indirectly, into the marine environment may bring about hazards to human health, harm living resources and marine ecosystems, damage amenities or interfere with other legitimate uses of the sea, even where there is no conclusive evidence of a causal relationship between the inputs and the effects.' See also Article 130r of the Treaty of Rome. On the concept see T. O'Riordan and J. Cameron (eds.), *Interpreting the Precautionary Principle* (London, forthcoming, 1994).

[63] Goldman, 'Resolving the Trade and Environment Debate', 1287–9; and id., 'The Legal Effect of the Trade Agreements on Domestic Health and Environmental Regulation' (1992) 7 *JELL* 11–56.

9.3.4. Subsidies

The question of subsidies is one of the most important in the future of the trade–environment debate, although the law and particularly the policy are still not well developed.[64] GATT Articles VI and XVI were augmented by the Tokyo Round Subsidies Code, and a further Agreement on Subsidies and Countervailing Duty Measures was reached in the Uruguay Round. If State A has laxer production-related environmental rules than State B, producers in State A will have an effective advantage over producers in State B in the internal market of State A, in the internal market of State B, and in third markets. At present none of these advantages are treated as subsidies.[65] If, however, State B subsidizes its producers to enable them to meet environmental compliance costs, these subsidies are subject to countervailing duties where goods are exported to State A,[66] and they are subject to possible GATT Dispute Settlement Panel proceedings (but no right of State A to impose duties) in respect of competition in third markets, but they are not subject to any GATT action for placing producers from other states at a disadvantage in State B's internal market. GATT does not establish substantive rules of environmental conduct: in particular, it does not incorporate a 'polluter pays' principle. The strong view within GATT is that weak environmental rules or enforcement in one country cannot be regarded as an actionable subsidy, nor indeed as a subsidy at all. This is seen as part of comparative advantage; and there is considerable concern that if it becomes possible to treat certain (lax) environmental conduct as a subsidy, pressure will mount to allow all manner of other societal variations to be treated as subsidies. In the case of active subsidies to meet compliance costs, proposals to treat certain such subsidies as non-actionable were made in the Uruguay Round, but the negotiating states saw greater problems in allowing further competitive distortions and in providing a non-actionable means to provide subsidies motivated by non-environmental considerations. The final Agreement on Subsidies and Countervailing Measures goes no further than rendering non-actionable one-off subsidies to promote adaptation of existing facilities to new environmental requirements, provided such subsidies are limited to 20 per cent of the cost of

[64] See generally J. Jackson, '*World Trade Rules and Environmental Policies: Congruence or Conflict?*' (1992) 49 *WLLR* 1227–78 at 1245–50.

[65] Some analyses discuss this issue in terms of 'dumping' or 'ecodumping'. As John Jackson has pointed out, however, dumping is normally assessed by comparing prices for export goods to reference prices or costs, often in the domestic market. Where environmental standards are lax domestic prices may also be low.

[66] For criticism of the possible adverse impacts of GATT on e.g. proposals to subsidize industry energy-conservation programmes, see e.g. Housman and Zaelke, 'Trade, Environment, and Sustainable Development: A Primer', 555, 565–6.

adaptation and meet other stringent conditions.[67] Certain research and regional development subsidies are also non-actionable.

The issues about subsidies are part of wider political and economic concerns in many states about competitiveness. The impact of differences in environmental standards on competitiveness is difficult to assess empirically: while environmental compliance costs in the highly regulated United States are much less than 2 per cent of total costs in most industries, environmental standards may have contributed slightly to productivity declines in some industries, and there is evidence both of migration to less-regulated locations for a few highly regulated manufacturing industries and of a gradual decline in the proportion of products from dirty industries among total exports from developed countries, while the comparable proportion for developing countries is rising.[68] The measurable effects on competitiveness have not been dramatic, and in many cases pale in comparison to other differences, but they may become more important as capital becomes more footloose. In any event they are politically salient, particularly where the concern is that manufacturing in high-standard countries will decline, and the choices appear to be acceptance of higher unemployment and a falling tax base or lowering environmental standards. The counter-arguments that firms in countries with higher standards will get a head start as global standards rise,[69] and that they will innovate to reduce resource use and become more efficient than their competitors, have not yet been supported by empirical work showing substantial advantages in major economic sectors.[70] The practical result of competitiveness concerns is a politically potent combination of environmentalist and pro-protectionist interests (compared by one commentator to the 'baptists and bootleggers' who supported prohibition of liquor in the United States),[71] often reinforced by other groups (e.g. labour unions) suspicious of absolutist versions of comparative advantage.

[67] The facilities must have been in operation for two years by the time the new environmental requirements are imposed; these new requirements must result in greater constraints and financial burden on firms; the subsidies must be directly linked and proportionate to a firm's planned reduction of nuisances and pollution; the subsidies must be available to all firms which can adopt the new equipment and/or production processes; the subsidies must not cover the cost of replacing and operating the subsidized investment, nor may they cover any manufacturing cost savings.

[68] A useful review of the empirical work is Richard B. Stewart, 'Environmental Regulation and International Competitiveness' (1993) 102 *Yale LJ* 2039–2106, esp. 2071–9.

[69] See e.g. M. Porter, *The Competitive Advantage of Nations* (London, 1990), 45–7.

[70] See generally Stewart, 'Environmental Regulation and International Competitiveness', 2079–84.

[71] David Vogel, in Low (ed.), *International Trade and the Environment*, 245.

9.3.5. Other Issues

The GATT/WTO system has begun to address other trade–environment areas of longstanding difficulty. The Working Group on Export of Domestically Prohibited Goods and Other Hazardous Substances proposed that the problem of absolute or conditional export bans on products banned or restricted in the market of the exporting state be resolved by making such measures GATT-legal without purporting to make them obligatory. Notification of such measures and of relevant domestic instruments would also be required.[72] The strategy is to extract the GATT/WTO system from the debate as to whether all such exports should be banned, thus restricting the ability of developing countries to obtain useful pesticides and other products, or whether exports should proceed with the consent of the importing countries, raising risks of damage to health which are not tolerated in the exporting state. Environmentalists have expressed concern about the impact on the environment of various other Uruguay Round measures. For example, there have been mounting complaints that the Uruguay Round commitment to more vigorous protection of intellectual property has not been accompanied by assurances of the affordable availability of environment-enhancing technology to developing countries, and is expected to have adverse impacts on biodiversity and on indigenous communities and farmers.[73] Major issues about product labelling, consumer information, and packaging have still not been fully resolved in the GATT/WTO regime or other bodies concerned with trade–environment issues.

9.3.6. Conflicts Between GATT and Environmental Treaties

The GATT/WTO rules apply to measures taken by one contracting party that affect the rights of another party. In most cases the measures involved are unilateral, but special problems arise where the measures are taken under the terms of an international treaty, a non-binding but legally significant instrument, or a rule of customary international law. Customary international law might be involved between GATT/WTO parties X and Y where, for example, State X alleges that State Y is responsible in international law for transboundary damage where a smelter just across the border in State Y is discharging noxious fumes which pollute State X, and, having failed to secure a remedy by negotiation, X bans imports of all products from the smelter pursuant to the

[72] GATT doc. L/6872 (2 July 1991).

[73] See R. Acharya, 'Patenting of Technology: GATT and the Erosion of the World's Biodiversity' (1991) 25 *JWT* 71–88.

right of non-forcible reprisal.[74] Major legal issues would arise were such a case to be raised in the GATT/WTO system. The more pressing practical issues, however, relate to conflicts with other legal instruments in the environmental field. A large number of environmental treaties oblige states to take trade measures, but the main concerns about GATT/WTO compatibility relate to the Convention on International Trade in Endangered Species of Flora and Fauna (CITES), the Montreal Protocol on Substances that Deplete the Ozone Layer, and the Basle Convention on the Control of Transboundary Movements of Hazardous Wastes and their Disposal. In each case there is prima-facie incompatibility with GATT where certain measures envisaged in the environmental treaty are taken by one GATT/WTO party *vis-à-vis* another.[75] Other treaties authorize and encourage states to impose trade measures, but leave states with considerable discretion as to implementation.[76] A similar range of provisions is found in non-binding but widely applied instruments. UNEP's London Guidelines for the Exchange of Information on Chemicals in International Trade, for example, envisage mandatory export restrictions. The prospect of trade measures imposed under an international environmental instrument being challenged in the GATT/WTO system raises a risk of serious conflict, particularly following reform of the dispute settlement arrangements to reduce the ability of states to block disposition of such complaints. Several strategies for reconciling legal conflicts of obligations require consideration.

9.3.6.1. Use of Public International Law

Public international law has a considerable reservoir of practice and doctrine on resolving apparent conflicts of legal obligations. The tendency in analyses of trade–environment conflicts has been to approach this material in a rather formal or mechanistic way which produces distorted results.

Customary international law on apparent conflicts between treaties is reasonably well represented by the Vienna Convention on the Law of

[74] See the *Trail Smelter* arbitral awards of 1938 and 1941 (US/Canada), *Reports of International Arbitral Awards* 3, p. 1905; and Principle 21 of the 1972 Stockholm Declaration, repeated verbatim in the 1992 Rio Declaration. On non-forcible counter-measures see the *US/France Air Services Agreement* arbitral award of 1978, *Reports of International Arbitral Awards* 18, p. 421; and O. Elagab, *The Legality of Non-Forcible Countermeasures in International Law* (Oxford, 1988).

[75] On CITES and the Montreal Protocol see Cameron and Robinson, 'The Use of Trade Provisions', 8–15. The trade restrictions in the Basle Convention might traditionally have been regarded as legitimate exceptions under GATT Art. XX(b), although the very broad definition of waste (including e.g. scrap metal) may render use of this exception problematic in marginal cases. However the *Tuna-Dolphin* decision raises doubts about export prohibitions imposed without the consent of a country interested in making imports.

[76] See e.g. the 1985 ASEAN Agreement on the Conservation of Nature and Natural Resources (not yet in force).

Treaties. The Vienna Convention focuses on consent as the basis of treaty obligation (leaving aside the complexities of *jus cogens*), so that in the absence of a contrary intention a treaty to which States A and B are parties continues to govern their relations notwithstanding subsequent conclusion of a contradictory treaty between States B and C.[77] This doctrine suggests that a GATT party ought to be able to insist upon compliance with GATT notwithstanding a widely accepted environmental treaty (e.g. the Montreal Protocol or the Basle Convention) to which it is not party. However there may be doctrinal reasons why this is not correct in a particular case, for example if an objective regime is created, if a state acquiesces in loss of its GATT rights, or if the environmental treaty can be construed as relevant subsequent interpretative practice or even as an authoritative interpretation of a treaty binding on all relevant parties. Practice is also more nuanced, and there do not seem to be major examples of a GATT party relying on GATT as against the terms of a widely accepted multilateral environmental treaty.

Where States A and B are both parties to apparently inconsistent multilateral treaties, the Vienna Convention refers to a number of approaches to construction, including those favouring the later over the earlier and the specific over the general. However, these are all subject to interpretation of the terms of the treaties and of any other materials indicating intentions of the parties. In the absence of other material supporting such a conclusion, it would be extraordinary if the relationship between the GATT and the Montreal Protocol changed because the GATT was adopted anew in 1994 and hence became later in time. Resolution of conflicts by means of interpretation depends heavily on the specifics of the case. One issue is whether the GATT has acquired any status as a fundamental document of the international community, or at least whether any of its principles has become quasi-constitutional.[78] Despite broad participation, it seems unlikely that states intend GATT/WTO rules to have a hierarchical superiority to other widely accepted multilateral treaties, and practice does not support such an approach.[79]

[77] The 1916 decision of the Central American Court of Justice in *Costa Rica* v. *Nicaragua* (1917) 11 *AJIL* 181, suggests that in an extreme case a state may by one treaty render itself incompetent to conclude another inconsistent treaty with a different state. In general, however, the competence of a state is treated as not being so diminished, and the validity of the later treaty is accepted, leaving open the possibility of liability for breach. See e.g. R. Jennings and A. Watts (eds.), *Oppenheim's International Law*, 9th edn. (Harlow, Essex, 1992), vol. i, ss.590–1; A. McNair, *The Law of Treaties* (Oxford, 1961), 22–33; C. Chinkin, *Third Parties in International Law* (Oxford, 1993), 73–80.

[78] Cf. *Military and Paramilitary Activities in and against Nicaragua* (*Nicaragua* v. *USA*), ICJ Rep., 1986, p. 14.

[79] See e.g. H. Zheng, 'Defining Relationships and Resolving Conflicts between Interrelated Multinational Trade Agreements: The Experience of the MFA and the GATT' (1988) 25 *Stan. JIL* 45; and E. McDorman, 'The 1991 U.S.–Mexico GATT Panel Report on Tuna and Dolphin: Implications for Trade and Environmental Conflicts' (1992) 17 *NCJICR* 461.

In the *Tuna-Dolphin Case* the panel commented that the GATT contracting parties acting jointly retained the right to address international environmental problems which could only be resolved through measures in conflict with the present rules of the General Agreement.[80] The meaning of this is not entirely clear. In context it appears not to refer simply to waiver or amendment under GATT/WTO procedures (which the panel had already discussed). Presumably the parties can act jointly only within GATT/WTO procedures, but the panel may have been referring also to more general action by virtually the whole international community.[81]

Where it is alleged that a rule of GATT is contrary to an existing rule of customary international law concerned with environmental protection, resolution of the conflict will again depend on interpretation. In the general case there are strong arguments for not upholding GATT/WTO rules as against a customary international law rule of environmental protection.

Conflicts may also occur between GATT/WTO instruments and non-binding but highly influential international environmental instruments, such as the FAO Code of Conduct on the Distribution and Use of Pesticides. In such cases the reasons why states have not proceeded to conclude a treaty would require investigation, to establish whether the extent and nature of support for, and compliance with, the non-binding instrument is sufficient to warrant regarding it as comparable to a treaty. Subject to this, however, technical status of the Guidelines would not itself preclude seeking to reconcile the conflict in accordance with international law and practice.

9.3.6.2. Waivers of GATT/WTO Obligations

GATT Article XXV enables the contracting parties by two-thirds of those voting (the two-thirds must include at least half the total membership) to waive a GATT obligation. The GATT/WTO Secretariat is resistant to use of waivers other than infrequently and for temporary purposes. Waivers granted in the past have not been to accommodate inconsistent multilateral treaties, and the Uruguay Round Understanding on Waivers gives no indication that broad multilateral waivers are contemplated.[82] Temporary waivers for major multilateral environmental treaties are nevertheless a practical and expeditious means of resolving

[80] DS21 (1991), para. 6.4. The panel's report was not put up by the parties for adoption by the Council, but it is nevertheless an influential source on the interpretation of GATT.

[81] *Contra* Cameron and Robinson, 'The Use of Trade Provisions', at 28.

[82] The Uruguay Round Understanding in Respect of Waivers of Obligations under GATT 1994 requires that any request 'shall describe the measures which the Member proposes to take, the specific policy objectives which the Member seeks to pursue and the reasons which prevent the Member from achieving its policy objectives by measures consistent with its obligations under the GATT 1994'.

some of the current conflicts. The voting requirements provide at least a limited check on use of minilateral agreements to evade GATT disciplines for dubious reasons. However the reality of the GATT/WTO system is that votes on waivers would be heavily influenced by extraneous political considerations. It may thus be desirable to adopt a code of practice on such waivers, or to base them on the advice of a more technocratic body. NAFTA deals with the issue of providing (Article 104) that in the event of a conflict between NAFTA and the specific trade obligations set out in CITES, the Basle Convention, the Montreal Protocol, and certain bilateral instruments, the obligations in the separate instrument 'shall prevail to the extent of the inconsistency, provided that where a Party has a choice among equally effective and reasonably available means of complying with such obligations, the Party chooses the alternative that is the least inconsistent with the other provisions of [NAFTA]'. For GATT purposes, however, a waiver or similar procedure is more flexible than an attempt to itemize a changing list of environmental treaties within GATT itself.

9.3.6.3. Amending GATT

Numerous amendments to GATT have been mooted by environment-oriented interests in recent years, often to incorporate some reference to environmental protection in Article XX. However the two-thirds majority (or in some cases unanimity) required to amend GATT is a difficult requirement to meet on a controversial matter; and in any event amendments bind only those states which ratify them. One result of the Uruguay Round is that amendment of other GATT/WTO instruments may have been rendered more difficult by reduction of some of the other pressures for revision, and by integrating most of the relevant codes into a single package. The political energy of states to contemplate major controversial amendments is not likely to be high for some years in the aftermath of the Uruguay Round.

Another possibility is the adoption of an environmental code. This would be binding on the GATT/WTO parties which chose to accept it, but its wider status would be limited in the absence of GATT articles of which it might constitute an interpretation.

A final means to reconcile trade–environment conflicts is through interpretation of GATT rules, either by the parties directly or through adoption of a Dispute Settlement Panel report.

9.4. IS THE GATT/WTO SYSTEM A SUITABLE FORUM FOR TRADE–ENVIRONMENT CONFLICTS?

9.4.1. Incorporation of Environmental Rules and Principles

A major limitation of the GATT/WTO system is that it presently operates with only moderate regard to substantive principles of international or national environmental policy and law. It is not easy for a trade regime satisfactorily to pursue the default strategy of detached neutrality with respect to environmental policies, framing trade rules in a manner that retains their integrity and purpose while neither recognizing nor impinging upon substantive environmental rules and principles. The European Union has responded to this dilemma by adopting substantive environmental rules, allowing member states some latitude to go beyond these, and seeking to integrate environmental protection into all relevant aspects of the substantive law of the Union.[83] The NAFTA system relies on political pressures within member states to ensure the adequacy of substantive environmental rules, but allows and encourages member states to adopt rules setting high levels of environmental protection, and establishes machinery to oversee domestic enforcement of domestic environmental rules. Neither model is likely to be suitable for the GATT/WTO system. It is too large and heterogeneous either to adopt comprehensive substantive environmental rules without years of acrimonious negotiation or to leave such matters entirely to individual member states with institutional oversight and conflict resolution from Geneva.

A more promising fourfold strategy for the GATT/WTO system may be to incorporate broad principles of environmental management developed in other international forums; to defer to specific environmental rules adumbrated in widely accepted international treaties or (perhaps) in soft-law instruments; to accommodate certain trade measures taken in pursuit of mutually recognized domestic environmental policies meeting certain international standards; and to work on harmonizing GATT/WTO rules and procedures with these principles and rules.

The first element of this strategy is the incorporation as mandatory, or at least as legitimate, of broad principles established in other international forums. The OECD is making some progress, through the joint working party of the Trade and Environment committees, which is addressing trade and environment aspects of such principles as national treatment, non-discrimination (MFN), transparency, proportionality,

[83] Treaty of Rome (as amended by the Maastricht Treaty), Art. 130r. See also Arts. 130s–t.

legitimacy of governmental involvement, polluter/user pays,[84] sustainable development, scientific assessments of risks, precaution, life-cycle management, and preservation of global environmental resources.[85] The last five of these principles, the most closely related to environmental management, involve complex problems of definition and application which have not been fully worked out in national practice and raise major difficulties at the international level. The OECD is not representative of the membership of the GATT/WTO system. In the absence of a global treaty on principles of environmental management analogous to, for example, the International Bill of Rights,[86] it will be necessary to refer also to other sources of baseline environmental policies drafted with the active participation of developing countries, possibly including Agenda 21, the current Lomé Convention, and the work of UNEP. Nevertheless, if suitable principles can be elaborated sufficiently to be operable, they could be recognized in the GATT/WTO system as relevant to the interpretation, application, and refinement of trade rules.[87]

The second element, which is at best a very long-term strategy in pursuit of a remote objective, would seek recognition by the GATT/WTO system of the prima-facie validity and legitimacy of measures taken pursuant to rules developed in general treaties, or possibly other instruments, concerning specific environmental problems. This is the approach already adopted with respect to technical regulations and standards in the Agreement on Technical Barriers to Trade. Stringent oversight of trade measures, including reviews based on necessity and proportionality, would be required to protect the integrity of the trade rules. The GATT/WTO system is still a long way from having such a system of review. The evolution of such bodies as the European and Inter-American Courts of Human Rights suggests that such an aspiration is not impossible, although precedents at the global level are not encouraging. Even

[84] For one limited approach, see OECD Council Recommendation of 26 May 1972 on Guiding Principles Concerning International Economic Aspects of Environmental Policies (Rec. C72(128), 11 *ILM* (1972), 1172), and OECD Council Recommendation of 14 November 1974 on the Implementation of the Polluter-Pays Principle (Rec. C74(223), 14 *ILM* (1975), 234). Under the 1974 Recommendation 'the Polluter-Pays principle . . . means that the polluter should bear the expenses of carrying out the pollution prevention and control measures introduced by public authorities in Member countries, to ensure that the environment is in an acceptable state. In other words, the cost of these measures should be reflected in the cost of goods and services which cause pollution in production and/or consumption'. The Council recommended that 'as a general rule, Member countries should not assist the polluters in bearing the costs of pollution control whether by means of subsidies, tax advantages or other measures.'

[85] Feketekuty (Chair of the OECD Trade Committee), 'The Link Between Trade and Environmental Policy', 201.

[86] The 1948 Universal Declaration of Human Rights, the 1966 Covenant on Civil and Political Rights, and the 1966 Covenant on Economic, Social, and Cultural Rights.

[87] For one approach to the use of principles in processes of interpretation and decision, see R. Dworkin, *Law's Empire* (Cambridge, Mass., 1986).

were it possible to overcome these institutional limitations, at present many relevant environmental policies are not covered by such treaties. There is scepticism about both the capacity of the international community to make comprehensive environmental rules and the desirability of it endeavouring to do so. On the other hand, environmental rule-making treaties already cover some areas reasonably well, and there is precedent for affirmative recognition of substantive international standards in the WTO Agreement on Trade-Related Aspects of Intellectual Property Rights, under which WTO members are obliged, *inter alia*, to conform to major parts of the Paris and Berne Conventions and to take other specific measures to protect intellectual property.

The third element is for the GATT/WTO system to encourage mutual recognition of domestic environmental policies meeting certain international standards, and to accommodate trade measures taken pursuant to such policies, subject to the necessary institutional oversight. This is the approach already taken in such areas as environmental subsidies and technical barriers to trade: in each case the Uruguay Round instruments establish WTO oversight bodies. It is common to refer to the relevant environmental standards as minima, but this masks the points that different approaches to environmental management may not be comparable on a single scale, and that international standards are unlikely to immunize every policy described by its practitioners as one of strong environmental protection.[88]

The fourth element, harmonizing GATT/WTO rules and procedures with relevant environmental principles and rules, entails some reform of GATT/WTO rule-making procedures. These have been less open to participation of environmental NGOs than some organizations dealing with environmental matters, and their deliberate pace is out of temper with recent environmental activism. National government departments making policy on GATT/WTO negotiations have consulted affected industry and trade groups, but in most cases have had little contact with governmental or non-governmental environmental bodies. Environmental expertise has not been common among GATT/WTO delegates or secretariat staff. The WTO Trade and Environment Committee is a successor to GATT's Working Group on Environmental Measures and International Trade, which was revived in 1991 after a twenty-year hiatus and made some progress on eco-labelling and other issues. One general issue facing the Committee is the extent to which member states, with great differences in

[88] Cf. the *European Community: Animal Hormones Directive Case*. The EC implemented a ban in 1989 on certain beef products where cattle had been fed natural growth hormones. Evidence that such products caused adverse human health impacts was not available. The USA imposed retaliatory import duties on EC exports. Standards Code proceedings did not produce a result. The standoff continued thereafter, with the *de facto* consequence that the EC in effect accepted a cost for its decision to continue the ban.

legal systems and policies, will be willing to make use of market-based approaches along with the familiar command-and-control regulatory models.

A further concern in rule-making as the GATT/WTO system endeavours to deal with trade–environment issues is the extent to which the system is able also to take account of goals of sustainable development. Arguments for the accommodation of environmental measures in the trade regime largely represent a Northern agenda, and depart in some respects from the compromise formulations on environment, development, and trade reached at the 1992 UNCED and particularly in Agenda 21. The longstanding issues concerning special treatment for developing countries, with which GATT has grappled since the Kennedy Round, arise again in relation to trade–environment questions, and come into conflict with the broad aim of the United States and other states to phase out special provisions for at least the more prosperous of the 'developing countries'.

9.4.2. Dispute Settlement Procedures

While the institutional structure and effectiveness of the GATT/WTO system could be better in many respects, the system does provide a highly experienced forum for addressing trade disputes. The dispute settlement process under Articles XXII and XXIII was used fairly frequently in the early years of GATT, with many of the original negotiators involved and an atmosphere almost akin to a club in which panel reports were often crafted in diplomatic rather than legal language.[89] After the admission of a significant number of developing countries interested in using dispute settlement to improve compliance by Western importing states, the EC (which was vulnerable to GATT challenges) and the United States both decried 'legalism' in GATT, and no GATT complaints were filed from November 1963 to December 1969. Dispute settlement activity (overwhelmingly among developed states) resumed in the 1970s, largely because of the demands of US domestic politics and the *de facto* resolution of questions about the compatibility of fundamental EC rules with GATT. Strengthening the dispute settlement process was a goal pursued with some success in the Tokyo Round, and the speed of the settlement process has been quickened in more recent years. The Uruguay Round negotiations produced agreement on a more legally oriented process,

[89] A very useful historical analysis and tabulation of the dispute settlement process is R. Hudec, *Enforcing International Trade Law: The Evolution of the Modern GATT Legal System* (Salem, NH, 1993). See also the annexe to E.-U. Petersmann and G. Jaenicke (eds.), *Adjudication of International Trade Disputes in International and National Economic Law* (Fribourg, 1992).

including establishment of an Appellate Body to hear appeals on points of law and legal interpretation, and a shift from requiring a consensus in the GATT Council to adopt a panel report to requiring a consensus in the new Dispute Settlement Body (DSB) to block the automatic adoption of reports of panels or the Appellate Body.[90]

The GATT/WTO dispute settlement procedures have been criticized by environmentalists for lack of transparency, lack of environmental expertise, and lack of effectiveness in constraining violation. There is NGO pressure to hold panel hearings in public and to make state submissions and panel reports public at an early stage. The GATT/WTO system is beginning to respond to some of these concerns, albeit slowly. In principle environmental expertise is available to panels in the same way as other technical expertise,[91] although the green socialization of participants in the whole dispute settlement process has been slow, and the Uruguay Round Understanding on Dispute Settlement makes experience or expertise in trade law or policy the only qualification for panel members.[92] The capacity to draw upon environmental expertise where necessary does not seem to have been significant in practice, and the GATT/WTO system is less explicit in this area than NAFTA.[93] There is considerable scope for further procedural improvement.

The GATT/WTO dispute settlement process may be invoked only by member states and the European Union. Unless members adopt domestic laws enabling private parties to force the state to investigate an issue and invoke the process, a great many domestic and international issues will enter into any state's calculations as to whether to take a matter forward. Although the Uruguay Round Understanding provides that 'requests for conciliation and the use of the dispute settlement procedures should not be intended or considered as contentious acts', potential defendants are sometimes able to find ways to signal to potential complainants that it is not desirable to go forward; such signalling of issue linkage (or, more bluntly, arm-twisting) may become more frequent with the shift to what is supposed to be an inexorable decision process in the DSB. Formal dispute settlement is a backstop to consultation and other means of settlement. In the early phases of the process considerable emphasis is placed

[90] Uruguay Round Understanding on Rules and Procedures Governing the Settlement of Disputes.

[91] GATT Tokyo Round Understanding Regarding Notification, Consultation, Dispute Settlement and Surveillance, para. 16; Uruguay Round Understanding on Rules and Procedures Governing the Settlement of Disputes, para. 13 and app. 4.

[92] Uruguay Round Understanding on Rules and Procedures Governing the Settlement of Disputes, para. 8.1. Broader but comparable qualifications are required for membership in the standing Appellate Body (para. 17.3).

[93] Under Arts. 2014 and 2015 of NAFTA, dispute settlement panels may request reports from an independent scientific review board and must take these reports into account as well as publishing them with the final decision. Panels may also solicit the views of NGOs.

on reaching a politically tolerable solution, although the Understanding makes reference to the desirability of negotiated settlements being consistent with the relevant WTO agreements. There is a long history of states using GATT-inconsistent or GATT-dubious understandings to end trade disputes,[94] and a number of GATT-inconsistent or GATT-dubious trade arrangements are allowed to endure without formal challenge for political reasons.[95] Some such results give satisfaction to environmentalists. For example, Ontario in 1992 sharply increased an environmental levy on beer cans (used mainly by United States beer producers) in order to encourage use of refillable bottles (used mainly by local producers). The high rate of recycling of cans meant the differences in environmental impact between cans and bottles were modest or negligible. The backdrop was a long history of protectionist actions concerning interprovincial and international trade in beer. After retaliation and counter-retaliation outside GATT, the settlement negotiated in 1993 allowed continuation of the beer levy, recognizing not that the environmental case overwhelmed trade law considerations but that both the United States and Canada were vulnerable to challenge for numerous entrenched measures of beer protectionism, and that each state had a greater interest in establishing a political climate conducive to gradual dismantling of these measures.

Once an issue reaches the stage of a GATT/WTO panel report, however, the goal of settling the specific dispute, while still important, is increasingly unlikely to displace the panel's obligation to evaluate the measures taken against the rules of the GATT/WTO system. At least since the enhancement of the quality of legal analysis and reasoning in panel reports in the 1980s, panels have attached importance to their roles in upholding the substantive standards of the system, and have recognized that they speak to a wider audience than simply the parties to the dispute.[96] The WTO Appellate Body is expected to share this approach.

The strongest inhibition on the development of case-law on resolution of trade–environment conflicts is that GATT/WTO panels have seen themselves as limited by their terms of reference: 'To examine, in the light of the relevant provisions in [GATT or the relevant WTO instrument], the matter referred to the DSB . . .' They have hitherto seen themselves as interpreters of GATT: the extent to which they will take account of other international law norms in the future is unclear, but may well be limited.[97] In any event they cannot rely directly on non-WTO rules as

[94] e.g. Orderly Marketing Arrangements, and 'Voluntary' Export Restraints.

[95] e.g. aspects of the Lomé Convention system, on which a Panel ruled adversely in 1994.

[96] On the tension between the functions of maintaining law and settling disputes in the work of international arbitral and adjudicative bodies, see C. Gray and B. Kingsbury, 'Developments in Dispute Settlement: Inter-State Arbitration Since 1945' (1992) 63 *BYIL* 97 at 114–19.

[97] In the *Tuna-Dolphin Case* (*Mexico* v. *USA*), the panel stated (para. 6.1) that 'its task

governing. There is thus a heavy weighting toward GATT/WTO rules where conflict of obligations issues are considered by Dispute Settlement Panels.

9.4.3. Enforcement of Standards

Enforcement of international trade standards involves a complex interaction of GATT/WTO institutional pressure, extra-institutional bilateral or even multilateral negotiation, unilateral retaliatory trade action, and domestic political structures. The GATT/WTO system has had great difficulty dealing with challenges to trade embargoes imposed for reasons of high politics.[98] In most other cases, however, once a matter has been formally raised the GATT/WTO process places considerable social pressure on infringing states to comply with substantive rules. In some situations national governments have welcomed adverse rulings under GATT as a means to overcome domestic pressures for maintenance of a GATT-illegal practice.[99] The Uruguay Round reforms increase the prospect that GATT/WTO bodies will be able in practice to set compensation for

was limited to the examination of this matter "in the light of the relevant GATT provisions", and therefore did not call for a finding on the appropriateness of the United States' and Mexico's conservation policies as such'. It is reported (para. 4.1) that Australia argued before the panel that a panel 'could not resolve conflicts between a contracting party's obligations under the General Agreement and its obligations under other instruments such as those in respect of the conservation of marine mammals'. The 1994 Dispute Settlement Understanding does provide for panels to 'make such findings as will assist the DSB in making the recommendations or in giving the rulings provided for . . .' This seems wide enough to permit reference to other relevant rules of international law.

[98] No useful decision was reached in *European Community, Canada and Australia: Trade Restrictions Applied for Non-Economic Reasons* (*Argentina* v. *EC, Canada, and Australia*), BISD 29 Supp., 23 (a complaint concerning the Falklands/Malvinas war embargo imposed by these states was never referred to a panel); *United States: Suspension of Most-Favoured Nation Treatment* (*Poland* v. *USA*), Complaint of 1 Nov. 1982 concerning US suspension of Poland's MFN status following suppression of Solidarity movement was never referred to a panel, GATT doc. C/W/401; and *United States: Trade Measures Affecting Nicaragua* (*Nicaragua* v. *USA*), GATT doc. L/6053 of 13 Oct. 1986 (complaint by Nicaragua against US embargo was referred to a panel but with terms of reference which proved too limited to reach a material result). In *United States: Imports of Sugar from Nicaragua* (*Nicaragua* v. *USA*), BISD 31 Supp., 67, a panel ruled that the US reduction of Nicaragua's sugar quota violated GATT Art. XIII, and the ruling was adopted by the GATT Council, but the US took the position that GATT had no role in such a dispute and ignored the ruling until sanctions were lifted in 1990.

[99] In a forthcoming book on *Contested Commitments in United States Foreign Policy, 1783–1989*, Robert Keohane draws attention to the successful use by the Reagan administration in 1986 of a GATT Panel ruling, adopted by the GATT Council with US acquiescence, to discourage Congress from re-enacting an 1891 law which protected the US printing industry by prohibiting import of various printed works written by US residents. *United States: 'Manufacturing Clause' in US Copyright Legislation*, BISD 31 Supp., 74 (1985). The EC requested authority from the GATT Council to retaliate under Article XXIII, but this request was still pending when the US law lapsed.

nullification or infringement of benefits under Article XXIII,[100] although the preference of defendant states for negotiations on such matters remains very strong.

Unilateral enforcement of trade standards under domestic legal procedures has become prevalent, and is likely to remain important. One aim of the Uruguay Round was to tie national enforcement action to the use of the GATT/WTO process: the long-term success of this ambitious reform will depend on highly effective operation of the GATT/WTO dispute settlement process combined with a major shift in member practices; the likelihood is that some independent enforcement action will continue. One influential theory holds that over and above unilateral attempts by states to enforce specific GATT rules, certain violations of GATT in unilateral enforcement of self-promulgated liberal trade standards beyond GATT levels make a positive contribution in forcing the evolution of GATT standards.[101] In states accustomed to committing such forcing violations, it is a short step for domestic groups interested in environmental protection to advocate violations of trade rules to promote acceptance of these goals. The perception of a degree of success for the United States with threats of trade sanctions in trade and intellectual property areas under s.301 and related legislation,[102] and the evidence of the effectiveness of threats of trade sanctions in the environmental field, for example in inducing South Korea finally to become party to the Montreal Protocol in 1992 despite the high costs to domestic industries, kindle enthusiasm for GATT-inconsistent unilateralism.

There is unresolved tension in the international trade regime between the elements of self-help and reciprocity on the one hand, and the aspiration for substantive rules of general applicability on the other.[103] Interests in environmental protection may rank lower than others and be bargained away in reciprocal if not necessarily equal negotiations, where community norms do not prevent this. Even where states rank their own environmental interests highest among their interests, unilateral pursuit of these individual interests through self-help will not necessarily achieve the best aggregate environmental results. If the interests of states become operational only where they suffer injury or lose a benefit, distortion may

[100] The only formal authorization of such measures before the completion of the Uruguay Round was in 1952, when the Netherlands was authorized to retaliate against an admitted US violation.

[101] R. Hudec, 'Thinking About the New Section 301: Beyond Good and Evil', in J. Bhagwati and H. Patrick (eds.), *Aggressive Unilateralism* (Ann Arbor, Mich., 1990), 113. See also Hudec, *Enforcing International Trade Law*.

[102] Section 301 of the Trade and Tariff Act of 1974, re-enacted and modified to become ss.301–10 of the Omnibus Trade and Competitiveness Act of 1988, and the Super 301 and Special 301 procedures.

[103] A useful study is C. Rhodes, *Reciprocity, US Trade Policy, and the GATT Regime* (Ithaca, NY, 1993).

occur through focus on transboundary impacts rather than domestic impacts in other states. Useful lessons may be drawn from the area of human rights, where the limited and partisan interest of third states in violations by any particular state diverges from the interests of the individuals and groups suffering violations. International human rights regimes were created using the standard forms of state–state obligations in multilateral treaties, but reciprocity has been gradually (although not completely) displaced by answerability to more-or-less independent international institutions.[104]

Tendencies to unilateralism in the trade regime generally, and with reference to environmental issues in particular, are not likely to disappear, but the GATT/WTO disciplines and other adjudicative arrangements will continue to play a constraining role, and any strengthening of the Geneva institutions will diminish demands for and the scope of unilateralism.

9.4.4. Alternative Forums for Addressing Trade–Environment Conflicts

The GATT/WTO system at present has no substantive prescriptive or enforcement competence in the environment field. For some environmentalists the relative cohesiveness and effectiveness of the GATT/WTO system is an asset which should be utilized by reorienting the system towards environmental protection. The overwhelming view of trade practitioners, however, is that the coherence and efficacy of the system are fragile, and that while trade–environment problems must be addressed, the GATT/WTO system should not move further than necessary beyond its areas of existing competence.

An alternative strategy favoured by many environmentalists is institutional emulation. The trade–environment debate has spawned post-UNCED proposals for a new Global (or International) Environmental Organization to match the GATT/WTO system, ranging from a powerful decision-making and implementation body incorporating many existing organizations[105] to a less grandiose institution modelled on the International Labour Organization with its distinctive tripartite structure of government, employer, and employee representatives.[106] While an environmental organization might well have been established had the idea been current in the period of institution building after the Second World

[104] See e.g. *Belilos* v. *Switzerland*, European Court of Human Rights Series A, no. 132 (1988).

[105] D. Esty, 'GATTing the Greens', Foreign Affairs (Nov. 1993), 32. See further Esty, Greening the GATT: Trade, Environment, and the Future (Washington, DC: Institute for International Economics, 1994).

[106] Charnovitz, 'Defogging the Debate', 513. See also H. French, 'Strengthening Global Environmental Governance', in L. R. Brown (ed.), *State of the World 1992* (Washington, DC, 1992), 155.

War, the sentiment of states has turned against enlargement of costly international bureaucracy. Many such proposals were mooted before the 1992 UNCED,[107] but the outcome was more modest: creation of the intergovernmental UN Commission on Sustainable Development (CSD) with limited resources, without superseding any existing bodies.[108] The difference of nomenclature between proposals for a GEO and the creation of the CSD highlights the continuing gap between the priorities of many Western environmentalists and the central importance of development to the majority of UN member states.

The decision-making process on policy questions will depend heavily on the forum in which particular decisions are taken, so the choice of forums will remain contested. The likely long-term role of the CSD is not yet clear, although there is scope for it to become a significant policy and review forum on the model of the Commission on Human Rights. As more systematic views about use of trade restrictions in environmental treaties develop, conferences negotiating such treaties may be able to draw on general policies rather than case-by-case outcomes, and such policies may funnel back into the GATT/WTO system.

The vision of a global structure patterned after the EU or NAFTA, with the GATT/WTO system either including a major environmental policy component or taking advice from and working in tandem with an environmental organization, seems remote. A new global environmental organization comparable to the European Environment Agency or the North American Commission for Environmental Co-operation is most unlikely in the near future. Adjudicative dispute settlement functions will almost certainly remain within the GATT/WTO, although other bodies such as the ECJ are also likely to find themselves obliged to interpret GATT/WTO instruments in adjudicating trade–environment conflicts.

9.5. CONCLUSION

A single 'neutral' forum for addressing trade–environment conflicts is not likely to emerge in the near future. Despite its limitations, the GATT/WTO system is the global institution most immediately involved in dispute settlement in which trade–environment issues are raised in their sharpest forms.

[107] See e.g. Hurrell and Kingsbury, *The International Politics of the Environment*, 33–5; and L. Kimball, *Forging International Agreements: Strengthening Inter-Governmental Institutions for Environment and Development* (Washington, DC: World Resources Institute, 1992).

[108] See generally P. Birnie, 'The UN and the Environment', in A. Roberts and B. Kingsbury (eds.), *United Nations, Divided World*, 2nd edn. (Oxford, 1993), 327–83.

GATT can be made more environment-conscious, including by amending the preamble, Article XX, and other provisions, and adopting an environment code. As to enforcement, the nature of constraint and coercion in the GATT/WTO process is complex, and cannot fairly be understood by simple reference to institutional forms and rules.

Some of the criticism of GATT, while useful in pointing to desirable improvements, has become disproportionate. First, environmentalist critiques sometimes lose sight of the value of much of the existing trade and of GATT's contribution to achievement of this through the disciplines of the GATT regime. Second, the significance of actual inhibition of worthwhile environmental measures attributable to GATT has been limited: major multilateral treaties on wildlife, hazardous wastes, ozone-depleting substances, and climate change have been concluded and operated without serious practical difficulties of GATT-compatibility. This is not to minimize the inhibiting and distorting effect of some GATT rules, both with regard to national measures generally and in bargaining in the shadow of the law with respect to unilateral and multilateral measures. Third, one of the achievements of GATT has been to place some constraint on tendencies to unilateralism in the trade field. When applied to environment this has been a source of irritation to the United States Congress and NGOs, but may well be seen as a blessing in many other parts of the world. Fourth, the GATT system leaves room to states parties to determine the levels of environmental protection applied within their territories: that is, it defers to national sovereignty. This form of pluralism has quite different objectives to those of a regional integration agreement, but arguably it is well suited to diverse circumstances around the globe and in particular to the needs of some developing countries. Fifth, GATT does not preclude the application of international environmental law among any group of consenting states. It may (although often will not) inhibit use of trade sanctions as a means of pressure for participation, but many other combinations of pressure (e.g. green conditionality) and incentives will be at least as effective.

Nevertheless, the GATT/WTO system is highly trade-oriented, and has a limited competence only. Other bodies with different patterns of experience, participation, and decision-making must be centrally involved in developing policy about environment–trade conflicts.

In the longer term, the wider problem of the challenges posed to international environmental law and to international trade law by the notion of 'sustainable development' may prove a source of greater difficulty than the present problems of resolving trade–environment conflicts.

10

Meeting the Cost of Environmental Regulation

JOHN CRIDLAND

10.1. INTRODUCTION

What are the effects of environmental regulation on business? Are there benefits as well as costs for business in embracing environmental policy, and how can we more effectively pursue the advantages and better manage the consequences? These questions are central to any debate about environmental regulation and economic growth. They are as relevant today as they were at the inception of current debate in the 1980s, but they are no nearer a definitive answer.

Three aspects of the debate have changed, however: acceptability, language, and urgency. Business and the environment is now accepted on the centre stage of public policy debate with a recognition that business is part of the solution rather than simply a key factor in the problem. Serious efforts by businesses to pursue spontaneous and voluntary environmental policies have established that greater degree of credibility. Secondly, we now have the language of sustainable development. Post-Rio it provides the framework for policy debate on environmental issues as disparate as land use planning and education and training. Thirdly, we have had recession and the need to foster recovery. 'Strategies for growth' are top of the political agenda. Constraints to economic growth, of which environmental regulation can be one, are thus less attractive.

Yet the answers to balancing environmental regulation and growth remain elusive. The European Community is urgently examining strategies which will allow the community to make progress simultaneously in attacking unemployment and environmental degradation. The Inspectorate of Pollution (HMIP) is seeking to overcome the difficulties which result from the Environmental Protection Act 1990 not defining 'environmental harm' which is central to its regulatory judgments. And the water regulator, the Office of Water Services (Ofwat), is expressing increasing concern at the impact of new environmental obligations on future bills for water. Most striking of all, the latest journal of the Organization for Economic Co-operation and Development (OECD) asks the question, 'Do environmental policies affect competitiveness?'

The Confederation of British Industry (CBI) is Britain's business voice. Its mission is to enhance the long-run competitiveness of business. Its environment programme seeks to promote voluntary efforts by business to enhance environmental performance and to ensure that the policy and regulatory framework within which business operates is consistent with the need to gain competitive advantage. The CBI speaks for businesses from all sectors, from firework manufacturers to insurers, and of all sizes, from the Post Office to the local printer. Its emphasis on competitiveness should bring a distinct but relevant contribution to making sense of sustainable development.

This chapter will first address issues of competitiveness and then explore ten key principles which CBI believes can reconcile environmental regulation and economic growth. It will then look briefly at experience with three current environmental topics: civil liability for environmental damage, water quality, and integrated pollution control. Finally we will address what business itself is doing to contribute to sustainable development.

10.2. COMPETITIVENESS

10.2.1. Competitiveness and the Policy-Maker

Competitiveness is appearing more prominently on EC agendas and is the subject of keen ministerial debate. With respect to the environment this is focusing attention on developing synergies between environmental concern and economic growth. The Commission sees no inherent conflict between the two. The argument runs that in market economies sustainable development can be promoted by the market signals which Governments give through taxes and charges.

With the Community facing 17 million unemployed, the commission notes nearly 50 per cent of the overall tax burden is placed on labour, whilst only 10 per cent of it falls on natural resources. Should not policy-makers promote jobs and environmental protection by penalizing undesirable activities and fostering those that are desirable? A consequence might be more efforts at taxing pollution and fostering innovation in clean technology. Such market instruments can be claimed to bring business gains in areas such as energy efficiency and waste minimization; the worldwide market for environmental goods and services was some 200 billion dollars in 1990 and is growing.

A continued concentration on environmental action should be good for business competitiveness. In Britain we have heard the same themes espoused by Ministers and an even greater concentration on economic instruments as the prime tool of future environment policy. The theory, then, is well established that environment policy should be good for business, despite a conceptual trend away from regulation and towards market measures. But what lies behind these claims?

10.2.2. Business Competitiveness and Environment Policy

The OECD claims that the relative stringency or laxity of environmental standards has little impact on the general competitiveness of nations because compliance costs only, on average, 1–2 per cent of total costs. This finding, if it is true, and if it remains true, would seem to bring little comfort to those Ministers stressing business opportunities or to business executives warning about costs. Yet the picture is a more complex one and each industry and sector has to be looked at on its merits, and it is here that the important gains and losses can be found. Those with strong innovation, investment, and marketing profiles may well gain whilst pollution-intensive, natural-resource dependent businesses, as well as those under competitive threat, may well suffer. In addition, in an increasingly competitive world all costs are critical, especially those that are controllable and avoidable.

In 1991 Britain spent some £14 billion on the environment, 2½ per cent of gross domestic product, and two-thirds of this comes from business. For 90 per cent of business, environmental regulation is the dominant factor in such expenditure, resulting in 60 per cent of all environmental investments in the chemical sector, for example, up to a fifth of total capital investment. Thus, coping with environmental regulation is a serious matter for business. It can be the opportunity to build new openings for the future, or one pressure too many. One business's opportunity is another's ossified market.

None the less, CBI experience of talking to member organizations would identify the following common threads which do provide a basis for future action.

- Well-run businesses are more likely to be able to cope with environmental regulation. Sound management results in clear strategy, accurate market assessment, and maximizing opportunities and action.
- It follows that there is much to be gained from voluntary environmental action in providing for spontaneity, creativity, and flexibility.
- Smaller businesses are nearly always likely to be faced with greater challenges and have less capacity to respond as they need to.
- All businesses need good regulation and good public policy. Policy-makers must offer greater certainty in the legal framework, more time to adapt to changing philosophies and priorities—especially in a decade of lower growth—and marked-based incentives which foster and promote action (rather than tax-based penalties).

10.3. PRINCIPLES FOR ENVIRONMENTAL REGULATION

Business and the environment is a relatively new debating area. It remains a voyage of discovery for many of those involved. If regulation and growth are, as governments claim, to be constant rather than conflicting priorities, then business must have a consensus with policy-makers on the rules of the game. To give meaning to sustainable development, the CBI has prepared a series of ten principles which should underpin policy development and regulation. They aim to encompass both the synergies which can be exploited and the trade-offs which need to be managed, and reflect the essential contribution which business brings to the debate—the innovative edge of wealth creation.

1. The CBI supports the goal of *sustainable development*, recognizing as it does that:
   - the impact of human activity on the natural environment must be prevented from causing irreparable degradation;
   - economic development itself is the prime source of environmental improvement—the means by which the considerable potential of advancing technology and better environmental practice is realized;
   - while industry can reduce the environmental impact of economic activity, individuals, their political leaders, and opinion-formers have a crucial contribution to make through their choice of living standards and consumption.
2. It follows that environmental policy, regulation, and measures to stimulate improvement should:
   - be based on constructive dialogue between business and government, on the best available scientific knowledge and analysis, on a thorough assessment of the technological options, and hence on a *realistic appreciation of the costs, benefits, and trade-offs* between different environmental objectives;
   - work with the grain of the *competitive free market*, and be conducive to resource-efficient economic activity achieving high environmental standards.
3. *Government's role* is to define broad goals and priorities consistent with concerted international programmes of environmental improvement. It should encourage environmental improvement through the setting of minimum standards and through business enterprise, innovation, and ingenuity in pursuit of commercial advantage in competitive markets.
4. The CBI supports a *precautionary approach* in cases where the science is still uncertain yet the risks are sufficiently great to justify the

encouragement of corrective action consistent with the economic use of resources and of best available technology. However, action beyond this should be based on a thorough assessment of risks, benefits, and costs.

5. Where scientific understanding permits quantifiable risk assessment, environmental protection should be promoted through the application of defined quality objectives. Regulation should be confined to the setting of minimum standards, leaving industry the freedom to find the best and most cost-effective means of achieving or surpassing them in individual cases.
6. Business-led, market-based voluntary action should always be the first recourse of government when seeking environmental improvement—this being made more credible and effective through systematic public reporting of environmental performance against objectives.
7. Economic instruments have a contribution to make as an inducement to environmental improvement. They should be applied in such a way as to reward success in meeting environmental standards cost effectively, while maintaining fiscal neutrality. Their application should be even-handed. Since economic development based on resource efficiency is the prime driving force of environmental improvement, the use of such instruments should not impair the competitiveness of British industry.
8. Environment *regulation* should offer businesses reasonable certainty, stability, and realistic timescales for efficient implementation. New legislation and regulation should be introduced only at a pace which can be implemented and enforced.
9. Environmental protection measures should be comprehensively and fairly implemented and enforced. The principle of subsidiarity should apply in this field, with action taken at a level of government relevant to the environmental objective concerned.
10. The monitoring of environmental quality is essential to the determination of the success of existing controls and the potential need for new or revised controls. The results should be in the public domain.

CBI would advocate that these principles have particular relevance to current debates on environmental objectives and regulation, and should be utilized to inform policy-makers in deciding whether proposals are likely to be effective in achieving their objectives.

10.4. THE CHALLENGES REGULATION FACES

Other chapters have addressed in detail many of the issues raised by current and proposed environmental regulation. Three priority areas of attention merit brief analysis here: proposals to change the regime of environmental liability, the choices which we face in the pursuit of water quality, and the way forward for integrated pollution control.

10.4.1. Environmental Liability

Many business leaders see the Government's review of the EC Green Paper on Remedying Environmental Damage as the number one environmental regulation issue at present. They face threats to their competitiveness, finance, and insurance as a result of recent developments in liability for damage tote environment. There is growing uncertainty about the liabilities which business may face in future and this is giving rise to concern that liability may be imposed on firms retroactively for past actions which were legal and acceptable at the time, with the possibility that those innocent of pollution may, none the less, be held liable.

Potentially the costs are vast and relate to the inheritance of the industrial revolution when environmental protection standards were not a priority.

None the less, it is estimated that there may be some 27,000 hectares of contamination in the United Kingdom amongst derelict land alone, and this does not include land which is in use. Dealing with this inheritance could well cost at least £20 billion.

Preventing lasting damage to the natural environment through human activity is of concern to all. Business recognizes that it has a central part to play in responding to this challenge. It is committed to working constructively with government, at national and EC level, in pursuit of systematic environmental improvement, and in the creation of a framework of policy, legislation, legal and commercial principles, and regulatory standards which is conducive to a positive and complementary relationship between economic development and environmental improvement. It recognizes that where business is at fault and causes damage to persons and to property it should face court action under civil laws. But liabilities for damages of an environmental nature pose unique problems which are becoming more acute, and which may sometimes require special treatment in regulation and law. With the rapid advance of technology, our ability to measure the impacts of human activity on the natural environment is increasing at an accelerating rate, raising the question of what is an acceptable level of contamination—and the associated remedial action—in relation to individual circumstances and proposed usage. At the same time, it becomes increasingly evident that the resources required to rectify the past contamination are potentially enormous—far in excess of the capacity of one generation to provide. Inevitably, this raises questions of priority. In some cases, the contamination may represent a significant hazard, calling for urgent remedial action. In others, the contamination may be contained and non-hazardous—at least in relation to some of the options for further usage. If so, it may be better to direct the resources elsewhere.

Against this background, there is growing uncertainty over the extent of businesses' environmental liabilities, and real concern that such unpredictable liabilities could harm companies in spite of their responsible observance of prevailing standards and good practice. One effect of this uncertainty is the increasing reluctance to purchase and develop contaminated land for continued industrial use, which in turn puts more pressure on the use of greenfield sites for industrial activity. More generally, and of crucial importance, the commercial risks deriving from unpredictable environmental liabilities are tending to impede the very process of innovation and the new investment which is the prime driving force for both economic development and environmental improvement—the means by which cleaner and more efficient technology and processes are introduced. Specifically, the financing and insurance of new industrial activity is an emerging problem in this regard.

In addition, business's confidence in the existing legal system has been shaken by the *Cambridge Water Company Case*. Had the House of Lords upheld the Court of Appeal's ruling they would have introduced a new element of strict and retrospective liability into British law. In this case small accidental spillages of a chemical prior to 1976 which subsequently seeped into a groundwater aquifer have been held to breach an EC Directive implemented in 1985. CBI members are conscious of experience in the United States with liability and Superfund legislation which has demonstrated how blunt a tool liability is, and the resulting diversion of resources into extensive litigation.

What conclusions can be drawn about the most sensible and productive way forward for environmental liability? First, society must be clear what the objectives of policy are. They should be to remove hazards to health, to prevent, where possible, future damage to the environment, to clean up past pollution and contamination and, perhaps of most immediate importance, to remove current uncertainty. Secondly, governments must set standards relevant to these objectives. These are being put in place through integrated pollution control, statutory water quality objectives and other measures. They are singularly lacking, however, in relation to identifying, evaluating, and remedying environmental damage. At present Dutch soil standards are widely used, but they seek to restore all land to a level at which it could be used for any purpose. To businesses this is an unrealistic and unsustainable objective. Agreed national and possibly European standards are needed, based on fitness for purpose. This would be a significant boost to practical efforts at tackling past pollution. Thirdly, policy makers must look for the most appropriate policy mechanism. Implicit in the EC approach is that civil liability can be used as a form of economic instrument to apply generalized pressure on business to raise standards of environmental performance. To business, this is illogical and unacceptable. Civil liability has proved to be a blunt and ineffective tool for this purpose in the United States, and policy-makers must not seek to use a system of civil law intended to provide injured parties with compensation as an environmental quality tool. A clear distinction is needed between the future, for which a fair and clear legal regime is needed, and the past, where efforts should concentrate on environmental standards and practical initiatives.

That legal regime must continue to be *non-retroactive*, and the United Kingdom's existing *fault-based* civil liability system should not be extended to include elements of strict liability. Where strict liability exists—as, in effect, it already does under regulatory law—it should be qualified by a state-of-the-art defence. The objective is to protect businesses from unaffordable liabilities due to actions which could not have been known to be harmful at the time they were taken. In response to the EC Green Paper, CBI members do not accept that a case is made for the *harmonization* of civil liability regimes across the Community. The imposition of this is impractical given the fundamental differences in the legal structures of the different Member States.

10.4.2. Water Quality

In the case of water quality, questions about cost and benefit are now being asked at an advanced stage of the implementation of key environmental programmes. In *Paying for Quality*, Ofwat attempts to estimate the future costs of implementing legislation relating to water supply and effluent disposal standards. This has raised the political profile of the debate on the right balance between costs and environmental improvements. The main costs are due to the EC's Urban Waste Water Treatment Directive (UWWTD) and revisions to the Bathing Water and Drinking Water Directives together with a proposed new Directive on surface water quality. In addition there are national initiatives, of which the most significant are the proposed Statutory Water Quality Objectives (SWQOs). The total bill together with existing obligations will be £45 billion to the end of the decade. Business, as a major user, contributes £1 billion per annum to water companies' revenues.

The consequences of this debate are illuminating. Ministers are still considering UWWTD regulations and the proposed SWQOs. They have real options to ameliorate the impact of the former, through designation of less sensitive areas, and to apply full cost and benefit analysis to the latter. What is striking is the absence of any adequate methodology for cost and benefit analysis, either domestically or in the European Commission. The result is incremental environmental improvement at disproportionate cost. Once again a key principle for environmental regulation has not been fully taken on board.

10.4.3. Integrated Pollution Control

The Environmental Protection Act introduced a range of new concepts for environmental protection without full definition. Its implementation has, as a result, been difficult. Regulators and employers have had a lot to learn. They have survived that process and identified many problems, but with IPC in fundamentally good shape. That has been indicated in the current deregulation initiative. What is only now being tackled is the persistent problem of definition and clarification of terms. BPEO, BATNEEC, the assessment of environmental harm, critical load factors, regulatory assessment levels—what do all these mean in practice?

In July 1993 HMIP presented proposals for assessing the environmental effects of a process, as well as for identifying the BPEO and site-specific BATNEEC. As with water quality, the developments are an essential basis for sensible target setting. They are long overdue and whilst business will undoubtedly want to see the HMIP model altered and refined, this development is welcomed.

10.5. VOLUNTARY INITIATIVES

Business too has a major contribution to make in the developing partnership between regulator and regulated. It must demonstrate that its voluntarily introduced environmental management systems are worthy of confidence from its external stakeholders. Irrespective of whether it is pursuing BS7750, the new EC Eco-Management and Audit, or voluntary initiatives developed by sectors—of which the best-established is the Chemical Industry Responsible Care Programme—such initiatives have a critical role in self-regulation, ensuring that the regulator should not need to interfere in the internal management of the business.

The CBI is convinced that this integration and interaction of voluntary and regulatory initiatives is a critical aspect of making sense of environmental protection and economic growth. We have established our own Environment Business Forum. Our mission is to promote good environmental performance within United Kingdom companies based on the benefits to the business of so doing. In essence those companies which are prepared to go beyond the 'minimum' required by current legislation should receive the appropriate credit of enhanced stakeholder confidence and ultimately of competitive advantage.

The overall objectives of the Forum are:

- to provide guidance on environmental management appropriate to any company, of any size and in any sector;
- to establish a network to carry the concept of the EBF throughout the United Kingdom and down to the smallest companies at the local level;
- to encourage partnerships for mutual benefit between larger and smaller organizations;
- to demonstrate the effectiveness of business-led voluntary action in protecting and enhancing the environment.

At the heart of the Forum is the Agenda for Voluntary Action to which forum members must commit themselves. This requires the following actions:

- designating a board-level director with responsibility for the environment;
- publishing a corporate environmental policy statement;
- setting clear targets and publishing objectives for achieving the policy;
- measuring current performances against targets;
- implementing improvement plans;
- communicating company environmental policy and objectives to employees, seeking their contribution to improvement and providing appropriate training;
- reporting publicly on progress in achieving the objectives;
- establishing partnerships, where appropriate, to extend and promote the objectives of the Forum, particularly with smaller companies.

The Forum is recognized internationally as the first national cross-sectoral initiative to encourage voluntary action by business. It is part of business's contribution to developing a sensible balance between environmental regulation and economic growth, a matter of importance to us all. The questions which opened this chapter will not be quickly answered, but they need to be tackled systematically and rigorously if we are to make progress towards sustainable development.

11

The Growth of US Environmental Regulation and the Cost of Compliance: A Model for Europe?

LOGAN G. ROBINSON

11.1. INTRODUCTION

This chapter looks at the costs of environmental regulation from the point of view of an important American industry, the automotive industry, one which is at the very centre of environmental concerns. There is no more dramatic initiation into the regulatory framework in the United States than to show the growth of federal environmental laws.

Note in particular the exponential leap in regulation following the establishment of the United States Environmental Protection Agency in 1970 (see Fig. 11.1). Since the creation of the EPA we have put thirty-eight major pieces of federal legislation on the books, shown in Fig. 11.2. Frankly, very few lawyers who are not engaged full-time in environmental work have any idea what most of the acronyms in the figure stand for, let alone their substance. Note that the list does not show the growth in pages of legislation—for example, the 1970 Clean Air Act was about fifty pages long, the 1990 Amendments to the Clean Air Act, about 800. Clearly no country can support this growth in regulation without enormous cost, as can be seen from Fig. 11.3. For example, with 70,000 chemicals on the EPA's Toxic Substances Control Inventory, it is estimated that the cost of cleaning up the hazardous waste sites subject to the Superfund programme could by itself reach an additional US$1.25 trillion for the decade. The EPA staff (at the federal level alone—there are equally large counterparts at both the state and local level) is itself the size of a large corporation. Although a comparatively young bureaucracy, only 23 years old, the EPA is described by many as 'the agency that ate America', as it now accounts for a seventh of the staff and a third of the spending of the entire federal regulatory apparatus. The ability of the EPA to spawn litigation is unprecedented. Four out of every five decisions made by the head of the EPA are challenged and litigated

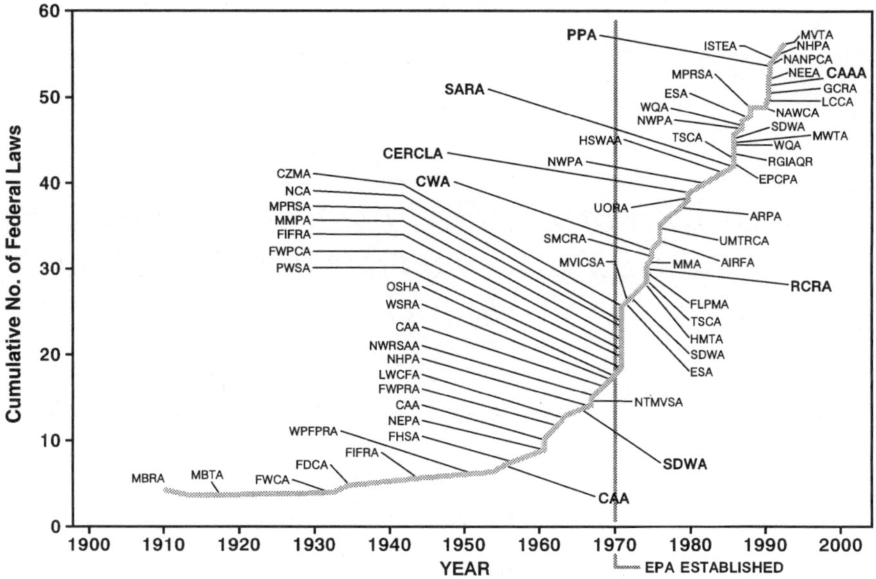

Fig. 11.1 Number of federal laws affecting auto industry

Hazardous Waste Discharge

Resource Conservation and Recovery Act (RCRA)
Comprehensive Environmental Response
Compensation and Liability Act (CERCLA)
SUPERFUND

Toxic Substances

Toxic Substance Control Act (TSCA)

Recycling

Pollution Prevention Act (PPA)

Air Emissions

Clean Air Act (CAA)

Water Emissions

Clean Water Act (CWA)

Vehicle Emissions

Corporate Average Fuel Economy (CAFE)

Fig. 11. 2 Some major new laws since 1970

- **Compliance costs will reach US$200 billion (British milliard) a year by 2005. For the entire 1990s estimated costs will total US$1.6 trillion (British billion)**
- **The EPA has a staff of over 18,000 people and a budget of US$4.5 billion (British milliard). This does not include state and local environment agencies**
- **Environmental compliance now represents more than 2% of GNP, affecting the price of US products**
- **US industry, as the most regulated, finds itself at a competitive disadvantage**

Fig. 11.3 Costs of regulation

by the permanent Washington environmental lobby. Thus, policy is actually made through a pastiche of court orders and settlement negotiations, not by the executive branch. Even the EPA's own employees are suing the EPA over the air quality in their Washington headquarters which houses 3,100 staff. And despite the enormous deficit on which the United States Government runs, the EPA adds people and budgetary authority every year.

Although two decades of intense regulation have achieved some results, the basic process shows severe impediments:

- The US system is one of 'command and control', and engenders an adversarial relationship with manufacturers.
- There is little concept of timing environmental compliance with facilitating economic goals, which seems to be much more the pattern in Japan.
- The market is not trusted to guide environmentally correct behaviour. For example, rather than taxing gasoline, as in Europe, so that consumers would naturally prefer small cars with smaller engines, the Government has forced manufacturers, through the 'Corporate Average Fuel Economy' (CAFE) laws, to produce a certain number of small cars whether the public has any interest in buying them or not.

- There are in general no 'credits' for over-compliance. Thus, there is no reward structure for going beyond current governmental mandates. In many cases the regulations not only mandate the performance standard, but also the technologies which must be used to achieve these standards. These mandated technologies may not only be sub-optimal, but also draw resources away from technical innovations.
- The inflexibility of the regulations forms a strong deterrent to remediation of existing facilities. Companies are induced to retain—but mothball—existing facilities, while putting new manufacturing investments into greenfield sites in former agricultural areas. Thus the inner cites, with existing older facilities, lose industry and jobs, worsening their plight.
- This problem—the high cost of de-activating and re-using urban manufacturing sites—is made worse for smaller businesses who must pledge their facilities. Lenders, fearing uncapped lender liability over environmental issues, are often unwilling to finance the purchase of any former manufacturing site. Thus reclamation is stymied, and the 'rust-belt' inner cities continue their role as the elephant graveyards of former manufacturing sites.

11.2. THE COST OF REGULATION

At Fig. 11.4 we can see the results of all this regulation and the financial impact it has had on the American consumer. Currently the cost per unit owing to emission and safety regulation is about $3,000. Similarly, the number of weeks an American *family* must work to pay for a new car is rising, with approximately 40 per cent of the differential from a 'comparable car' of the late 1960s attributable to added mandatory safety and emissions equipment.

Note that the graphs in Figs. 11.5–7 are deceptive to some extent as they are phrased in terms of median *family* income: in 1967 it was rare to have two income earners in a family, now it is commonplace. But for this profound sociological change, the number of weeks of family income to pay for a new car would be very much higher.

Having shown some startling figures about the cost of compliance with increasing United States environmental regulation, and mentioned some significant flaws with the approach these regulations have taken, we should not conclude that the American automobile industry—and Chrysler in particular—is uncommitted to environmental responsibility. The fact is, mandated or not, it is not just the EPA that wants a green revolution—customers want cleaner cars, workers and neighbours want

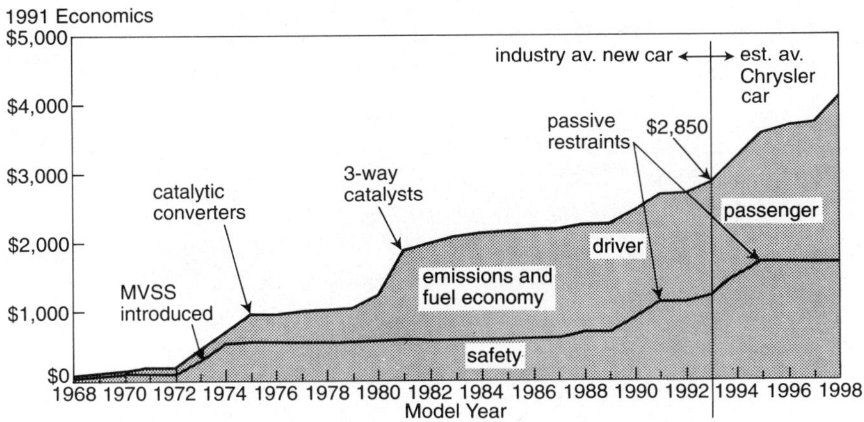

Emissions price increases include changes to improve fuel economy

Fig. 11.4 Cumulative retail price increases for safety and emissions equipment

cleaner factories, and as a corporate citizen, we want these things too. Also, in the late 1970s, Japanese competitors caught Detroit napping when oil prices skyrocketed and they had the technology to offer smaller, fuel-efficient cars. Having very nearly gone bankrupt at that time trying to sell unpopular vehicles, Chrysler is determined to be in the forefront of the new environmentally driven technologies.

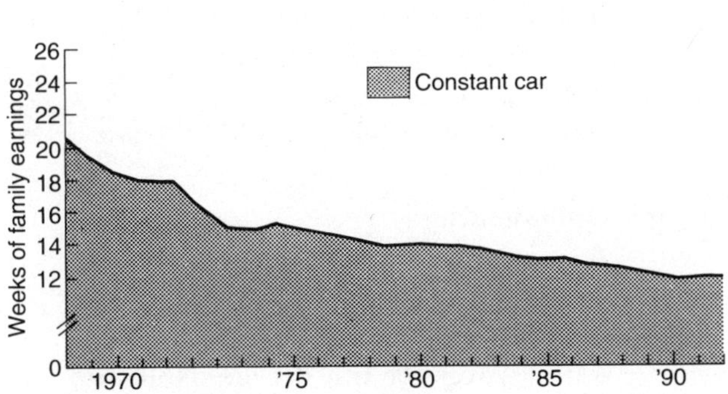

Fig. 11.5 Affordability of autos (1)

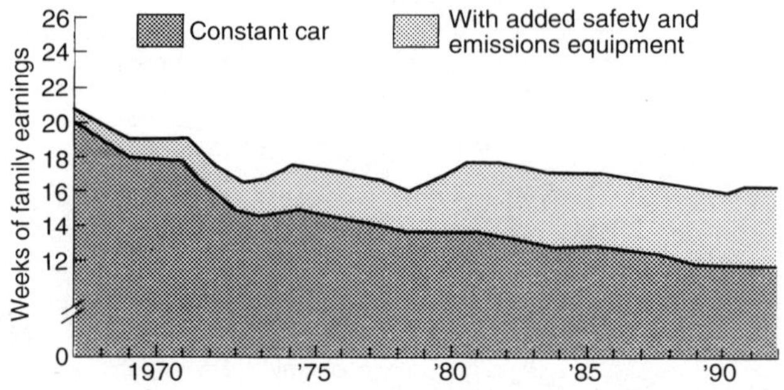

Fig. 11.6 Affordability of autos (2)

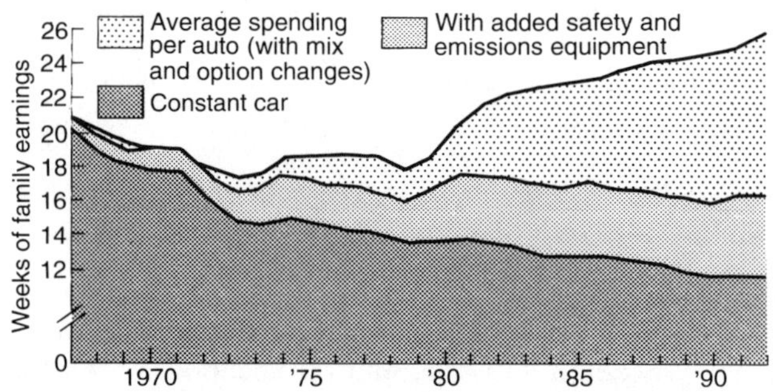

Fig. 11.7 Affordability of autos (3)

11.3. VEHICLE EMISSION TRENDS AND ALTERNATIVE TECHNOLOGIES

Now let us look at the results to date—focusing on the key area of vehicle emission—and then at some of the options for the future and where Chrysler is in developing these technologies.

There are three major sources of air pollution (see Figs. 11.8, 11.9, 11.10):

Volatile organic compounds,
Oxides of nitrogen,
Carbon monoxide.

Note that in the case of each category of pollutant, the percentage caused by motor vehicles is down over the last decade. Note also that total emissions are considerably down as well, making the motor vehicle reduction even more dramatic.

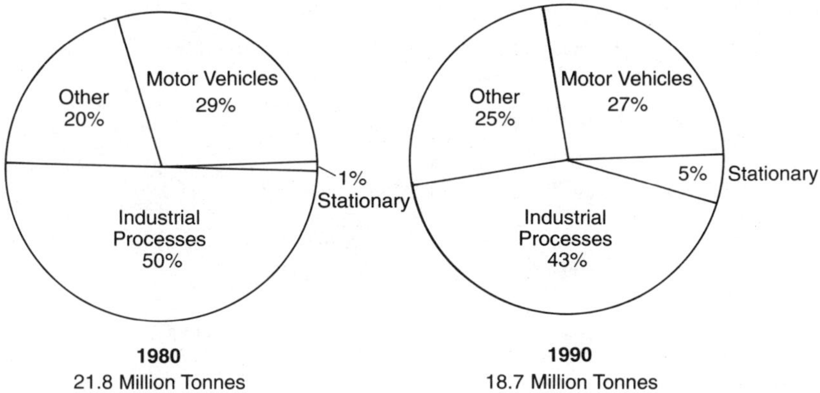

Fig. 11.8 Major sources of air pollution: volatile organic compounds

The improvements summarized in Fig. 11.11 show that, over the last twenty years, despite a huge increase in vehicle miles travelled (VMT), emissions are on a steady decline. Improvements in vehicle emissions have been so noteworthy that Chrysler received an EPA citation for its work in stratospheric ozone protection.

Fig. 11.12 shows some alternatives for the future. Methanol is particularly interesting as its octane rating is so high that it is the fuel of choice for Indianapolis racing-car drivers. Chrysler has developed a Methanol Concentration Smart Sensor that permits a car to accept any fuel-tank mixture of unleaded gasoline and M85, an 85 per cent methanol mixture, with no noticeable difference in performance. Without this flexibility of

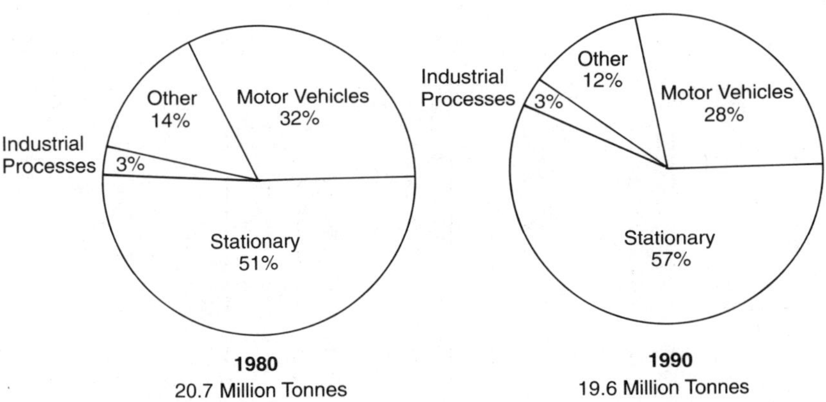

Fig. 11.9 Major sources of air pollution: oxides of nitrogen

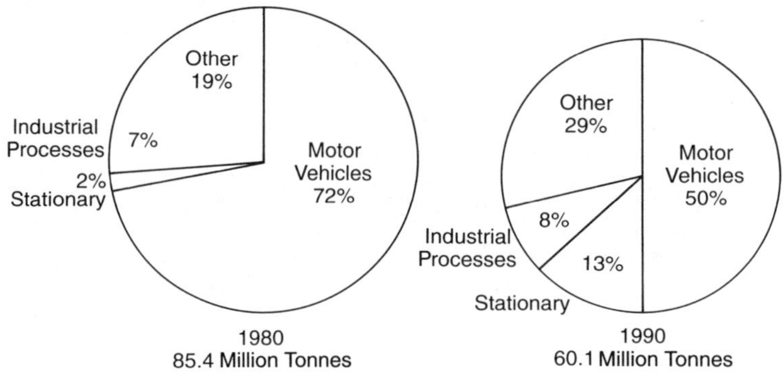

Fig. 11.10 Major sources of air pollution:

fuels one always confronts the 'chicken and egg' problem. The automotive industry says, 'We can make the cars, but there's no fuel available,' while the oil industry says, 'We could supply the stations with methanol, but there aren't any cars that can use it.' The sensor, which can also be used for ethanol fuels, is no bigger than an audio cassette tape. The United States Government recently agreed to purchase 5,000 such vehicles.

Chrysler has also modified a few of these vehicles to run on compressed natural gas (CNG), but probably the best-known alternative is the electric vehicle. This concept is not all theory: Chrysler is this year delivering fifty Dodge Caravan Electrics, the nation's first federally safety-certified electric vehicle, to utilities around the country. While it will still be some time before electric vehicles become a practical reality for consumers—issues such as battery weight, range and reliability must be solved—there is no substitute for the field experience that is being gained through actually having a fleet on the road.

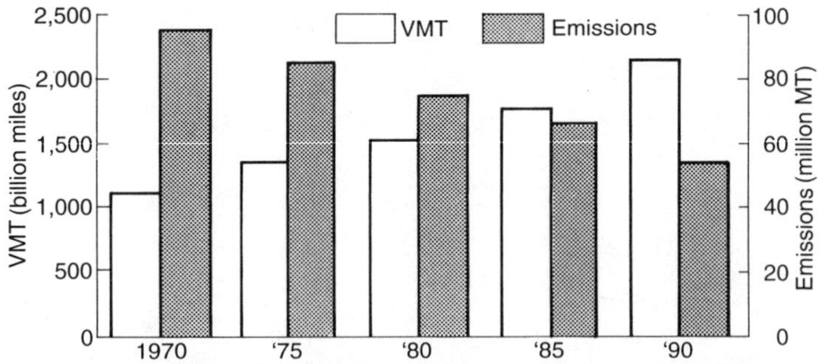

Fig. 11.11 Emissions vs. vehicle miles travelled

	Vehicle changes	Emissions reduction potential	additional fuel cost per gallon
Accelerated scrappage	None	Moderate, one-time	None
Reformulated gasoline	None	Moderate, one-time	\$.02 to \$.12
Methanol (M-085)	\$400	Moderate, increasing	\$.15 to \$.60
CNG	\$1,200 to \$1,500	Moderate to high, increasing	–\$.20 to –\$.30
Heated catalysts	\$1,400	Moderate, increasing	None
Electric	High	High, increasing	–\$.60 to –\$.80
Taxes	None	Depends on tax level	Amount of tax

Fig. 11.12 Alternatives for reducing vehicular emissions

So, in summary, we can see some of the possibilities for the future. Much of the research and development in the United States automotive industry in environmental technology is being done in joint ventures among Chrysler, Ford, and General Motors. These would not have been possible before the National Co-operative Research and Development Act of 1984, which gives limited anti-trust immunity to so-called 'pre-competitive' research and development joint ventures. The initial one was for polymer-based composites—which became the first joint venture of any kind among the so-called 'Big Three' car companies. That became the model, and there are now fifteen such partnerships, from the Advanced Refrigeration Consortium to the Vehicle Recycling Partnership.

11.4. CONCLUSIONS

Near-term emission problems are best addressed by:

- accelerated scrappage
- reformulated gasoline
- taxes

Mid-term solutions are costly:

- ethanol
- methanol
- CNG
- heated catalysts

Long-term global warming is best addressed by:

- more research and development
- electric vehicles?

Index

Location references are to page numbers; numbers in italic indicate diagrams or charts